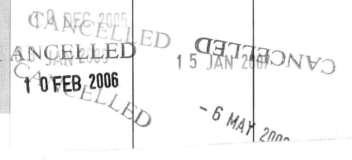

SERIES IN TOURISM AND HOSPITALITY MANAGEMENT

Key Textbooks

Series Editors:
Professor Roy C. Wood The Scottish Hotel School
University of Strathclyde, UK

Stephen J. Page Massey University, New Zealand

Series Consultant:
Professor C.L. Jenkins The Scottish Hotel School, University of
Strathclyde, UK

Titles in this series:

**Behavioural Studies in Hospitality
Management**
R. Carmouche and N. Kelly
ISBN 0 412 60850 2, 232 pages

**Managing Human Resources in the
European Tourism and Hospitality
Industry**
A strategic approach
T. Baum
ISBN 0 412 55630 8, 280 pages

**Interpersonal Skills for Hospitality
Management**
M.A. Clark
ISBN 0 412 57330 X, 232 pages

Hospitality and Tourism Law
M. Poustie, N. Geddes, W. Stewart and J.
Ross
ISBN 0 412 62080 4, 320 pages

**Business Accounting for Hospitality and
Tourism**
H. Atkinson, S. Berry and R. Jarvis
ISBN 0 412 40808 8, 452 pages

Economics for Hospitality Management
P. Cullen
ISBN 0 412 60540 6, 224 pages

**Marketing Tourism, Hospitality and
Leisure in Europe**
Susan Horner and John Swarbrooke
ISBN 0 412 62170 3, 728 pages

Managing Wine and Wine Sales
J.B. Fattorini
ISBN 0 412 72190 2, 200 pages

Wildlife Tourism
Myra Shackley
ISBN 0 415 11539 6

Torism and Public Policy
C. Michael Hall and John M. Jenkins
ISBN 0 415 11354 7

Transport for Tourism
Stephen J. Page
ISBN 0 415 10238 3

Urban Tourism
Stephen J. Page
ISBN 0 415 11218 4

Books in the series are available on free inspection for lecturers considering the texts
for course adoption. Details of these, and any other Chapman & Hall titles are
available by writing to the publishers (2–6 Boundary Row, London, SE1 8HN) or by
telephoning the Promotions Department on 0171 865 0066.

Managing Packaged Tourism

Relationships, responsibilities and service quality in the inclusive holiday industry.

E. Laws
Napier University, UK

INTERNATIONAL THOMSON BUSINESS PRESS

I(T)P An International Thomson Publishing Company

London · Bonn · Boston · Johannesburg · Madrid · Melbourne · Mexico City · New York · Paris
Singapore · Tokyo · Toronto · Albany NY · Belmont CA · Cincinatti OH · Detroit MI

Managing Packaged Tourism

First published by International Thomson Business Press

 I T P A division of International Thomson Publishing Inc.
The ITP logo is a trademark under licence

British Library Cataloguing-in-Publication Data
A catalogue record for this book is available from the British Library

First edition 1997

Typeset by Photoprint Typesetters, Devon
Printed in the UK by Clays Ltd, St Ives plc

ISBN 0-41511-347-4

International Thomson Business Press
Berkshire House
168–173 High Holborn
London WC1V 7AA
UK

International Thomson Business Press
20 Park Plaza
13th Floor
Boston MA 02116
USA

http://www.itbp.com

Contents

List of case studies

List of tables

List of Figures

Series Editors' Foreword

The International Thomson Business Press Series in Tourism and Hospitality Management is dedicated to the publication of high quality textbooks and other volumes that will be of benefit to those engaged in tourism, hotel and hospitality education, especially at degree and postgraduate level. The series has two principal strands: core textbooks on key areas of the curriculum; and the *Topics in Tourism and Hospitality* series which includes highly focused and shorter texts on particular themes and issues. All the authors in the series are experts in their own fields, actively engaged in teaching, research and consultancy in tourism and hospitality. Each book comprises an authoritative blend of subject-relevant theoretical considerations and practical applications. Furthermore, a unique quality of the series is that it is student oriented, offering accessible texts that take account of the realities of administration, management and operations in tourism and hospitality contexts, being constructively critical without losing sight of the overall goal of providing clear accounts of essential concepts, issues and techniques.

The series is committed to quality, accessibility, relevance and originality in its approach. Quality is ensured as a result of a vigorous refereeing process, unusual in the publication of textbooks. Accessibility is achieved through the use of innovative textual design techniques, and the use of discussion points, case studies and exercises within books, all geared to encouraging a comprehensive understanding of the material contained therein. Relevance and originality together result from the experience of authors as key authorities in their fields.

The tourism and hospitality industries are diverse and dynamic industries and it is the intention of the editors to reflect this diversity and dynamism by publishing quality texts that enhance topical subjects without losing sight of enduring themes. The Series Editors and Advisor are grateful to Steven Reed of International Thomson Business Press for his commitment, expertise and support of this philosophy.

Professor Roy C. Wood   Stephen J. Page
The Scottish Hotel School   Massey University – Albany
Strathclyde University, UK   Auckland
                                                 New Zealand

Series Consultant
Professor C. L. Jenkins
The Scottish Hotel School
Strathclyde University, UK

Acknowledgements

This book could not have been written without the support, advice and encouragement of many people. The case studies of particular organizations, and the chapters on the timeshare industry and charter airlines depend entirely on the detailed knowledge and expertise of the managers who discussed them at length with me, and I gratefully acknowledge the assistance of the following:

Peter Allport, Marketing and Sales Director, Haven Leisure
Pierre Claus, Executive Secretary, ANTOR
Brian Coupland, Chairman, Frames
Peter Cox, Commercial Manager, Air 2000
Bob Duffett, PSARA
Glynn Huggins and Eric Huggins, Kes Tours
Kevin Ivie, Marketing Director, First Choice
Mike Kay, Aviation Solutions
Barbara Le Palley, Senior Planning Officer, Canterbury City Council
Ian Raitt, Dubai Commerce and Tourism Promotion Board
Malcolm Wood, Head of Resort Services and Market Development, RCI UK and Ireland.

Among the many tourism enthusiasts and experts who have helped in this project I wish to express my gratitude to two main groups. The first are my students and colleagues, many of whom have contributed to the development of the ideas advanced in this book over a period of several years. The second group includes all the experts who have presented their views for discussion and debate at meetings of the Tourism Society, the Chartered Institute of Marketing Travel Industry Group, the Institute of Travel and Tourism and the Travel and Tourism Research Association. I extend my thanks to all these, particularly those who made the time to comment on early drafts of the case studies and some of the chapters. Any remaining errors are my own responsibility.

I also wish to thank Barbara Conroy for her support and advice.

Preface

Since Thomas Cook in 1841 took advantage of a then new form of transport to organize his first tour, a day visit by chartered train to Loughborough from Leicester, transport and tourism have transformed people's ability to make leisure visits to distant places. Thomas Cook's original objective was to promote the temperance movement of which he was a member, but he soon came to realize the business potential of packaging transport with meals, activities and accommodation, and the company he founded continues to be a leader in tourism and the inclusive holiday sector (Swinglehurst, 1982).

During the next century, the inclusive holiday industry developed in a variety of forms including guided overseas tours and domestic holiday camps with occasional interruptions caused by major wars until, in the 1950s, it began to take on its modern form of air charter-based inclusive holiday packages. Two decades later, with the deployment of jet aircraft into charter service, its most rapid phase of expansion began, and by 1990 some 12 million overseas package holidays were being sold annually in Britain alone while about a third of all travel abroad by US residents was on some form of organised package (Sheldon and Mak, 1987).

The main emphasis throughout this book is on inclusive overseas holidays by air as this form of holiday is the characteristic mode of popular long-distance holidaytaking. It is typified by large-scale resort development in destination areas, by charter airline travel linking many points of tourist origin with a wide range of destinations, and by the creation and management of packaged holidays by tour operators based in holidaymakers' countries of origin.

Tour operators deal in holiday concepts. They select destinations, resorts and hotel or other accommodation, and package these elements with the other basic component of holidays, the journey between home and destination. On arrival in their holiday centres, clients are encourage to undertake group activities such as excursions, shopping and entertainment arranged by their tour operator, and this has led to rather homogenized holiday products which do not fully recognize the individual and specific place values of the various destinations.

Increasing efficiency, returns to scale, industry competition and the highly open entrepreneurial forum for tour operators, charter operators, travel retailers and resort developers led to a spectacular reduction in the real price of holidays. When expressed as a proportion of average UK take-home pay, a two-week overseas holiday has become much more affordable since the mid 1960s. At the same time, increased familiarity with overseas destinations resulting from personal experience and from coverage in the media, both in news reports and through advertising or informational pieces, has resulted in overseas holidays becoming widely accepted as a standard part of the family's annual budget rather than an exceptional item.

Holidays are now readily available and affordable to many people in Western and other industrialized societies, and many of these are taken in different countries. Most governments throughout the world have policies aimed to further develop their inbound tourism, motivated by the employment and foreign currency benefits it brings, or by the exposure to foreign influence for themselves and their citizens. A key aspect is the widespread practice in the industry of emphasizing low prices. This has been successful in expanding the market, thereby filling the expanding capacity of resorts around the world, but the policy has resulted in several problems which are increasingly being recognized by local and national governments, leaders within the industry and other interest groups. In particular, concern has been expressed about the effects on destination communities of rapid and insensitive expansion of their tourism sectors and unsustainably low profit margins for the companies involved. The policies which led to the growth of the inclusive holiday industry now require re-evaluation and perhaps revision if it is to continue the pace and scale of its development.

By collaborating with each other and other organizations, retail travel agents and tour operators are able to offer easy access to distant destinations from countries of tourist origin, in particular by providing packaged holidays enabling clients to buy all the elements needed for their holiday in one transaction. The demand for these inclusive holidays has been stimulated by the industry's marketing, including its advertising and pricing practices. These have tended to emphasize the brands of the tour operators and retail travel agents, while often presenting stylized and general images of the destination areas. This has led to the commoditization of the holiday industry – many of its products are now very similar in style, and this homogenization has encouraged clients to discriminate between the destinations offered in holiday brochures by price (Urry, 1990; McCannel, 1992; Boniface and Fowler, 1993).

It is no longer satisfactory for policy-makers to regard tourism as a trivial activity. During the second half of the twentieth century tourism has become one of the major industries in the world. The number of people travelling abroad for all reasons in 1992 was 476 million (WTO, 1994). The proportion of United Kingdom population who had ever taken an overseas holiday rose from 34% in 1970 to 70% in 1990 (BTA, 1992).

Technological developments such as jet aircraft and CRS/telecommunications systems have enabled tour operators to increase the scale of their activities, extend the range of destinations offered and reduce the costs of holidays. In combination with improved standards of living (especially higher discretionary income, longer paid holidays and changing demographics and patterns of work), this has resulted in much wider social access to holidays and demands for enhanced infrastructure to cope with the increasing numbers of travellers. The holiday industry's development has also coincided with greater general awareness of overseas travel resulting from television and media coverage of heritage, ecology and other place-related topics.

This book introduces a critical evaluation of the holiday industry from several perspectives, illustrated with a range of case studies. It examines the nature and evolution of inclusive holiday concepts, evaluates the marketplace responses to low-price holiday offers and focuses attention on the consequences for all organizations in the holiday industry system of their interdependence, arguing that the analytical and policy focus should be the entire industry. The objectives of the book are, firstly, to evaluate the factors which constrain the holiday industry's ability to function systemically as a network of long-term business relationships, creating the types of holiday products and experiences which are enjoyable for clients, rewarding for entrepreneurs and staff, and welcomed by destination area residents, local business and politicians. Secondly, this book provides a framework within which to understand the developing maturity of the industry as it moves into the third millennium, when a further rapid expansion of demand can be anticipated resulting from the ability of people from Eastern European and Asiatic countries to travel widely for recreation.

The evolution and structure of the inclusive holiday industry

In this section, Chapter 1 considers the varied factors which have contributed to the growth of the inclusive holiday industry in Britain, providing in outline a historical context to the creation and management of packaged holidays.

The techniques which underlie modern packaged holiday organization and marketing were established by the early entrepreneurs, particularly Thomas Cook. The issues which confront the contemporary inclusive holiday industry, and result from its greatly increased scale and some of its business practices, were already becoming apparent by the mid 1970s. The industry's operational practices, the relationships between organizations in the holiday industry system, the impacts of mass holidaymaking on destination areas and the quality of holidaymakers' experiences are the subject of the ensuing parts and chapters of the book.

The evolution of the inclusive holiday industry | 1

INTRODUCTION

Tourism, like most social activities, can be more fully understood by identifying the events which led up to contemporary situations, and considering changes in the relationships between key elements of the system over time. The history of inclusive holidays is quite brief, but since the end of the Second World War it has enabled significant numbers of people from the wealthier nations to travel for leisure throughout the world.

EARLY ORIGINS

By the end of the nineteenth century, although travel was much slower than now and relatively more expensive, much of the present-day form of tourism was becoming evident, with organized groups of travellers paying a professional organizer to make the arrangements for their leisure itineraries around Europe or further afield. One of the most successful entrepreneurs was Thomas Cook whose contributions to the development of the industry are outlined in Case study 1.1, although many other travel organizers became established about the same time in Europe and America, the core business activities common to them all being the packaging of travel, accommodation and excursion arrangements.

Winter sports had also begun to feature as a travel motive. The first holiday for that purpose is said to have been organized by Sir Henry Lunn to Chamonix in 1898. Within a few years the growing interest in skiing had encouraged the Grindelwald authorities to extend the new cog railway up to Kliene Scheidegg, to facilitate the sport of downhill slalom skiing. Thus, the holiday industry's demands were beginning to alter the infrastructure and environments of destination areas. However, as Table 1.1 indicates, the mass market for overseas holidaytaking could not develop fully without several enabling factors external to the

Table 1.1 Factors in the growth of foreign holidaytaking

Supply factors:
- technological developments in transport
- improvements in telecommunications
- development of computerized reservations systems
- tourism entrepreneurs' creativity
- investment in tourism infrastructure development in destination areas

Demand factors
- increases in standards of living in the countries of tourist origin
- increased awareness of destinations
- lifestyle changes
- demographic changes

industry itself, notably fast and affordable long-distance transport, and a large number of people wanting to holiday abroad, able to afford both the time and expense, and with the confidence to travel.

CASE STUDY 1.1

Thomas Cook

The early origins of mass tourism can be traced back to the middle of the nineteenth century, when in 1841 Thomas Cook, a Leicester based printer and temperance preacher, claimed a place in modern social and business history as the innovator of the package tour holiday. Although the first excursion he organized was in the form of a day excursion by train, it had many of the features found in modern inclusive holidays, with the notable exception that his original motivation had been to provide his clients with a diversion from the evils of drinking! Swinglehurst (1982) has described how, as a sales incentive, Thomas Cook added two brass bands, a gala and tea with buns. The tour attracted 570 customers, paying a shilling each for the journey between Leicester and Loughborough.

The subsequent development of his company foreshadowed many practices which were to become common in the industry. Thomas Cook owned a print shop, so when he decided to run a weekend trip from Leicester to Liverpool four years later, he produced as an aid to sales a brochure: 'A handbook of the trip to Liverpool'. Before this trip, Cook spent several days in Liverpool, assessing the merits of various hotels and restaurants and organizing local excursions. As a result of the popularity of these trips, he decided to operate further excursions to more distant destinations. An advertisement at the time exactly defined Thomas Cook's view of the tour agent: 'The main object of the conducted tour apart from being able to calculate the exact cost before starting is to enhance the enjoyment by relieving the traveller of all the petty troubles and annoyances from a journey.'

In 1855, he began to organize excursions to Europe. Initially, he lost money on the project, due to the high cost of crossing the Channel. However, he subsequently negotiated reduced rates for the Newhaven–Dieppe crossing with the ferry operators, promising them many more customers, and declaring in his advertisements for the trip that his arrangements meant that the journey to Paris was quicker and cheaper than travelling to Edinburgh! In 1863, he began to promote touring holidays, whose itineraries were largely based on the two leading guidebooks of the day – Murray and Beidecker. But instead of the leisurely, individualistic and often quite erudite upper-class travellers who followed one of the grand itineraries around Europe, Thomas Cook's tours were fast paced, usually stopping only for one night at any attraction, and his middle-class clients were relatively numerous and less well read. These features sometimes puzzled local hotel and transport staff or the guides who were accustomed to rather different clients, and apparently resented these 'vulgarians'.

Cook continually expanded the range of destinations offered, and was very successful in Egypt. Its antiquities have attracted scholars and travellers throughout recorded history, but with the imminent opening of the Suez Canal, he began to feature Egyptian tours in 1890. He rapidly developed a local infrastructure of tourism businesses (notably a fleet of Nile paddle steamers) to support the high level of interest, and by the end of the decade tourism had become the second most important industry in Egypt after agriculture, and Thomas Cook was referred to as 'the uncrowned King of Egypt'.

Another of his innovations stemmed from his philosophy of providing a full service to his clients and the lack of a developed banking system. As the number of travellers increased, he devised the 'Circular Note', a form of letter of credit which his network of contracted hotels agreed to accept in payment for the services his clients required while travelling. This also offered his clients protection against theft while travelling in remote and sometimes dangerous areas, as well as the certainty that they could pay for their needs. The concept has evolved into the modern traveller's cheque system.

The period when Thomas Cook became successful coincided with the introduction of steam powered trains and ferries, providing greater certainty in transport schedules, as well as increased speed and passenger capacity. Thomas Cook & Co. continues to be a leading travel retailer and supplier of travel services, although at the time of writing it is part of a large banking group.

Based on Swinglehurst (1982) and Brendan (1990).

THE DEVELOPMENT OF MODERN OVERSEAS HOLIDAYS

The predominant modern form of international leisure tourism is the air charter based inclusive holiday, a concept which had its origin in the conditions in Europe following the Second World War. During the war, many servicemen had been engaged in foreign military campaigns, in Europe or further afield, and many had developed an appetite to return in peaceful times to countries and peoples for which they had formed a particular affinity (Milligan, etc.). After the war, military equipment, including aircraft, became surplus to requirement, and could be purchased relatively cheaply. In addition, the war had provided many people with training and experience in aircraft operations. These two factors, the wish to travel and the technical means to do so, provided the basis for the earliest air inclusive tours. The first is said to have been organized by Vladimir Raitz who set up Horizon Holidays in September 1949. His first tour actually took place in May 1950, when 17 professional people travelled to Calvi, in Corsica for a fortnight's holiday which was priced at £32.50. The group flew in a war surplus Dakota and are reported to have stayed in ex-army tents (Davidson, 1989). However, other informal sources have suggested an earlier origin, citing a number of *ad hoc* charter-based overseas holidays to Europe organized by British entrepreneurs and operated during the 1930s.

The coronation of Queen Elizabeth II in 1953 dramatically boosted the ownership of TV and prosperity was gradually increasing in Britain. However, most holidaytaking was still to nearby coastal resorts such as Blackpool or Margate, usually with travel by train, and staying either in guesthouses or holiday camps such as those founded by Butlin in 1936 at Skegness. The concept of holiday organization and style of service at these establishments has been the basis of many humorous postcards and has provided material for music hall comedians and television series. During the 1950s overseas holidays gradually grew in popularity, although only a small minority of the population was able to take advantage of this new form of leisure, as Britain was still enduring postwar austerity including government restrictions on the export of sterling.

THE INTRODUCTION OF JET AIRCRAFT

The concept of overseas holidays received another boost, and its form shifted significantly, with the advent of jet-powered commercial aircraft. Initially developed for scheduled airlines, these aircraft so improved services in terms of speed, load carrying ability, range, reliability and comfort that within three years of the first commercial jet flights by the Comet and the Boeing 707 (in 1958), most of the major airlines sold their pre-jet fleets at knock-down rates. These superseded propeller aircraft were bought cheaply by the emerging African and

Asian national fleets, and by tourism entrepreneurs in Europe. Although many of the new airlines quickly failed, some, such as Eur- avia, succeeded. This became the predecessor to Britannia, the first charter airline to be integrated with a tour operator.

Euravia's boss, Ted Langton, had established Universal Sky Tours after running a UK domestic 'hot-bed' holiday company. The basis of this operation had been a regular coach route from the North of Eng- land to fill beds in Cornwall and Devon left vacant by departing holi- daymakers who returned home on the same coaches. This back-to-back transport operation minimized travel costs while maxi- mizing the tour operator's use of bed spaces, and the concept became the blueprint for his package holiday operations to Spain. Langton initially bought blocks of seats on charter services, but he was dis- appointed with their standards. Instead, he took advantage of the cheap aircraft on the market, buying three Constellations from El Al for £90 000. This price included spares, full overhauls and the cost of reconfiguring the planes into higher density charter seating at a time when the overhauls alone were worth £60 000. Langton's first group flew from Manchester to Palma on Saturday, 5 May 1962. Subsequen- tly,the company was one of three acquired by a Canadian press mag- nate, Lord Thomson. Summing up his reasons for the purchase of Universal Sky Tours, Riviera Holidays and Britannia Airways, Lord Thomson forecast that the group of travel companies had 'substantial growth prospects'.

Several factors were contributing to the increasing interest in over- seas holidays. By the mid 1960s, Britain was enjoying increased pros- perity, longer paid holidays, a greater choice of TV programmes, many featuring foreign cultures and wildlife, wider car ownership and the relaxation of currency export restrictions.

Charter airlines were soon able to contract jet aircraft, and linked with the development of outbound markets and the proliferation of resorts around the Mediterranean, the pace of growth of the holiday industry again quickened. The greater speed and range of jet aircraft, together with their lower seat-mile operating costs (discussed in more detail in a later chapter), increased the spatial distribution of the indus- try. This had two aspects: an increasing number of points of origin, and a greater reach, increasing the range of destinations available. In the mid 1990s, there are now some 22 British airports from which charter flights operate to destinations in Europe, throughout the Mediterra- nean, the Canaries, the Middle and Far East, the Caribbean, the American continent and Australasia (CAA, 1994). CAA data records 2.7 million inclusive tour (IT) holidays were taken in 1970, rising to 6.25 in 1980, and to some 12 million by 1990. Figure 1.1 presents a model illustrating the growing scope and extent of overseas holiday- taking.

Jenner and Smith (1993) have described the central importance of aircharter travel in the following terms:

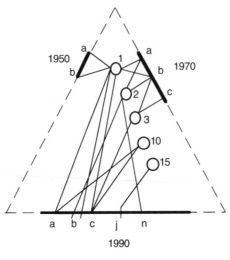

Key :

1, 2, 3 ….	Departure airports (UK)
a, b, c, ….j….n	Destination airports (overseas)
1950, 1970, 1990	Length of 'destination' line indicates relative number of inclusive holiday clients (not to scale). Distance from origin airports indicates relative length of holiday journeys.

Figure 1.1 The growing spatial distribution of charter flights.

Throughout the 1970s and 1980s charter air travel has been the driving force of the North European holiday business. Since 1975 air charter traffic throughout Europe (which is primarily geared to Mediterranean holiday resorts) has exceeded scheduled traffic when measured in revenue/passenger miles (RPMs) … The flow has primarily been from the UK and Germany to Spain, although UK to Greece and Scandinavia and Benelux to Spain are also growing fast.

Case study 1.2 presents a profile of a successful independent tour operator.

CASE STUDY 1.2

The Holiday Club of Upminster

Harry Chandler was highly respected by his peers in the industry, both because of the vision and vigour with which he had developed his company and because of the leadership he gave on industry issues. In 1937, shortly after leaving school, he cycled to Berlin from London, and on his return he persuaded an audience at his old school in the East End that they too could afford a foreign holiday. Subsequently, he organized and accompanied a group to Schwangau, travelling by train and cross-Channel ferry. A week after returning with the first group, he took out another tour. He charged ten guineas (£10.50) for third-class rail travel between London and Augsburg with onward coach travel and full board at the hotel. By booking a party of 20 people he obtained group discounts and free places on the train. The following year, he provided optional second-class travel for a supplement of £2 10s (£2.50). However, by 1938, war was in prospect for Europe, bookings fell off and he could no longer obtain group discounts for the journey.

After war service, he returned to Europe to settle an unpaid prewar hotel bill, and the warmth of his welcome encouraged him to restart the travel business in 1947. He produced a two-page leaflet featuring a line drawing of the hotel Waldheim in Sarnen, but this brochure had to be printed in Germany due to the lack of paper and ink in Britain, a copy being sent to every address on his prewar mailing list of clients. His business plan was to attract 250 customers, and to earn £1 profit on each. The first postwar tours were modelled very closely on his prewar tours, but the European railway system was still in disarray and the journeys were slow and indirect so he arranged for breakfast to be served in the first-class lounge at Basle station. During 1947 he organized eight groups. Most of the clients were women, so when any group was half complete he refused further bookings unless they included some men in the party, thus coincidentally implying that the holiday was popular and thereby encouraging bookings.

In the face of severe currency export restrictions, he introduced a scheme for clients to book excursions using a master ticket system which meant that they were able to pay in advance. This also had the added advantage of earning him commission on his clients' resort activities. One of the popular excursions was a shopping trip to Lucerne, where the holidaymakers visited shops which also paid 10% of sales made to groups.

Encouraged by the success of his first season, Chandler developed a five-year business plan of controlled expansion, adding Weggis in 1948, Ponteressa in 1949, Seefeld in 1950 and Menton in 1951, setting himself a target of 200 to each centre. For 1951, he increased his target to £5 profit per passenger, totalling £5000, an objective which he achieved.

He continued to improve the service he offered, including reserved seats, baggage transferred by porters between trains and ferries, meals provided on trains, and small booklets giving information and tips about the five centres.

In 1953, he provided clients with the option of night flights by BEA, SwissAir and Air France following the introduction of turbocharged aircraft. But in 1956 he gambled on charter flights between London and Basle, using 44-seat Metropolitan aircraft chartered at a cost of

£660 for each rotation. This offered a massive saving over the scheduled-based costings used in the brochure which he had already had printed, but the risk was whether his company could generate sufficient sales to fill the 44 seats. Previously, the average party size was ten per trip, determined by the number of beds booked in the hotel Karwendlehof, Seefeld, and the size of the Alpine postal transfer coach. However, the arrangements proved popular, and in addition, Chandler was also able to sell a combination of rail and air travel at the beginning and end of the season to make use of the otherwise empty first and last flights.

In 1960 Chandler began to charter 90-seater DC6s to the Italian Riviera, and Constellations for routes to France using spare time on aircraft normally flying the Atlantic, enabling him to offer first-class seats for a supplement. He also chartered a Caravelle jet airliner, flying from Heathrow to Basle on Saturday mornings, and to Perpignan or Nice on alternative Saturday afternoons.

He adopted another innovative approach in 1965, sharing a chartered BAC 1-11 with Lord Brothers to Faro. However, this new resort area had a very limited number of hotels, and the series sold slowly. Sidney de Haan, the boss of Saga Holidays, had some villas nearby, and they decided to experiment by extending the season into the winter months. The villas also had private swimming pools, as Renee Chandler explained during an interview broadcast on the *Breakaway* programme in 1995. This was significant because it enabled the company to provide clients with higher standards of accommodation than they had in their own homes, thus enhancing the aspirational appeal of the product.

In 1971, the relaxation of Schedule One (one of the rules governing the air transport industry) enabled the return flight to Faro, with a fortnight's accommodation, to be sold for £37.00, the same as the single fare to Faro. This, and the opening of additional properties in the area, boosted business, and by 1972, Chandler was operating four aircraft into Faro weekly. By the mid 1980s, his company was bringing in 35 000 holidaymakers annually, with aircraft operating at 90% load factors.

After the collapse of the tour operator Fiesta in 1963, Harry Chandler flew to Perpignan in the company of his local MP, Godfrey Langden. He made available the empty seats in his return charter flight to clients of the failed tour operator, while the Chairman of ABTA (Tubby Garner) organized similar support from other member companies. The scandal surrounding Fiesta's failure and the disappointment and financial loss it had caused to many of their constituents led to the issue of holiday companies' operations being raised in the House of Commons with a view to imposing regulations on the industry: '. . . Godfrey Langden was able to tell colleagues in the House of Commons that not all tour companies were tarred with the same brush.' Chandler had earlier proposed a reciprocal booking scheme in which ABTA members agreed only to trade amongst themselves:

1965 Stabiliser. To avoid accusations of creating a closed shop, ABTA had to lower its membership standards, thus avoiding a government-imposed regulatory system on tour operators.

Based on Carter (1985).

THE SIGNIFICANCE AND EFFECTS OF THE MODERN INCLUSIVE HOLIDAY INDUSTRY

Within a span of four decades, the varied forms of international leisure tourism have become established as one of the dominant economic and social activities of the late twentieth century. By the end of the 1980s, British tour operators, retail travel agents, airlines and hotel groups and many other organizations were geared up to produce and sell some 12 million overseas package tours annually. However, by the mid 1990s, the volume of overseas holidays sold by British tour operators had dropped to about 10 million, and a range of problems were becoming apparent.

The key social achievement of the industry is its ability to provide easy and affordable international travel to large numbers of people, thus broadening their experience of the diversity of human culture and other environments and ecologies, in an affordable, leisure-oriented context. But this depends on packaging the elements of travel, accommodation and destination activities. A result of the packaging of travel opportunities is that tourists tend to go to the same places, meeting other holidaytakers from similar backgrounds, and sharing with them their experiences of the cultures and places which they visit because the tour operators (or their ground handling agents) also organize these elements of the holiday (Dulles, quoted in Gee et al., 1984). These factors may insulate or buffer tourists and local residents from full and effective contact with each other (Laws, 1995).

It is the mass nature of inclusive holiday operations which gives rise to four particular consequences with profound effects on destinations. Firstly, their requirement for standardized large-scale accommodation, entertainment, shopping and other amenities has resulted in the development of many very similar, homogenized resorts around the world (Krippendorf, 1987). Secondly, the scale of these activities imposes heavy and often quite localized pressures on the environments and ecology, in some cases modifying these primary features which attracted tourists to the area (Edgington and Edgington, 1990). Thirdly, the presentation of destination areas' culture and history, both in brochure images and during resort-based activities such as dance groups, is often selective and simplified, thus reinforcing stereotypes and sometimes modifying the behaviour of residents (Pi-Sunyer, 1989). The fourth factor, the economic consequences of tourism, is often complex, combining both positive and negative effects through the development of a waged sector, opportunities for small enterprises, and, through the multiplier effect, stimulating wider prosperity. However, tourism also imposes heavy demands for infrastructure, and modifies both the employment and retail sectors (Bull, 1991).

CYCLICAL NATURE OF THE INCLUSIVE HOLIDAY INDUSTRY

Even within its brief history, tourism has exhibited the characteristics of a cyclical industry. The pattern is that a higher level of demand is stimulated by price reductions or the relaxation of controls over international travel (for example, the V card restrictions on exporting currency from Britain were only withdrawn in 1969). In the resultant boom, tour operators charter more planes and book additional hotel rooms. In turn, this stimulates investment in air fleets and in the construction of new hotels or even entire resorts. Local entrepreneurs respond to their free-spending visitors by expanding or adapting existing businesses to meet their needs or by developing new enterprises such as taxi firms, restaurants, shops, guiding or sports instruction bureaux. However, the market clearing mechanism operates imperfectly, and in the short run the expanded aggregate industry supply often exceeds the total demand for holiday services. The industry's typical response to overcapacity is discounting, but this short-term, market-clearing measure has had unfortunate long-term effects, undermining the industry's stability, profitability and probity, as indicated in Case study 1.3. Perhaps more seriously, the opportunistic investment in resort development has spoiled the environments of many holiday destinations.

Furthermore, despite the industry's impressive four-decade record of growth, a variety of factors can occur both in origin and destination markets to depress demand. These include economic retrenchment, strikes, the outbreak of disease or civil unrest and unusual weather conditions. Examples of the latter include seasons when snow cover in the Alps is unusually limited, thus destroying the winter holiday market, or a very hot summer in the Northern origin markets which greatly reduces the demand for overseas sun belt holidays. Table 1.2 summarizes the factors affecting the level of demand for holidays.

CASE STUDY 1.3

Clarksons

Despite its spectacular growth (perhaps paralleled only by car and television ownership, both of which have contributed significantly to the general interest in travel) the holiday industry has already experienced some major company failures, and these have had important results for the subsequent regulation of the industry. One of these was Clarksons, a company founded by Tom Gullick. Another senior industry manager, Colin Collins, has described the growth and subsequent failure of Clarksons:

> Gullick would pound the pavements of the City looking for business house deals. He then chartered a plane to take his clients to the Brussels Trade Fair. Next he introduced day trips to the Dutch bulbfields, which expanded into short tours. These were followed up by another of his loves, three or four day wine tours to France. From there, the natural progression was city breaks but he did not bother selling through agents. Gullick sought out the treasurers of Women's Institutes, charged them with the responsibility of collecting the half crowns from their members and gave them a free seat on the tour for their pains.

In 1967, Clarkson produced its first all-jet brochure to Spain based on a single Dan Air Comet, and at that time it began to sell through the retail travel trade. Part of its success resulted from the innovative racking arrangements it negotiated with retailers; the policy of displaying only selected brochures in return for higher commission has become a major feature of agency agreements.

Clarksons stimulated hotel construction in the resorts it used: between 1969 and 1973 Clarksons added 47 brand new hotels in Spain to their programme. The company guaranteed would-be hoteliers a certain level of capacity as a basis for the local entrepreneurs to obtain finance from bankers in order to start building.

By 1974, when the company failed, it was carrying 750 000 holidaymakers and had its own airline. Tour operator failures were quite common, but the scale of Clarkson's operation had major implications for the industry and was a contributing factor in the introduction of financial protection for holiday company clients.

Table 1.2 Factors affecting the demand for overseas holidays

Encourgaing	Discouraging
Encouraging	
Increasing prosperity	Economic depression
Financial windfalls (e.g. Tessas maturing)	
Earlier retirement	Fear of unemployment
Longer holidays	Weak exchange rates
Lifestyle	Good weather
Destination factors	
Improved access (airport)	Political turmoil, riots
Low cost	Earthquakes or other natural
Good quality of service and standards	disasters
	Expense

IMPERATIVES TOWARDS COMPANY INTEGRATION

Many of the major companies trading during the 1990s had started as small, localized holiday packagers, buying the travel they needed from seat brokers and booking hotels through ground agents or direct in response to customers who booked the holidays which companies had advertised locally. In many cases, these operators had originally been linked to church groups or student societies, but as they grew, the need for greater control of the quality of services led to them taking an ownership stake in the companies supplying services, or forming selective strategic alliances. Bywater (1992) has reported that, of the top 20 holiday companies in Europe, 19 had travel agency businesses and 19 were also involved in outbound tour operating. Most are involved in inbound tourism to their home countries, most are predominantly leisure based, but some are also involved in the business and incentive travel sectors. Eleven have hotels, six have airlines, and most of the others have strategic alliances with an airline. Some own, or have an alliance with, a cruise line. Only two of the top 20 companies do not have international trading and marketing alliances, selling only in one national market. The volatility of this industry is such that, of the top 20 package travel operators in Europe in 1986, one had failed, and eight others had been taken over by 1991. Three of these, Horizon Holidays, Portland Holidays and Blue Sky Holidays, were taken over by Thomson (Bywater, 1994). Table 1.3 indicates the market share of the leading British holiday companies and shows how their seasonal trading strengths differ. As Table 1.4 shows, a high proportion of Europeans take holidays, but the patterns of domestic and foreign holiday-taking differ.

Table 1.3 Market power of leading UK holiday companies

	Year to September 1994	Winter season 1993–4		Summer season 1994	
	Rank	Passengers carried	Rank	Passengers carried	Rank
Thomson	1	1 169 233	1	2 727 017	1
Airtours	2	691 855	2	1 735 503	2
First Choice Travel	3	462 034	3	1 042 269	3
Avro	4	271 838	4	703 915	4
Iberotravel	5	146 785	6	514 296	5
Unijet	6	189 981	5	397 591	7
Cosmosair	7	128 186	7	406 346	6
Best Travel	8	64 544	12	317 926	8
First Choice	9	82 688	8	211 305	9
Sunset Holidays	10	39 985	19	171 559	10
Kuoni	11	81 012	9	91 767	13
Crystal	19	70 162	10	38 327	30

Source: CAA (1994)

OBSTACLES IN STUDYING THE INCLUSIVE HOLIDAY INDUSTRY

The rate of change in the industry, its comparative newness, the high degree of competition and the ease with which competitors can copy any product or service innovations account for the difficulty of obtaining accurate current data from tour operators and retail travel agencies. This is also a consequence of the relatively small size of even the major tour operators in comparison with other industries, despite the scale and significance of the tourism industry.

> Only a minority are listed companies, and only a handful of others voluntarily comply with international accounting standards . . . This is an industry where the major companies are quite small in international terms – TUI, the biggest tour operator in Europe, is barely large enough to be included in the list of Germany's top 200 companies . . . More than half, including 11 with annual sales in excess of ECU 300 million – do not normally make their annual accounts publicly available.
>
> (Bywater, 1994)

Many factors have contributed to the development of the industry, including the development of technology and the vision of entrepreneurs linking these new business opportunities with an evolving market for inclusive holidays. As it has increased in size, significance and sophistication, the need for self-regulation and legislation to control the excesses of the industry has become apparent. The discussion so far is summarized in Table 1.5 which shows the key steps in the evolution of British inclusive holidays.

INCLUSIVE HOLIDAYS AND OTHER FORMS OF TOURISM

Tourism embraces a wide range of motivations for travel, including recreation, business and visiting friends and relatives (Holloway, 1994). The main elements of the industry, transport and accommodation, are utilized for a variety of purposes, while the destination-based entertainment and catering provision can generally be enjoyed by locals and

Table 1.5 Key steps in the evolution of inclusive holidays

Period	Technological developments	Entrepreneurship	Market conditions	Regulations
First Elizabethan			Queen Elizabeth encourages travel by leading scholars to study foreign conditions	
C18th		Publication of *A study of the curative effects of Sea Water* by William Russell.	Developing interest in inland, later seaside spas.	
C19th	Improvements to roads and stage services, followed by development of rail network throughout Europe. 1820s, first regular cross-Channel ferry service.	1839 Samual Cunard founds British and North American Steam Packet Co. 1841 Thomas Cook's first train excursion, Leicester to Loughborough. 1851 Six million visitors to the Great Exhibition in London. 1862 Brighton receives 132 000 visitors by train in one day. 1855 Thomas Cook's first Paris Exhibition tours. 1867 Thomas Cook issued hotel coupons and organizes visits for 75 000 clients to Paris exhibition. 1872 Thomas Cook takes first group of tourists around the world. 1879 First Continental tour organized by Cycling Tourist Club. 1988 Polytechnic Touring Association organizes cruises to Norway (£8 8s) 1898 Henry Lunn organizes a party to Chamonix.	Slowly increasing awareness of leisure travel opportunities among middle classes.	Factories Act 1833 gives young workers eight half-day holidays per year.
Pre-Second World War	Development of international phone and telegraph systems. Early growth of air transportation. 1931 Southern Railways introduce SS *Auto Carrier* on cross-Channel service. 1934 Erich Korstam's first T bar ski lift increases the number of runs a skier can make in a day by a factor of five.	Henry Lunn formed Public Alpine Ski Club, the travel organization for the Free Churches, and later the Hellenic Travellers' club specializing in study visits to classical sites in Greece. 1922 Cunard's *Laconia* undertakes first world cruise. 1937 Butlin's Skegness camp opens.		

Period				
1945–1960		1949 Vladimir Raitz takes 35 clients to Sardinia by DC3 for 35 guineas each. 1950 Horizon's first charter holiday to Corsica. 1952 Tourist class fares offered on scheduled transatlantic flights.	Post war austerity. Coronation: growing TV ownership and interest in overseas travel. 3% of population have travelled abroad. Louis Ricard exhibits first bikini in Paris fashion show in 1946, named after The South Pacific atoll used for nuclear tests.	Vladimir Raitz obtains ARTAC licence for Palma. Sterling travel allowance gradually increases from £40 to £250. 1959 airlines allowed to market chater fares.
1960s	American Express charge card introduced. Boeing 737 operational.	1963 Caledonian and Donaldson Line introduced first inclusive tour to US (£149.65) Fiesta collapses. 1963 Hapimag introduces timeshare concept. 1965 International Thomson Organization, seeking cash flow, buys several tour operators. Short city breaks introduced by Time Off and Travel Scene.	Increasing demand for overseas holidays. More people travel to/from UK by air than by sea.	TOSG discusses bonding holiday companies. 1965 Stabiliser introduced. 1969 Currency control removed. 1969 Development of Tourism Act creates statutory Tourist Boards.
1970s	Increasing number of airports able to handle jets located near major resorts.	1971 Thomson introduced £13 weekend packages to Majorica. First price war between Clarksons and Thomson reduces rpofit to £1.50 per head. 1973 Court Line purchases Horizon and subsequently collapses (1974) causing 100 000 holidaymakers to loose their deposits. 1974 Jan and Cristel DeHaan incorporate RCI, the timeshare exchange company. Thomson, Intasun and Horizon each create own charter airline. Ilkeston CoOp introduces 10% voucher discount, leading to ending of RPM and the development of added value offers.	1970 2.7 million passengers use charter flights for their holidays.	1973 *Jarvis v Swan* establishes the liabiliyt of the industry for 'general damages'. 1975 ATRF established as existing £3.5m bond insufficient to cover Court Line. £2 per client levy, subsequently reduced to £1.
180s	Twin jets licensed for long-haul routes, making Far East, Caribbean and Australia viable holiday destinations.	1980 Harry Goodman promotes Miami holidays for £200. 1982 Collapse of Laker. Second price war. Fly free Caribbean cruises introduced. Package holidays increasingly commoditized, reducing prices and quality. 1985 Thomson declares at the Sorrento ABTA convention, 'We will not be undersold'.	1980 6.25m charter passengers. Traditional 70% summer holidays sold by end of January gradually eroded by price reductions for late bookings.	1982 Stabiliser ruled to be in public interest.
1990s		1991 Collapse of ILG, second largest UK tour operator. Gulf war. Third price war.	1990, m charter passengers. 1995 m charter passengers.	1992 Package Travel, Package Holidays and Package Tours Regulations.

domestic visitors. Figure 1.2 shows some of the overlapping features of the various elements of the tourism industry, and points out that the destination areas where both general tourist and inclusive holidaymakers activities take place should also be understood from the perspective of the areas where residents live.

Hunt and Layne (1991) have examined the problems of definition which cause confusion in the American tourism industry. Their purpose was to clarify the definitions of tourism used by US state and city administrators. They cite other writers (notably Smith, 1988), who regarded 'a single, comprehensive and widely accepted definition of tourism – [as] beyond hope of realization. Practitioners must learn to accept the myriad of definitions and to understand and respect the reasons for those definitions.' Even the more limited field of the inclusive holiday sector of tourism raises problems of definition, and many of the terms used in everday discussion, by the industry's managers and by academics lack clarity of meaning. This difficulty reflects the rather overlapping and fuzzy nature of the concepts and businesses practices in this new and quite dynamic industry. The meanings of terms used in this book are defined on their first use, and for convenience of reference, they are presented together in a glossary at the end of the book

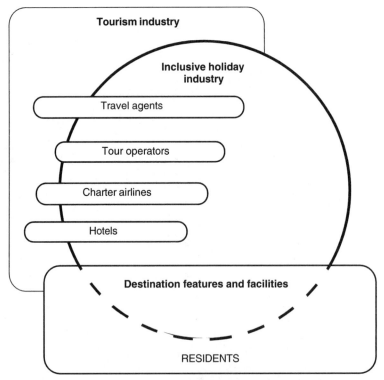

Figure 1.2 Tourism and the inclusive holiday industry.

which also shows related terms together with variants used to avoid repetition.

Hooper (1995) has distinguished six forms of travel package: fully inclusive packages comprising travel plus accommodation and selected ground services; escorted services when a group is accompanied by a guide; theme packages which include a special event; add-on pricing in which an airfare is sold together with related services such as hotel accommodation at a favourable rate; joint promotions where travel is sold with unrelated services; and independent packages allowing the traveller to choose his or her own departure date and the components of the holiday. This book is mainly (but not exclusively) concerned with the first and second forms noted by Hooper.

RECENT AND FUTURE DEVELOPMENTS

The rate of development of the industry, and the scope of its operations, has exhibited a number of steps related mainly to the introduction of new technology. Recently, it again picked up pace when the more economical twin engined jets were licensed to fly routes which took them more than 90 minutes from an airport, thus enabling them to operate long-haul flights. This has begun to open up the Far East, America, the Caribbean and Australia to European markets for inclusive holidays based on charter flights and to reduce their prices. While it is risky to predict the future, it seems likely that the next major developments to affect the industry will come from the increasing power and sophistication of other forms of technology, as widespread commercial and domestic access to computerization and telecommunications will perhaps have the effect of 'unpackaging' the way that inclusive holidays are currently presented.

The stereotypical model of an inclusive holiday as very similar to all others, with a coordinated pattern of activities arranged for participants by the operator, is being superseded by greater variety and differentiation between holidays, by an emphasis on service quality and by a growing concern with managing the effects of the industry on destinations (Krippendorf, 1987; Poon, 1993). Bywater (1992) argues that the underlying reasons for increased individuality in holiday arrangements on the demand side are a growing confidence amongst holidaymakers about overseas travel and consumers' wishes for greater differentiation in their purchases. The suppliers' responses include offering clients greater choice, more variety and the opportunity to undertake a wide variety of specialized activities.

FURTHER READING

Cooper, C., Fletcher, J., Gilbert, D. and Wanhill, S. (1993) *Tourism Principles and Practice*, Pitman, London.
Krippendorf, J. (1987) *The Holiday Makers*, Heinemann, London.

Moynahan, B. (1983) *Fools Paradise*, Pan Books, London.
Swinglehurst, E. (1982) *Cook's Tours: The Story Of Popular Travel*, Blandford Press, Poole.

Swinglehurst (1982) provides an informed and entertaining review of the history of Thomas Cook, together with insights into the operation of inclusive holidays. Moynahan (1983) raises many of the practical and ethical issues confronting the industry which are analysed in Krippendorf (1987), while Cooper, Fletcher and Wanhill (1993) provide a wide ranging introductory analysis of the importance and functioning of the tourism industry.

SUGGESTED EXERCISES

1. Interview an elderly relative, and write a report contrasting their recollections of early holiday experiences with your own. Explain the differences.
2. Interview the manager or proprietor of a long-established locally based holiday company (travel retailer or tour operator) and write an account of the way the industry's ways of operating have changed.
3. Consult the back issues of a local newspaper or similar source in a tourist destination and discuss the changing impacts of tourist activity reported in the area.

Analysing the inclusive holiday industry

PART
2

> Theories and models provide an abstract way of visualizing complex situations, and they also offer a framework to analyse the interactions between the elements which make up a functioning system. A variety of approaches are available to aid in understanding the holiday industry. In part, this is the result of the varying backgrounds in management, economics, anthropology, geography, psychology and so on which researchers have brought to this relatively new area of study. In a more fundamental way, this diversity also reflects the complexity of the industry, and of the wider tourism phenomenon of which it is a part.
>
> Chapter 2 examines the relationships between companies providing various elements of the services needed by the inclusive holiday industry, while Chapter 3 opens the important discussion of how their interdependence affects the quality of service which holidaymakers and others experience from the system's functioning.

Systems, network and stakeholder perspectives on the inclusive holiday industry

2

INTRODUCTION

The inclusive holiday industry consists of several discrete elements, notably the various accommodation providers and other destination-based businesses, transport, tour operators and travel retailers. The success of the industry depends on how effectively they work together to create satisfying holiday experiences for their clients. The industry's success can be considered from the perspectives of each organization involved in supplying elements to the industry, and from that of residents in destination areas. This chapter argues that in many of these respects, the industry must be regarded as immature, since the major tour operators and the chains of retail travel agents often fail to pay sufficient regard to the advantages of cooperating with other elements of the industry for mutual benefit, and focus instead on short-term competition with other companies, to the detriment of all but a few.

The purpose of this chapter is to provide readers with a fuller and more systematic perspective on the industry, enabling the interrelated nature of its members' contributions to be more fully appreciated.

THEORETICAL MODELS OF THE INCLUSIVE HOLIDAY INDUSTRY

Concepts are the building blocks for models, but although any particular concept presents the analyst with an ordered view of the subject under scrutiny from a particular perspective, it has limitations. Two in particular need to be noted. In the first place, a model is a simplification. It generalizes from reality and does not provide a complete consideration of all factors relevant to each situation, rather it stresses the common elements which are found in different situations. Secondly, any model, theory or concept is based on assumptions. Many of these can be made explicit, or can be teased out of the argument offered, but others are deeply imbedded in the cultural values from which the researcher constructed his (or her) theory. As such, these assumptions are seldom visible, either to researchers or to others who read and attempt to apply any theory, because they often share a similar cultural background.

Models such as those presented in this book can be used in one of two main ways, either to explain events which have occurred, or to predict what may occur in the future. This match to reality is the traditional test of a model's strength, and as weaknesses or limitations are revealed, the need for a new theory or model is demonstrated, and so theory progresses to deeper levels of understanding and application.

THE BASIC HOLIDAY MODEL

An inclusive holiday has three key elements: return travel, accommodation and a range of activities at their destination for the vacationers. The industry provides the services of packaging and distributing holiday products; its functions are often described in terms of supply and distribution channels in which tour operators select and package the great variety of tourism services available at destinations, for sale through travel agencies to their ultimate clients.

This can be illustrated by adapting the standard model of wholesalers and distributors linked in a channel which has typically been applied to fast-moving consumer goods or manufactured products (Bucklin, 1967). Figure 2.1 shows that individuals have the choice of making their reservations direct with the hotel and airline of their choice, or they can use the expertise and facilities of a full service travel agent to undertake their bookings. The alternative method of purchasing a holiday, now used by some 10 million people annually in Britain, is to buy a packaged holiday. In this case, the tour operator contracts for the seperate elements of a holiday and customers have the choice of making their booking direct with the tour operator or through the services of a travel agency. Increasingly, these are specializing in selling selected inclusive holidays, and are therefore sometimes referred to as 'holiday shops'.

POWER RELATIONSHIPS AND THE GROWTH OF THE INCLUSIVE HOLIDAY INDUSTRY

The organizational members of the supply and distribution channel contribute to the value chain of any industry (Porter, 1980) in several

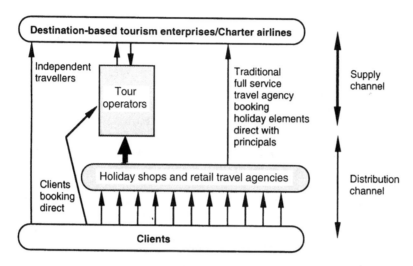

Figure 2.1 Holiday industry channel organization.

ways, but together they bridge the distance and communications gaps which separate producers from their consumers. Through their brochures and high street presence, tour operators and travel agents provide readily available information about a wide range of destinations spanning the globe, while airlines, hotels and tour operators together gain a detailed and rapid understanding of consumers' fast-changing holiday preferences through the information requests and bookings which travel agents undertake for their clients.

However, as a subsequent chapter will show, distribution channels are often characterized by an imbalance of power, and they tend to be dominated by particular types of company. In the inclusive holiday sector it is generally the vertically integrated groups which have determined decisions about the specifications, supply and pricing of holidays. Their power is the result of their relative size and sophistication, in relation to both suppliers and distributors. Their skills in packaging and promoting the concept of inclusive holidays has enabled them to dominate many destinations because of the large volume of business which they have been able to supply on a regular basis. This has stimulated expansion of resorts, hotel building and small-scale entrepreneurial investment in tourism-related enterprises. The end result is that these areas' economies have become dependant on tourism. Similarly, most travel retailers are dependant on tour operators for products to sell, and also rely on their greater promotional and advertising power to create the demand which brings clients to their holiday shops seeking brochures and holidays to book.

INTERDEPENDANCE IN THE INCLUSIVE HOLIDAY INDUSTRY

The inclusive holiday industry is really rather more complex than suggested by the channel model (Figure 2.1), and the approaches which are examined in this book emphasize the significance of the network of relationships between companies which underpins the holiday industry system. This also recognizes that it is the tour operator whose business skills bring together the varied elements which together constitute an inclusive holiday. But, as a later chapter will demonstrate, it is the consumer whose experience of the holiday determines whether the tour operator has succeeded in unifying the separate elements so as to provide a satisfying holiday. A particular problem worth noting at this point is that the varied nature of tourists (their differing backgrounds, experience, interests and holiday motivations) imply that they are seeking varied benefits, and consequently it is unlikely that everyone taking a particular holiday will experience the same level of overall satisfaction, nor will they experience the individual elements in the same way.

Additional insights into the complexity and the dynamics of the relationships between inclusive holiday industry participants can be obtained by adopting the theoretical perspectives of network and alliance theory or relationship marketing (Gummesson, 1994; McKenna, 1991), and by viewing the holiday industry systemically. Gummesson examined the question: 'What do you learn if you look at marketing as relationships, networks and interaction, and what can you do with this knowledge?' He argued that a relationship exists between 'at least two parties who are in contact with each other', and that 'networks appear when the relationships become many, complex and difficult to overview.'

As will become apparent in the case study of RCI, the timeshare exchange company, with which this book concludes, the approach can lead to the selective development of the most effective working relationships with resources being invested in their increased efficiency, and can operate through personal contact and through information technology.

Gummesson further points out that even the most powerful companies such as IBM cannot 'develop, manufacture and market their products and services on their own. They enter into alliances with customers, competitors and middlemen, and others to gain time and cost advantages and to access markets. The corporations add to each other's resources for the benefit of all stakeholders.' He contrasts this perspective on management philosophies with the more familiar idea of competition: 'Competition means winning over somebody, even destroying others, showing who is the biggest, the best ... The fight has a value in itself. Short-term greed may overrule long-term survival.'

The network of relationships and dependancies which link travel retailers, tour operators, charter airlines, hotels and other destination-

Table 2.1 Interdependencies in the inclusive holiday system

System member	Destination	Tour operator	Principals	Travel agent
Destination		Tour operator provides regular batches of visitors	Quality of visitors' experiences depends on standards of hotels etc.	Staff knowledge of and enthusiasm for destination can be critical factor in clients' choice
Tour operator	Depends on primary features (climate, scenery, culture, infrastructure). Ability to exploit these commercially depends on the range and quality of tourism services offered		Major expense for tour operator; also critical in ensuring customer expectations met	Sales agent directing high street clients to specific tour operators' products
Principals – hotels and airlines	Depend on destinations for primary appeals and for social or technical infrastructure, such as sewers roads, educational standards of staff and airport facilities	Tour operators provide flows of customers throughout season to specific destinations at agreed prices		Generally minimal for holiday products as their services are embodied in tour operators' products
Travel agent	Depends on destinations for briefings, staff familiarization tours and point-of-sales materials	Dependant on tour operators for creating a market through advertising, for staff training, brouchures and CRS for sales		Depends on hotels and airlines for sales support and staff training

based interests is illustrated in Table 2.1, although it should be noted that both competition and collaboration are integral features of the inclusive holiday industry.

DIRECTION AND CONTROL IN THE INCLUSIVE HOLIDAY INDUSTRY

Although some dominant companies have emerged in the inclusive holiday industry, notably the large vertically integrated groups, there is no strong leadership of the industry. The Association of British Travel Agents (ABTA) represents the industry's interests to government, provides a framework for equitable relationships between tour operators and travel agents (its two main membership categories), and mediates between them and their customers as a case study in Chapter 5 demonstrates. However, it does not represent all elements of the industry, nor does it offer a vision for its future development. A similar criticism could be levelled against most, if not all, industries, but in the case of tourism it has a particular poignancy. The lack of agreement on issues, priorities, policies and responsibility poses a threat to travel agencies, tour operators and destinations. Table 2.2 indicates how the leadership roles which classical management theory defined for organizations might be applied to the inclusive holiday industry. The points raised here are discussed later in this book.

SYSTEMS THEORY

Systems theory emphasizes the interdependency of the elements which together make up the industry, notably the tour operators, travel retailers, airlines, hotels and destination organizations and communities (Mill and Morrison, 1985; Leiper, 1990; Laws, 1996). Systems analysis also focuses attention on the consequences for all stakeholders and the environment within which the industry operates of the way the system functions, and the results of any policy or operational changes. These approaches highlight as critical issues for examination the mutual dependency of all organizations in a holiday system, rather than the legitimate but lower order issue of competition between individual member companies.

In order to provide a framework for the examination of the complex relationships within the holiday industry, a systems method is now adopted in this book. The origins of systems thinking lie in the biologist Bertolanffy's insight into the complexity of living organisms. He

Table 2.2 Classical leadership roles – application to the inclusive holiday industry

Role	General meaning	Application to the inclusive holiday industry
Plan	Forecasting and planning action	Capacity driven by aircraft fleet size (international) and by hotel space (destination)
Organize	Developing people and resources	Limited policies, generally at a local level or for particular sectors of the industry
Command	Leadership and motivation	Strong in major companies and some destinations
Coordination	Harmonizing plans and resources	Limited, but some efforts to coordinate the elements in the holiday industry system
Control	Ensure conformance to the vision and plan	Subject to external and short-term factors such as economic, political and weather conditions which affect both trading policy and results

Based on Fayol (1930).

argued that an organism's functioning is best understood in the context of the conditions it exists in, while the inputs it needs for its existence may be set against what it contributes to the ecology of which it is a part in order to obtain a measure of its efficiency. Over time, the organic system also grows and develops, reaching a level of maturity at which homeostasis operates to maintain its optimum size and operating efficiency, until eventually it declines, atrophies and dies.

The systems approach has since been applied to social organizations such as businesses. The method brings a range of advantages to scientific enquiry including the abandonment of one-dimensional thinking, and it facilitates a multidisciplinary perspective reflecting the superordinate systems within which phenomena such as tourism occur. These include economic, social, technological, political and ecological contexts to tourism management decisions. It is arguably superior to the more common scientific approaches which are concerned with the analysis of a situation by breaking it down into its component parts. In contrast, the systemic approach is interested in the interactions between its components, and is particularly relevant when people are a significant part of the operation.

Kaspar (1989) advocated the systems approach in analysing tourism because of its advantages over other methodologies. He pointed out that a theoretical image of reality can be gained in three ways: by reductionistic, holistic or systemic approaches. Reductionism dissects a whole entity into separate, isolated units. That method places the focus on the elements of a system rather than the interrelationships between them, but is characteristic of many introductory tourism texts and can be found also in more advanced academic and management research. Holism represents the contrary approach; it regards the whole as non-separable and therefore non-analysable. Kaspar quoted Kuhne's view that 'these limitations are sufficient to abandon both approaches and to search for a perspective which enables one to grasp the peculiarities of the whole and the specific properties of the parts at the same time.'

A system is therefore merely an ordered set of components; each component is affected by being part of the system: its behaviour is constrained by the needs and conditions of its setting, and the entire system is affected if one component changes. Taking a view of a system is to recognize particular systems boundaries; setting a clear boundary around the system under investigation emphasizes the inputs and outputs for investigation. Outside the boundary of any system are a range of other entities which influence its activities, and which are affected by them: the system is itself part of the environment for other systems. The systems view of any organization suggests that it exists to carry out the activities and processes related to achieving its aims, and that it controls its activities and communicates with the environment about it in order to obtain resources and attract support for its products.

Business organizations can be seen as purposeful social systems, taking resources from their environment and using the skills of their employees to produce outputs to satisfy their clients, and the organization's own objectives. Although the systems approach can be applied to the separate operating units of the industry such as tour operators, travel retailers, airlines, hotels, and tourist attractions at destinations, it is at its most powerful when focused on the complex issues of destinations (Laws, 1995) or, as in the case of this book, the entire industry. A systems approach enables the goals, organization, resources and output decisions of management to be examined, in order to understand the effects of their decisions on other groups affected by the organization's activities. Constraints such as competition and regulatory environments may also be studied to gain an understanding of how levels of efficiency and operational standards are brought about in the industry.

Three stages can be identified in general models of system processes. Inputs are required in the form of equipment, skills, resources and clients' demands for the industry's outputs, holiday packages. But a system's outputs also include the profit and work which it creates and the effects of its operations on other interests, notably those of the destination's residents. The intermediate stage of systems analysis connecting inputs with outputs is concerned with the internal processes whereby organizations transform those inputs into outputs. The various components or elements of the system are interlinked, and the efficiency of the system operating within its boundary will be affected by changes to any of the elements of which it is composed. Figure 2.2 shows how these systems concepts can be applied to the inclusive holiday industry.

The holiday industry system consists of elements (or subsystems) in the form of natural or primary destination attractions such as climate, supported by secondary features (Jansen-Verbeke, 1991). The secondary elements include hotels, guest houses and the range of attractions, shopping and catering in the city centre. Additional elements are the information services available to visitors, catering, and car and coach parking. Destination inputs are managerial and technical skills including recognition in the local planning process of the need for a positive framework for tourism management leading to a continuity of approach, investors' resources, and the expectations and attitudes of its tourists and residents.

The model recognizes the significance of external factors such as changing competitive conditions or improvements to the transport network. The method focuses attention on the outcomes of the system's functioning for particular stakeholder groups during a given time period. Evaluation of the outcomes against the costs of inputs and policy objectives provides the basis of feedback, thus introducing a future-time dimension to the model.

A further level of systems analysis focuses on the various subsidiary systems which contribute to an organization's overall functioning. For effective management two aspects need to be clearly understood: the effects on outputs of any change to its inputs, and secondly the ways in which its processes are organized and controlled. Control over the quality and consistency of a system's outputs requires regular monitoring of its products, and an effective feedback channel between the monitoring and decision-making subsystems within the organization. Efficiency in the system's operation can be evaluated by measuring outputs against the inputs required to produce them, by examining the quality of the outputs and by considering the way each process contributes to the overall service. Systems theory argues that the efficiency of an industry's operations will be affected by changes to any of the elements of which it is composed. For effective management, three aspects need to be clearly understood:

- the effects on outputs of any change to its inputs;
- the ways in which its internal subsystems and processes are linked;
- how the subsystems and processes are controlled.

Overall, a judgement can be made about the stage of development, or maturity, of the industry. It is the opinion of this author that the inclusive holiday industry is at present immature, as it neglects (with notable exceptions) the interests of destination residents, while few of

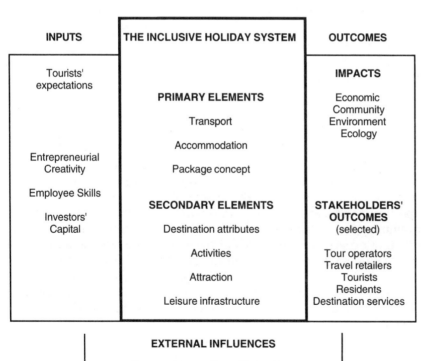

Figure 2.2 General model of the inclusive holiday industry system.

its member organizations earn a realistic profit, either on their investment or their turnover.

SOFT SYSTEMS THEORY

Kirk (1995) has pointed out that systems theory has traditionally been applied to 'hard' engineering situations with clear and unique outcomes, but notes that the socio-technical features of services also benefit from systems insights when these are expanded to include human ('soft') issues where there is less certainty (Kirk, 1995). The interdependency of the elements which together make up the holiday industry can best be understood from the perspective of a soft, open, systems model (Checkland and Scholes, 1990). The 'systems' aspect of this type of model has the advantages of focusing attention on all the major inputs needed to provide tourism services, and on the outcomes of tourism processes for all groups with interests in the industry. The 'soft' feature of the approach is concerned with the interactions of tourists, staff and residents in tourist destination areas. The model is 'open' because it recognizes the legislative, cultural and technological contexts for tourism processes. A further aspect highlighted by this analytical framework is the consequences of tourism for the area's environment. On a theoretical level, systems theory provides a way of focusing the insights from many social sciences on tourism industry processes and their consequences: Krippendorf (1987) has pointed out that the relationships between ecological and other effects and the phenomenon of mass tourism 'cannot be identified if they are viewed from a narrow multidisciplinary angle.'

STAKEHOLDERS IN THE INCLUSIVE HOLIDAY SYSTEM

Viewing tourism as a system, as shown in Figure 2.2, gives the advantage of identifying people involved in it: the managers, staff, residents and tourists, and the systems model provides a framework to understand the effects on these stakeholders of the system's operation. The appropriateness and quality of the tourism system can be assessed by examining the outcomes for each stakeholder group, that is the satisfaction experienced by clients of the system; the remuneration, work satisfaction and career development of staff; the profit and growth of the system which can be regarded as proprietor and managerial outcomes; and the benefits or problems which the industry creates locally which are the outcomes for residents. Table 2.3 illustrates these points.

The holiday system model focuses particular attention on the role of management in matching an organization's processes to the needs of the various groups with a stake in the tourism industry, stressing the many organizations involved in supplying tourism services, as well as the interests of holidaymakers, and tour operator, travel agency and

Table 2.3 General stakeholder outcomes of the inclusive holiday industry

Stakeholder	Positive outcomes	Possible negative outcomes
Holidaymakers	Relaxation; new and pleasurable experiences	Stress from delayed flights; disappointment with features of the destination, accommodation weather, other holidaymakers
Tour operators	Profitable business	Complaints from clients; operational difficulties
Travel agents	Profitable business	Complaints from clients on return profit
Hoteliers	Profitable business	Low contract room rates; rowdy groups
Destination residents	Improvements to economy; work opportunities; development of infrastructure and environment	Congestion; increased prices, noise, aldulteration

hotel staff, managers and proprietors. An additional and fundamental issue highlighted by soft systems analysis is the impact of tourism on destination residents, an issue considered in detail in Laws (1995).

TOURISM GROWTH AND DESTINATION DEVELOPMENT

The tourism industry, of which the inclusive holiday industry is a part, offers many opportunities for entry, both to entrepreneurs and staff. In part, this results from the diversity and speed of development of the tourism industry but it also reflects two related trends. The vision which drives the continuing development of tourism services offers scope for entrepreneurial initiatives, while the increasing scale of tourism operations provides a major source of new employment in many countries. The organizations supplying tourism services include public and private enterprises, and range from large to small in scale. Entrepreneurial opportunities to establish a business can be found in most sectors of tourism, but small-scale companies are most common in catering, consultancy, attractions management and travel retailing or tour operating.

However, through enabling the regular arrival of large numbers of people with money to indulge their interests and few constraints on their time, the holiday industry also creates a significant opportunity climate in the destination areas. Many smaller-scale businesses are established when their entrepreneurial founders see a coincidence of market openings with their own skills and interests and are able to exploit these on their own financial resources. Others, perhaps people retiring or made redundant from a career but therefore with a small amount of capital, see an opportunity to relocate to an attractive area with which they may already be familiar as tourists. This has a number of important consequences for destination communities, including changes in local retailing, higher prices, the squeezing out of local staple products and colourful, noisy street outlets.

Many start-up enterprises have a short life because their managers lack the resources or the skills needed, and small resort-based businesses are generally unable to significantly influence the flow of business, depending on attracting people who are already visiting. A study of the formation and operation of tourism enterprises in Cornwall found that a major feature of the tourist industry there was its fragmentation into many small independent units dependent on marked seasonal peaks in July and August (Shaw and Williams, 1987). The authors commented: 'The success of tourism depends ultimately on the efficiency with which local businesses respond to new situations.' They found that, in the hotel and guest house sector, 60% of establishments had new owners and 28% had only been in operation for two years at the time of the survey.

> Family and personal savings were the two major sources of capital ... This pattern of capital formation ... is suggestive of firms being controlled by relatively inexperienced business people who may have little or no conception of the need to draw up management strategies for their businesses ... although 35% had some professional or vocational training, mostly related to former activities [rather than] managing a tourist business. Less than 8% had held previous occupations relating to tourism.
>
> (Shaw and Williams, 1987)

OTHER COMPANIES SUPPLYING TOURISM SERVICES

The limitations of a reductionist approach to the management of the holiday industry can be seen particularly clearly in the consequences of tour operations for other members of both the supply and distribution channels. As a subsequent chapter will show in more detail, the issues for channel members (Bucklin, 1967) are about dominance and control. Retail travel agents have traditionally been regarded as weak because of their small size relative to the tour operators and their reliance on the tour operator for products to sell, although they are developing ways of gaining influence, for example by refusing to rack the brochures of tour operators paying low commission, or those about which many complaints are received.

An aspect of competition leading to changes in channel dominance is the effect of discounting in favouring the larger companies, particularly the multiple-branch retail agents. 'Discounting advantages are quickly negated by competitive response, but then there is no doubt that multiples take bookings from independent agents. Through acquisition of extra retail outlets and through heavy discounting, the major multiples are steadily increasing their share of business' (Heape, 1994).

Discussing the advantages of larger companies, Heape also pointed to the fact that the tour operators who own retailers do not pay extra commission on the sales made by their retail partners. 'Therefore their products can be priced very competitively compared to other operators.'

Traditionally, economists have argued that incumbent firms in a market gain advantages from insurmountably high fixed costs barring entry to a market. Baumol and Willig (1981) defined entry barriers as 'anything that requires an expenditure by a new entrant into an industry, but requires no equivalent cost upon an incumbent'. Another feature of contestable markets is that exit costs are minimal as other businesses, incumbents or new entrants, will be willing to buy the business assets. Price discounting provides the package holiday with a tool for structural changes by undermining the profitability of some companies to the point where it is no longer viable for them to stay in the industry. A director of Airtours reported that 'I have about 20 proposals a week land on my desk from companies who want us to purchase them because they know we have lots of money and are ambitious' (Skidmore, 1995). Sheldon (1986), discussing the relationship between industry structure and pricing policy, noted a polarization in the industry, with a few large firms and many small ones, and pointed to the relative short lives of many small companies. However, several large tour operators have failed, and many mergers or acquisitions have been recorded in the industry.

OTHER DESTINATION EFFECTS

The effects of tourist activity on the areas that become tourist destinations must be one of the primary focuses of attention in considering the maturity and functioning of the holiday industry. Underlying the success of the industry is the fact that one of the primary motivators for travel is the intrinsic appeal of the areas visited, but this is often obscured by the range of advertising appeals and the price-based marketing which together have resulted in a much lower emphasis by consumers on destination preferences in favour of the current 'best deal'. Against this is another fact: the increasing resistance found in some areas to the development of mass market tourism in their localities. Rationales for the resistance may be found in religious beliefs, in the fear of damage to unique cultures or environments, and in a reluctance to see the profitable businesses which more selective tourism has supported undermined by a new wave of low-cost high-volume operators. Figure 2.3 illustrates some of the contrasting views of residents and tourists of a destination area.

More attention must therefore be focused on the fact that pricing decisions by tour operators and travel retailers have consequences not only for the companies which take them, but also for their partners, the hotels and destinations who are the principal suppliers of the holiday

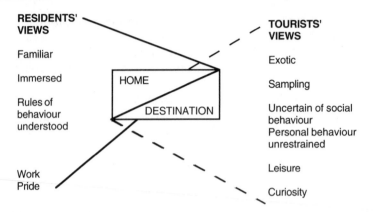

Figure 2.3 Contrasts between tourists' and residents' attitudes to a destination. Source: Laws (1995).

experience. The rapid growth of the industry during the 1960s and 1970s resulted in a proliferation of hotel developments, particularly in the Mediterranean resorts. Many of these hotels were built to low design criteria, and they were often aesthetically unappealing in the context of idyllic settings. As the hotel stock grew, and as more destinations became accessible, tour operators were able to drive contract room rates down. The cumulative effect of repeated seasons of low contract rates paid by tour operators to hotels has eroded their ability to improve standards of service or invest in upgraded facilities, but this period has coincided with a period of increasing consumer awareness (Morgan, 1994; Vellas and Becherel, 1995). More effective deployment of consumer rights has alerted media attention to the dissatisfaction and complaints arising from low standards in holiday accommodation. Hoteliers have responded by showing a preference to deal with tour operators who do not exert such severe cost controls, notably those from other European countries. This has given rise to the phenomenon of one set of guests in a hotel being afforded preferential treatment in terms of better rooms or a more varied dinner menu, further exacerbating the dissatisfaction.

Hoteliers have also responded by adopting overbooking policies (Lamnert *et al.*, 1989), because the slender margins on room revenue leads to a need to sell all available capacity and to take the maximum advantage of the additional sources of revenue from clients, such as bar sales. Overbooked hotels result in the need for tour operators to switch their clients, often after arrival in the resort, to alternative hotels, and often results in complaints or claims for compensation by disgruntled clients.

A number of stages can be postulated linking the inclusive holiday industry with destination developments. After tour operators and destination organizations stimulate interest in a particular destination, its existing facilities for tourists come under pressure from increased demand. This increased rate of local tourist activity acts as an economic signal, stimulating investment in an increased supply of such facilities as accommodation. However, in the absence of effective fore-casting and planning, it has often happened in the past that an over-supply of rooms has resulted. This situation has the effect of depressing room rates and, together with their own efficiency gains, enables tour operators to reduce the price of their packages, thereby increasing the volume of demand for that resort, and at the same time to meet their aspirations to grow their businesses or to increase their share of the outbound market.

Increasing tourist arrivals creates pressure on the area's infrastruc-ture and often has a range of negative effects resulting from the regular arrival of large numbers of visitors. At the same time, yields for local businesses tend to be low because of the low spending characteristics of visitors. The overall effect is to reduce standards of service and the quality of experiences for both visitors and residents. Two choices now face those responsible for policy in the destination. They can either permit the continuing iteration of this model, allowing the building of further hotel capacity and other facilities needed by yet more visitors putting further pressure on the local area. Alternatively, they can take the radical steps needed to break the destination's dependency on high-volume low-revenue business by changing the nature of the holi-day experience offered in the destination. This requires the upgrading of resort facilities and changes in the nature of demand for them. These steps require effective control over local building and trading standards, and cooperation with the tour operators which promote the destination.

Case study 2.1 discusses improvements to Majorca's tourism industry demonstrating how cooperation in emphasizing the quality of custom-ers' experiences offers the promise of long-term benefits to all organi-zations participating in a holiday system.

CASE STUDY 2.1

Destination improvements in Majorca

Majorca was one of the first destinations for mass tourism in the Mediterranean, but visitor numbers began to fall at the end of the 1980s, suggesting that it was losing its appeal due to over-familiar-ity, falling standards relative to alternative Eastern Mediterranean or long-haul destinations, and adverse publicity in its main origin mar-kets featuring the unruly behaviour of some visitors.

Majorca's problems were exacerbated since 90% of its visitors were clients of charter-based inclusive tour operators (WTO, 1994) bringing high-volume low-yield business. Furthermore, pressure dur-ing the 1970s and 1980s from the large overseas tour operators had forced hotel rates down, and although this strategy succeeded in attracting large numbers of visitors, the low room rates meant that hotels could not afford to modernize or refurbish their facilities in line with competing destinations. The situation was further worsened since another response to the increased arrivals through the 1980s had been the building of low grade hotel stock, and as a result Majorca gained a reputation for building activity, blocked views and the spreading of hotels to previously unspoiled areas. These difficulties of environmental deterioration were compounded by frequent and highly publicized flight delays from Northern Europe across French airspace and the tour operators' tendency to alter clients' accommodation arrangements on arrival.

Coordinated approaches were adopted to improve visitors' experiences and to obtain increased financial benefit from each visitor.

- From 1985 onwards, development controls limited building permits to four-star or better properties with a maximum height of three storeys, and required 30 square metres of land per guest.
- In Magaluf, measures to improve the quality of the environment included tree planting, pedestrianization and a public sea-front esplanade to replace privately owned hotel and cafe frontages.
- A wider customer mix was sought by attracting tour operators from the Netherlands and Switzerland, and by inviting quality press visits to other aspects of Majorca, drawing attention away from the established resort areas near Palma in favour of the modern, architecturally more sensitive resorts on the east coast.
- Overseas youth tour operators cooperated by repositioning their services as well organized and behaved. Large same-sex groups were prohibited, and representatives' roles were redefined – they no longer lead drinking competitions!
- Thomson embarked on a programme to invest £10 m in ten three-star properties. Detailed specifications were prepared covering food, facilities, entertainment, room decor and service standards expected from staff.

The improvements to Majorca's tourism standards should be seen in the context of the Spanish government's four-year improvement plan (1991–95) for tourism, focusing on the appropriate development of the industry in the light of Spain's heritage and other resources (Jenner and Smith, 1993). The objective is to improve the product rather than expand capacity.

Based on Laws (1995).

A STAKEHOLDER ANALYSIS OF THE INCLUSIVE HOLIDAY SYSTEM

If the holiday industry is considered as a system in which all component elements are interrelated, any test for the effectiveness of any holiday system should include the assessment of outcomes for all stakeholders, not just tourists and the companies which comprise the holiday industry. Indeed, it is becoming evident that the relative priority given to the benefits accruing to tour operators and their clients can no longer be sustained. The key factor in the long-term success of the industry is the destinations which attract and entertain visitors, and in turn support the enterprises which profit from organizing their visits. Many destinations are being overwhelmed by the pressure of visitor numbers, and more importantly by the changes which their behaviour causes for the population, culture and ecology of destinations. In many such cases, the 'destination' is rather fragmented and uncoordinated and is therefore unable to provide a framework for systematic, long-term development. They are therefore open to exploitation and abuse of their attraction, although this is generally not the operators' intention.

Nor should most destinations be considered solely as centres of tourist activity. In fact it is doubtful whether this is valid for even the most extreme cases of enclave resort development, but it is particularly important for historic and cultural centres such as Europe's walled cities. Many of these are attractive centres for visitors, but because of their small size and their layout, large numbers of visitors quickly disrupt their traditional small-city functions. This was the situation in Canterbury, one of Europe's most visited walled historic cities. Case study 2.2 examines the city's responses to the pressures of its visitor industry.

CASE STUDY 2.2

A stakeholder analysis of visitor management initiatives in canterbury

The Canterbury City Local Plan (1981) recognized the pressure which large numbers of tourists placed on the attributes of the city which attracted them in the first place, and the concern was echoed in the 1994 Canterbury District Deposit Draft Local Plan. These documents form the statutory basis for the city's visitor strategy, but its implementation requires the coordination of many local council functions, especially Planning, Conservation, Highways and Environmental Health, with those undertaken by Kent County Council as the strategic highway authority.

A sensitive approach is required to the key problem in Canterbury, the physical constraints imposed by its narrow medieval street patterns and its buildings. In order to further develop a sustainable policy approach to Canterbury's tourism, the city council has set up a partnership with the commercial sector, amenity groups, the Cathedral, the county council and Christ Church College. The Canterbury City Centre Initiative has been established as a legal entity which aims, through the PATHS (*Proactive Approaches to Tourism Hosting Strategies*) and PEACE projects (*Partnership for Environmental Action and Commercial Enterprise*), to develop a sustainable management strategy for tourists and shoppers which complements the qualities of life of Canterbury's residents by involving the tourist trade and residents in its evolution.

The Canterbury City Centre Initiative (CCCI) has four main objectives:

- to identify and respond to the needs of residents and visitors;
- to stimulate the prosperity of the business community;
- to add value to the experience of visiting Canterbury;
- to preserve the character of the city.

These aims are being achieved through the CCCI's management structure which consists of:

- a management board of directors drawn from the partners;
- two steering committees – Strategy and Monitoring;
- several single-issue task forces drawn from the wider community according to expertise, e.g. coach management, residents' issues;
- a dedicated Canterbury Visitor Manager, provided by Canterbury City Council;
- a Research Fellow to oversee the monitoring, based in a local college.

The CCCI draws together all those who have an interest in managing Canterbury's visitor infrastructure and is a forum for communication between them about their own work. The partners continue to implement their respective management tasks, and jointly fund the CCCI to carry out tasks which no one else is doing or those which need a coordinated approach. Examples of its work include the appointment of several 'Visitor Shepherds' located at the new coach park, the waymarking of visitor trails and the provision of maps to distribute mass tourist groups onto four designated routes between the new coach park and the town centre. Other management measures in the town which have a bearing on the PEACE project are concerned with improvements to parking, coach groups, and congestion.

Coach groups

Coaches are an increasingly dominant means of bringing visitors to Canterbury, particularly from the continent of Europe which accounts for over 75% of the city's annual coach visits. Four to five hundred coach groups arriving weekly are not uncommon, and recent price wars between the cross-Channel ferries and the Channel Tunnel have increased the pressure. Canterbury's original coach park at Longport, with just 40 spaces, was unable to cope with the demand and presented a poor first impression of Canterbury, compounded by a

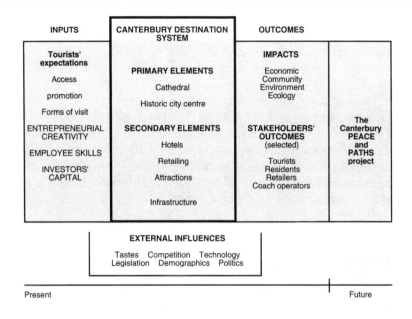

Figure 2.4 A soft, often-systems model of tourism in Canterbury.

dangerous road crossing on which several tourists have been injured or killed.

As a result of forecasts during the early 1990s of increasing coach group visits, an urgent decision was taken to move the coach park during the winter of 1994/95, ready for the main 1995 season. The only available large site capable of holding in excess of 100 coaches was at Kingsmead market site on the east of the city centre. Logistically, this is not the ideal location as the main coach arrivals to the city come from the west, although there is a steady recorded increase in coaches arriving from the ferry terminal at Ramsgate. The Kingsmead coach park is seen as a temporary solution whilst a more permanent arrangement is investigated. Nevertheless, it is being used as an opportunity to test the efficacy of various visitor management techniques, and to see whether good quality facilities would attract coach drivers to the new coach park: it is hoped that they will no longer drop passengers illegally in the streets. The effectiveness of the four tourist trails is also being evaluated, as is the contribution made by the Shepherds to the success of Canterbury's visitor management strategies.

As the Kingsmead coach park is a long walk from the city centre, approximately 20 to 40 minutes depending on the agility of the passenger, the project will also evaluate 'People-Mover' provision for the elderly and disabled, possibly using gas-powered shuttle buses. Financial help for this programme is being sought from the European Union's LIFE programme for the environment.

The PATHS project will develop a methodology for pre-booking tour coach visits to Canterbury through collaboration with Brugge in Belgium and St Omer in France on the development of Proactive Approaches to Tourism Hosting Strategies. This will involve market research, especially on school parties arriving from Nord-Pas de Calais, focus groups with schoolteachers in France and coach operators' workshops to be held in Brugge, Canterbury and St Omer. The objective is to involve coach tour operators and their drivers in accepting the concept and benefits to be achieved by pre-booking and a move towards general acceptance of the idea that it is not unreasonable for tourists to expect a 20 minute walk to reach the centre of any of Europe's historic towns.

The main attraction in Canterbury is the Cathedral. This too experiences severe pressures from visitors and has developed visitor management policies appropriate to a Church. The first recorded visitor management task was to ensure that the medieval pilgrims approached St Thomas à Becket's tomb on their knees! The modern concern is to ease the flow of visitors around the main points of interest in the Cathedral. The religious and architectural importance of the Cathedral attracts many school parties, both from Britain and abroad, and these groups were identified as a major cause of complaint by others who used the Cathedral. A scheme, 'Operation Shepherd', was developed with a number of tactics to control the entrance of groups. In the first year 1992, only 13% of groups booked their visit to the Cathedral but in 1993, 45% of school groups pre-booked. In June 1995, an entrance charge of £2.00 was introduced for all tourists visiting Canterbury Cathedral and its Precincts, although local people can continue to enter free with the benefit of a pass. Close monitoring of this new policy approach is being undertaken, but it is too soon to assess its impact on the Cathedral and the city.

Table 2.4 Problems and improvements for selected stakeholders in Canterbury's tourism system

Stakeholders	Indicative tourism problems	Current improvements
Coach operators	Restricted and underdeveloped parking	New coach park
Cathedral	Crowds detract from experiences of visitors and worshippers	
Tourists	Congestion; limited range of attractions	Signing, shepherding, pedestrianization; new attractions
Residents	Congestion	Attract tourists into less visited areas

Enhancing the city's tourist appeal

To increase the range of attractions in Canterbury, the city council encourages private projects such as Canterbury Tales, housed in a renovated church and portraying the experience of Chaucer's pilgrims on their journey to Canterbury. The council has also invested in a museum explaining Canterbury's heritage more formally, and it operates a Visitors' Bureau in partnership with the Chamber of Trade. Figure 2.4 presents an open, soft systems model, and Table 2.4 presents a stakeholder analysis of tourism in Canterbury.

Monitoring the initiatives

Control over the quality and consistency of a system's outputs depends on an effective feedback channel between the monitoring and decision-making subsystems of the destination. These functions are based on market research to understand the expectations of visitors, and techniques to assess the impacts of tourism. The Canterbury City Centre Initiative includes independent research on its effectiveness conducted by a researcher based in a local college, and entails a base study to establish the nature and extent of tourism in Canterbury and the monitoring of the evolution of the City Centre Initiative.

Source: Le Pelley and Laws (1995).

SERVICE QUALITY IN THE INCLUSIVE HOLIDAY INDUSTRY

The key to any organization's success is its understanding of how the individuals who are its potential clients make decisions to spend their resources of time, money and effort, and of the benefits they seek from so doing. Within any company, marketing's strategic role is therefore to bring the organization around to an awareness of the needs of its customers and to develop ways of delivering its services effectively. In a complex industry such as tourism where clients rely for their satisfaction on the efforts of a wide range of very diverse companies, the issue is much more challenging, because satisfying experiences in tourism require both the coordination of many service elements contributed by each company and its staff, yet retaining, even emphasizing, their individual styles of service. The next chapter addresses the question of service delivery and service quality in the inclusive holiday industry.

FURTHER READING

Checkland, P. and Scholes, J. (1990) *Soft Systems Methodology in Action*, John Wiley & Sons, Chichester.

Leiper, N. (1990) *Tourism Systems*, Massey University Press, Palmerston North, New Zealand.

Mill, R.C. and Morrison, A.M. (1985) *The Tourism System*, Prentice Hall, Englewood Cliffs, New Jersey, p. 89.

Laws, E. (1995) *Tourist Destination Management: Issues, Analysis and Policies*, Routledge, London.

Laws (1995) and Mill and Morrison (1985) provide a context to the operations of the inclusive holiday industry by analysing the effects of tourist activity on destination areas, adopting systems theory. Leiper (1990) also applies systems perspectives to the analysis of interdependencies in the tourism industry. Checkland and Scholes (1990) provides a detailed critique of soft systems theory.

SUGGESTED EXERCISES

1. Reflecting on a holiday which you have experienced, draft a systems model showing its main service elements and discuss how the quality of your holiday was affected by different organizations.

2. For any tourist destination with which you are familiar, evaluate the effects of tourism on its various stakeholders and discuss your findings.

3. Interview the manager of an independant travel agency and report on his or her views of the extent to which the holiday industry's member organizations are mutually interdependent.

Service quality in the inclusive holiday industry

3

INTRODUCTION

Managers in all types of enterprise recognize the significance of providing satisfying products and services to their customers. Similarly, there is a widespread emphasis on ensuring the quality of an organization's products, and seeking improvements in specifications and performance. This chapter reviews the theories underpinning service industry management practices and considers the meaning and nature of quality and customer satisfaction as applied to inclusive holidays.

SERVICE THEORY

A major focus of practitioner and academic interest is product or service reliability, and there is increasing recognition of the operational significance of the distinction between services and products. Many experts have pointed to the distinguishing characteristic of services, showing how they depend on face-to-face delivery when service staff are in direct contact with the clients. In contrast, the manufacturing of most products occurs 'offstage', remote from the public. Although managers may wish to specify precise standards for their services, just as a production manager in a factory setting would expect to, in reality each service transaction is itself a variable dependent on the performance of staff when in contact with the client. From this point of view, the service is a dynamic event during which client and staff may try to influence each other in many ways as they interact. Inclusive holidays share the attributes of service sector products, the key features of which are listed in Table 3.1.

In contrast with manufactured products, it is less clear that criteria set by managers for tourism service standards can be achieved consistently. The difficulty revolves around the two basic functions in service systems, termed Type A and Type B by Laws (1986). Type A

Table 3.1 Service features of inclusive holidays

Service characteristic	Significance for inclusive hoildays
Intangibility	Client cannot see or sample holiday until it is taken, although may rely on previous experience; distinctive service features cannot be patented
Inseparability	The holiday is created in the presence of the holidaymaker
Heterogeneity	Each holiday a client takes differs from other holidays, and each client on one holiday experiences it in different ways
Perishability	Unsold seats and beds cannot be stored for later sale
Ownership	The customer does not obtain ownership of the holiday or its elements; payment is made for access to and use of the facilities

Based on Cowell (1986); inclusive holiday factors added.

factors are the technical aspects of running a restaurant, hotel, transport operation or tourist attraction and are similar to the 'hard' systems elements discussed earlier. Type B factors are the interactions between staff and clients which characterize the delivery of tourism services and have much in common with the 'soft' features of systems. Other writers, for example Grönroos (1980), have distinguished between technical and functional quality, the latter meaning how the service is delivered, and have pointed to the need for managers to evaluate their customers' attitudes to 'each element in the bundle of service attributes'.

Differing though connected implications flow from the recognition of these two factors in tourism management. Type A factors are the technical factors which often form the main basis for the service which managers design, but while Type A factors are generally under the direct control of managers, the Type B factors are more complex. They include the skills and motivations of staff, their ability to interact effectively with clients, and the highly variable expectations and behaviour which different clients bring to the service episode and its constituent elements. Both Type A and Type B factors must be considered in designing an effective service delivery system, or in diagnosing difficulties and evaluating improvements to existing services.

MANAGEMENT RESPONSIBILITY FOR QUALITY IN THE SERVICE SECTOR

Writing in 1984, Shostack drew attention to a general criticism of the service sector:

> The development of a new service is usually characterized by trial and error. Developers translate a subjective description of a need into an operational concept that may bear only a remote resem-

Table 3.2 Definitions of service quality

- Technology-driven and product-oriented definitions – similar to the consumerist gap Type A technical management concerns.
- Fitness-for-use definitions, market driven and customer oriented focusing on customer utility and satisfaction – this is similar to consumerist gap Type B service management.

Based on Gummesson (1988). Comparison with consumerist gap terminology added.

blance to the original idea. No one systematically quantifies the process or devises tests to ensure that the service is complete, rational, and fulfils the original need objectively. No R and D departments, laboratories or service engineers define and oversee the design. There is no way to ensure quality or uniformity in the absence of a detailed design. What piecemeal quality controls exist address only parts of the service.

A great deal of management theory, and increasing managerial effort, has since then been directed towards achieving improvements in the efficiency of service sector organizations. Some tourism companies are noted for their success in enhancing the levels of service offered to their clients, notably SAS (Carlzon, 1989) and British Airways (see Laws, 1991 for details of the organizational turnaround led by Lord King and Sir Colin Marshall, and for an examination of how they monitor customer experiences). The roles for management in service delivery systems are fundamentally concerned with designing and resourcing an appropriate delivery system.

> Examples of poor service are widespread, in survey after survey services top the list in terms of consumer dissatisfaction ... Faced with service problems, we tend to become somewhat paranoid. Customers are convinced that someone is treating them badly, managers think that recalcitrant individual employees are the source of the malfunction. Thinly veiled threats by customers and managers are often first attempts to remedy the problem, if they fail, confrontation may result.
>
> (Shostack, 1984)

Two approaches for analysing the quality of services have been suggested by Gummesson (1988), as Table 3.2 indicates.

TECHNICAL APPROACHES TO TOURISM SERVICE QUALITY

The technical approach to quality emphasizes the performance criteria which are often specified for service delivery systems. Thus, airlines publicize the proportion of their 'on-time' arrivals and aim to open the plane's doors within two minutes of 'engines off'. Commenting on technical performance goals, Locke and Schweiger (1979) identified seven important characteristics of effective programmes. These suggested that the goals set must be specific, accepted, cover important job dimensions, be reviewed, with appropriate feedback, be measurable and challenging, but attainable. Just as the performance criteria for a car, its speed, acceleration and fuel economy, are built into the early stages of its design the operational goals set by a holiday company's managers are embodied in the design or blueprint of its service. The design stage is the first opportunity to influence customer satisfaction (Walsh, Roy and Bruce, 1988).

One strategy which service managers often adopt in their search for consistent service is to eliminate employee discretion and judgement whenever possible (Sasser, Olsen and Wycoff, 1978). This approach relies on the specification of tasks to a standard of performance expected by management, and then provides them with a basis for measuring the effectiveness of staff performing services. Hollins and Hollins (1991) also advocate a process of continuous improvements, relying on a view of the service as a chain of events which the customer experiences sequentially.

Increased standardization implies a reduction in the discretion allowed to individual employees, although this contradicts clients' expectations of being treated as individuals with needs which may vary during the many events of which a service is composed. Efficiency goals may clarify performance targets for staff but can conflict with the customer's expectation of warm and friendly service. Underlying this approach are the twin assumptions that consumers experience any service as a sequence of events, whereas managers tend to regard their service as a set of elements which require skilled coordination, and an understanding of the customers' perspectives.

CUSTOMER ORIENTATION IN HOLIDAY SERVICE MANAGEMENT

The second service quality approach discussed by Gummesson (1988) is fitness for use. In the case of tourism services this can best be understood in terms of customer expectations of satisfaction against which they match their subsequent individual experiences during the service. Case study 3.1 shows how Jan Carlzon set about improving the ability of Vingressor to provide holidays meeting its clients' needs.

CASE STUDY 3.1

Vingressor

Jan Carlzon has described how he became Chief Executive of Vingressor during troubled times. 'In June 1974, at the age of 32, I sat down behind the desk in the president's office of Vingressor, a subsidiary of the Scandinavian Airlines System . . . I had authority over 1400 employees, many of them roughly the same age as I . . . The

1973–74 oil crisis had escalated air travel prices so much that passengers shied away from charter trips.' He acknowledged that most production-oriented executives would have cut back on service. 'But this would only bring in less revenue . . . instead we chose to squeeze costs, resturcture the organization making it more flexible and able to handle more customers should the market bounce back.'

One market segment had attracted the managers' attention as providing additional demand that was not being effectively served. Managers had realized that senior citizens were becoming an important category of consumers in the travel business. The company undertook research to understand what senior citizens thought about holidays. 'We . . . concluded that senior citizens were fearful of travelling abroad and therefore would want to stay in special hotels filled only with other Swedish senior citizens.' Their research indicated that their clients preferred 'an apartment style suite with a living room where they could entertain their new friends and a kitchen equipped with a special Swedish coffeemaker and Swedish coffee.' In order to provide these services, special arrangements were made with selected restaurants 'to serve Scandinavian dishes suited to our guests' cranky stomachs. And since we assumed that older people prefer getting out and seeing the sights to sunbathing on the beaches, we arranged a wealth of brief excursions, interspersed with plenty of restroom breaks.'

As a further step in their research, they invited a group of people from a Stockholm retirement club to comment on the holiday concept. 'Not a single retiree expressed interest in our wonderful project . . . we stubbornly invested $100,000 in brochures.' Carlzon commented that: 'It is after you discover what your customers really want that you can turn to establishing business goals and a strategy to achieve them.' During his first year as president, Vingressor earned the largest profit in its history.

Based on Carlzon (1989).

Kotler (1982) has defined services as 'an activity that one party can offer to another that is essentially intangible and does not result in the ownership of anything'. In other words, the people who work to create and deliver touristic experiences have extensive contact with their clients. Anecdotal evidence supports this view – people often discuss the rapport (or otherwise) which they struck up with the waiter, barman or courier (as well as with other holidaymakers) during the holiday. The quality of these relationships and the style of service delivery are just as significant in tourists' satisfaction and enjoyment as the efficiency with which the services are performed.

A familiar example is the difficulty and dissatisfaction which all other passengers experience when one client on a coach tour is consistently late in returning to the vehicle after a sightseeing stop, irritating other customers and presenting the courier with a delicate problem. One way of understanding its origin is through the technique of service blueprinting, because the duration of the stop is an element of the service design, and it is apparent from the customer's behaviour that the specification does not meet his or her needs. However, it is a responsibility of managers to ensure that the features of their service satisfy as many as possible of their clients, and an element of compromise is necessary as discussed later in this chapter. The view that service quality is produced in the interaction between a customer and the service organization's staff has been referred to as 'interactive quality'. This has been explained as meaning that quality derives from 'the interaction of personnel with customers as well as that between customers and other customers' (Lehtinen and Lehtinen, 1982).

A related problem is that customers' behaviour and perceived attitudes can please or distress staff. Supportive customer behaviour has been shown to correlate positively with job satisfaction and performance, whereas instrumental behaviour by clients has negative outcomes for staff (Bowen, 1983). He defined instrumental behaviour as 'telling staff how to perform their tasks'. Similarly, Lovelock (1992) has cited Bony's definition of service as 'a deed, a performance, an effort'. The performance is experiential; it involves the customer during a period of time and the way that the customer participates helps or hinders the process. Normann (1991) referred to the points of interaction in a service episode as 'moments of truth', a phrase which Carlzon adopted for the title of his perceptive book (1989) in which he demonstrated that each of the many occurrences is used by customers to judge the quality of the service. Baum, in another book in this series, has written in detail of the human resource issues which confront the tourism industry, and of the policies it has adopted.

CUSTOMER SATISFACTION

Marketing theory argues that customers' experiences with any purchase give rise to outcomes for them varying from satisfaction to dissatisfaction. This reflects a divergence from the standards of service which clients had anticipated, as the following abbreviated quotations indicate: 'The seeds of consumer satisfaction are planted during the prepurchase phase of the consumer decision process' (Wilkie, 1986). It is against this individual benchmark that tourists measure the quality of their service experiences. 'Satisfaction is defined as a postconsumption evaluation that the chosen alternative is consistent with prior beliefs and expectations (with respect to it). Dissatisfaction, of course, is the outcome when this confirmation does not take place' (Engel, Blackwell and Miniard, 1986).

Dissatisfaction has also been defined as a state of cognitive or
tive discomfort. The consumer has allocated some of his reso
spending money and time, and built up an anticipation of satisfa
but if his judgement of the service he received is that it was not
his standard, he will experience cognitive dissonance (Festinger,
The response to any dissonant experience is an effort to corre
situation while other people decide to avoid it in the future.
nificant problem for managers, however, is that individuals resp
it in different ways.

Other authorities have examined the process by which consumers
understand quality; it is generally regarded as being a comparison of
their perceptions of their experiences against the service standards
they expected.

> The outcome of the evaluation process through which the con-
> sumer automatically goes may be viewed as an operational defini-
> tion of service quality ... Thus, quality is not inherent in the
> properties of the product or service itself, but is a function of the
> consumer's CS/PS (consumption specific/product specific) values
> which govern expectations and perceptions.
>
> (Klien, Lewis and Scott, 1989)

It is critically important to ensure that the facilities and services promised in advertisements actually are provided to the tourists they attract.
Unless the expectations which led them to purchase a particular vacation are matched by their experiences during the holiday, dissatisfaction will be the result.

Formal analysis highlights the significance of evaluating holidaymakers' experiences and examining them against the expectations which
led to their purchase of a particular service. Various factors have been
identified (Ryan, 1995), which, in combination with individual personality and a customer's previous experience, determine customer expectations. These include formal marketing communications such as
advertising messages or brochures, the opinions of friends or other
people who have experienced the service, and significantly, the price of
one service relative to the alternatives.

Consumer satisfaction is the outcome when expectations are matched by service experience, conversely, dissatisfaction occurs when
there is a mismatch and expectations are not fulfilled by the service
delivered (Engel, Blackwell and Miniard, 1986). Aggregate dissatisfaction amongst many consumers is a serious matter to the firm providing
a service, as the implication is that customers will take their future
business elsewhere. They are also likely to discuss their negative experiences with friends thereby further undermining the company's marketplace credibility (Laws, 1991).

Dissatisfaction can be understood as cognitive dissonance (Festinger,
1957), a psychological condition making it unlikely that the customer
will purchase from that supplier in the future. In extreme cases, the
customer will complain formally, thereby imposing a burden on the

company to which it will have to respond in a considered way (in case the dispute reaches court or an arbitration process for ultimate resolution). The company may decide (or be ordered) to pay the disappointed client financial compensation. Arbitration involves the travel retailer as the first point of recourse and this has introduced a new dynamic into the network of organizations contributing to the package holiday industry. Letters to the travel trade press indicate that, increasingly, travel retailers are reluctant to act as agents for tour operators which are the subject of frequent complaints by customers. Court cases, or those pursued through the consumer pressure groups and on radio, TV or press consumer programmes, also attract widespread attention, thereby further threatening the company and ultimately undermining the credibility and desirability of the industry's products (Rogers, 1993).

MANAGING SERVICE SATISFACTION

From this point of view, two primary functions can be identified for service sector managers. One is fundamentally concerned with designing and resourcing an appropriate delivery system which also defines the parameters for service encounters between staff and customers. The second function is concerned with staff selection and training, and beyond that, the development of an organizational culture which empowers staff to solve problems on behalf of customers within the company's cost or profit policies, and rewards them for contributing to customer satisfaction. The first management function, service design, underpins successful service delivery; it minimizes dysfunction and maximizes effective service transactions, providing satisfying experiences for customers. Thus, the service interactions (Type B) are relatively unstructured, and therefore the outcomes of actions are less predictable. These have been described as 'messy' problems. 'Problem situations, for managers, often consist of no more than a feeling of unease, a feeling that something should be looked at, both from the point of view of whether it is the thing to do and in terms of how to do it' (Checkland and Scholes, 1990).

The effects of service failure become evident when clients complain to resort and hotel staff, or to tour operator and travel agency staff when they return home. Berry (1991) has examined the range of costs caused by quality problems. Table 3.3 indicates that three levels of management responsibility can be identified.

Table 3.3 Costs resulting from quality problems

- **Prevention** – training and planned procedures to get the service right the first time
- **Appraisal** – routine inspection and quality audits
- **Correction** – dealing with customers' complaints

Source: Berry (1991).

An organization incurs costs from any service failure, but implementing a quality control system also incurs costs. These costs result from actions taken to get a service right from the start, auditing that it is correctly delivered and the expenses of responding to any failure (Lockyer and Oakland, 1981). From a managerial perspective, the technique of service blueprinting discussed later in this chapter can assist in auditing an existing service to locate problems with the service delivery system (Leppard and Molyneux, 1994), and it can also be helpful in evaluating the benefits of alternative remedial actions.

Apart from the physical or psychic consequences for customers and staff of unsatisfactory services, the costs include disturbance in the running of departments and a reduction in future sales levels resulting from dissatisfaction. Further costs are incurred in implementing preventative measures to reduce future dissatisfaction, including the redesign of service delivery systems or training and motivational programmes for staff. Taken together, this discussion demonstrates that the nature of the service design and the quality of contact between clients and staff can enhance or detract from three managerial goals:

- achieving customer satisfaction;
- achieving staff satisfaction.;
- achieving the organization's objectives.

CUSTOMER-ORIENTED TOURISM MANAGEMENT

Holiday company managers need to know what their clients regard as the components of a satisfying tourism experience in order to provide it effectively. In a sense, tourists 'measure' the quality of services which they receive against the expectations they formed ahead of travel when they selected, purchased and then anticipated their journey (Laws, 1986). The process by which consumers understand quality is now regarded as a comparison of the service standards expected against their perceptions of what they experience. The outcome of the evaluation process may be viewed as an operational definition of service quality, implying that the critical aspects of quality are not just inherent in the properties of the service itself (Garvin, 1988). Quality is also a function of the consumer's experiences and the personal values which govern their expectations (Engel, Blackwell and Miniard, 1986).

Weaknesses can occur at all stages of tourism services, beginning with the formation of customers' expectations created by the influences of many tour operators and destination agencies. They have a tendency to exaggerate the uniqueness or the high quality of the services they offer, thereby increasing the likelihood of disappointment, a problem which is exacerbated by the lack of coordination between the many organizations providing services to tourists within a destination. Table 3.4 demonstrates the ways in which various inclusive holiday industry suppliers can influence customer satisfaction.

Table 3.4 Influence of inclusive holiday industry suppliers on customers' satisfaction

Phase	Purchase decision	Return journey	Holiday
Main contacts and influencers	**Tour operator, travel agent**	**Airport, airline**	**Hotel, tour operator**
Other influences	Media, NTO, friends	Ground handler, check in, security, ATC, flight caterers, cabin crew, customs and immigration	Meeting and transfer staff, hotel reception, other hotel staff, resort representative, excursion guides and drivers, shops and restaurant staff
Timing	Several months prior to departure	During holiday	

The complexity of managing tourism services for quality and customer satisfaction can be contrasted with the challenges confronting manufacturers. The producer can specify manufacturing criteria which can be measured objectively. A range of quality control techniques ensure that each unit will match the intended performance specifications with a very high degree of consistency. These specifications become a basic component in the advertising claims (together with cost, lifestyle appeals and so on). Customers then decide whether these characteristics are what they seek, and subsequently evaluate the performance of a product against what was claimed for it (although in the case of technically complex products technical expertise may be required to know whether full performance is being delivered). Thus, the advertised (or implied) product attributes are important criteria by which the client is presumed to judge the quality of his or her purchase.

Satisfactory service experiences call for a systematic approach to quality control. This suggests both that the organization should be designed around an appropriate holiday and service concept, and that its management should focus on quality issues relevant to their clients, as Case study 3.2 on Haven Leisure indicates.

CASE STUDY 3.2

The Haven Leisure Holiday Centre Business

Recent data indicates that the growth in holidaytaking by Britons over the previous two decades is mainly overseas, while the overall UK domestic holiday market has been static, although it is larger in volume. Factors influencing the decision to holiday in Britain include family finance and ease of access. Additionally, the intrinsic attractions of Britain's varied scenery and culture are reason enough for many people to take their holidays, especially short breaks, within the country. An overseas holiday is generally twice as expensive as one taken in Britain. For many families (particularly those with pre-teen children) and for senior citizens a holiday taken in the unfamiliar surroundings of a foreign country, with the associated uncertainties of a long and complicated journey, is sometimes too stressful to contemplate.

Some 22% of domestic holidays in the UK are taken in caravans or chalets, and in total this sector provides more accommodation than hotels. Of the 30 million British people who take holidays of four nights or more in the UK, 7 million stay in the organized form of the caravan and chalet sector, holiday centres. These provide clients with a package combining accommodation, site facilities, activities and entertainment. The concept of holiday centres is said to have been originated by Billy Butlin, who established his first holiday camp at Skegness in 1936, marketing it on the basis of a 'week's stay for a week's pay'.

Establishing the Haven brands

In 1986, the Rank Organization acquired a holiday centre company, Haven, to add to its own Leisure Holidays for its portfolio of hotel and leisure companies. In 1990, Rank acquired Mecca which included the Warner holiday centre brand. Haven is the brand for the UK operations, Haven Europe is used for overseas holidays, while Haven Leisure is the holding company for these brands. In the five years following the acquisition of Mecca, some £120 million was invested into Haven, in upgrading the accommodation and holiday centre facilities, and the capacity of the computerized reservations system was doubled.

The objectives set for the holiday centre business were to maximize yield and to sustain the holiday centre product within a market which was mature and static. It was decided to operate three brands: Haven, with 41 self-catering parks offering four types of family holiday; Warner, offering 11 half- or full-board family villages; and a separate product for the 37 French and Spanish self-catering parks.

In a presentation to CIMTIG in 1992, Peter Allport, Haven Leisure's Marketing and Sales Director, explained that the rationale for this approach was that it capitalized on customers' loyalty both to particular sites and to the people who staffed them, while distinguishing the brands to the travel trade. In order to communicate these new brands, guests staying at the holiday centres were presented with leaflets and a poster (bundled with a copy of the *Star*). A dinner was hosted for the managing directors of key travel agent accounts, while receptions were staged for travel agencies' staff in the six marketing regions. Five thousand launch packs were mailed to ABTA agents, and 26 merchandisers visited 3000 of them providing in addition to the normal support a video which customers could view in the shop or borrow. All consumer advertisements for the new brands' brochures contained prices, a contact phone number and an injunction to book through a travel agency. The brochure launch was supported by a coordinated campaign in the trade press which included a corporate profile insert.

Subsequently, a mystery shopper campaign was conducted, visiting 350 retailers, and this confirmed a very high awareness of the new brands. Later, the Warner brand was spun off as a specialist brochure, providing year-round short breaks and holidays in the UK with the strap line 'Holidays just for adults'. The emphasis in this brand is on relaxation in good company, with fine food and accommodation in stately homes and castles as well as holiday centres selected for their scenic locations.

Haven's holiday centre products

Haven Leisure is one of the four major UK holiday centre operators, the others being Butlins, Pontins and Center Parcs. Within the holiday centre sector, the four major companies have much in common, although Center Parcs is easily distinguished by its Dome, which represents a very visible form of differentiation. Most holiday centre clients know the product well, and choose on the basis of the service offered by each company. Peter Allport described Haven Leisure's distinguishing features as 'the mix of accommodation and entertainment, driven by the needs of children in the families for which it caters'. Although C1C2DE clients are the core of Haven Leisure's business, it is essentially classless, attracting clients who closely match the UK demographic profile.

In 1995, Haven Europe's brochure offered clients self-drive holidays in sited mobile homes and tents to attract families with older children from the ABC1 socioeconomic groups. The Haven UK brochure offered three categories of holiday centre:

- **character villages**, centred on an old manor house or equivalent, or sited in a particularly appealing location where the emphasis is on accommodation standards, and clients are offered the opportunity to 'dip into' on-site entertainment;
- **all-action centres**, emphasizing entertainment included in the price of the holiday;
- **family parks**, offering high standards of accommodation at locations around Britain's holiday coasts.

Although most of the clients stay at one holiday centre, 28 of Haven's resorts also provided accommodation for clients touring Britain with their own caravan or tent.

A range of special offers are featured in the brochure, including 'Fortnight's Delight', a discount for booking two consecutive self-catering weeks either at one centre or staying somewhere different for the second week, 'Under 5's Specials', 'Group Discounts' and 'Single Parents'. These and other offers are available only when booked before 31 January.

Since the intended market for Haven Holidays is primarily families with children, and over half its guests are children, the company provides special facilities for them and their parents. These include the 'Tiger Club' which provides holiday adventures for 5 to 11 year olds organized by experienced leaders. Children receive a club badge and membership card and can win prizes. This proved a very popular element in the holiday centre product, and was extended in 1995 to include two new sections, 'Animal Crackers' for young children and 'Jungle Rangers' for the 8 to 11 age group. This split resulted in part from Haven's policy of monitoring its younger guests through the mechanism, of 'The Tiger Club Board' set up from Rory Award winners who are encouraged to tell Haven's directors what they want. The *Travel Weekly* Corporate Profile featured a photograph of the Tiger Club Board at the CBI (Confederation of British Industry) conference. The 'Rory Road Show' features jungle characters such as Anxious the Elephant and visits many of the holiday centres. This is linked with the Jungle Club and provides children with 'Rory Awards' for winning competitions.

Teenagers join 'All The Rage' (ATR) which provides them with computer games, disco dancing, blind date and other activities and facilities under the guidance of club leaders called Havenmates. The brochure describes them in this way:

> It takes a really special kind of person with bags of personality to cope with the teen scene, and we choose them very carefully. Young, friendly and switched on to the same wavelength as the youngsters, they know how to coax the most out of them, boost their confidence and ensure they have a really great time in their own way – so all the family has a happy holiday!

Entertainment for adults is another major element in Haven's product, and the centres provide late-night cabaret, resident live bands, competition time, discos and resident live bands, as well as summertime spectaculars. The brochure points out that the 'unsung heroes' of a holiday are the 'Havenmates' who plan, organize and host the entertainments.

Haven offers a series of 'Starburst weekends' during which guests can enjoy stage and TV stars live. Those appearing during 1995 included Freddie and the Dreamers, Keith Harris with Orville and Cuddles, Joe Pasquale, The Grumbleweeds and The Crankies.

The Mill Rythe Centre

As Table 3.5 indicates, the brochure provides examples of a typical invoice for half-board and self-catering holidays, thus emphasizing the fully inclusive nature of the product. It provides a clear, colour-keyed map showing the locations of each of three types of centre, indicating at the same time on which page of the brochure they can be found. It describes Mill Rythe in the following terms:

Table 3.5 Typical half-board holiday invoice

Haven accommodation for 1 week from 3 June 1995 at Mill Rythe Family Holiday Park		
2 adults @ £214 each		£428
2 children First child	Free	
Second child		£ 99
Full English breakfast every day	Included	
3-course dinner every day	Included	
Colour TV	Free	
Bed-linen and towels	Free	
Great entertainment	Free	
Tiger Club for 5–11 year olds	Free	
ATR Club for 12–17 year olds	Free	
Indoor funpool	Free	
Adventure playground and fun palace	Free	
VAT at 17.5%	Included	
Total holiday cost		**£527**

Mill Rythe on Hayling Island is the place to come for a great family holiday. With plenty to do by day plus spectacular evening entertainment and late night discos, we've arranged everything.

In addition to the Tiger Club including the Jungle Rangers, the kids will love the Indoor Fun Palace. With larger than life Snakes and Ladders, and Biff bags, they can play among board games galore. Meanwhile, teenagers can enjoy the variety of activities offered by ATR.

After a delicious 4 course dinner it's time to take in an evening of sparkling entertainment, with dancing, shows and visiting cabaret.

Later, things liven up in Hudson's Bar – a popular evening rendezvous with attractive bars, discos and late night entertainment . . .

There are 41 activities and amenities listed, including abseiling, laser pigeon shooting, snooker and darts, and seven children's facilities. This holiday centre offers full board for a supplement, and a range of accommodation including single, double, twin and 3-, 4- or 5-berth chalets. There are also Ambassador chalets and hotel-style blocks. The main season at Mill Rythe runs from late May to mid September. Full-board themed short breaks are also offered from April through to October. Themes include traditional jazz weekends, family breaks, a cockney weekend, the swinging sixties and a cabaret spectacular. The Centre also provides Christmas and New Year breaks.

Holiday centre accommodation

The core of Haven's product is the accommodation it offers, and the brochure provides illustrations of typical caravans, chalets and sited tents. These include exterior and interior photographs and schematic drawings of the interior plans. Haven features two classes of new caravan in 1995, 'ComfortPlus' models which have added insulation and double glazing, and 'Ambassador Caravans' 12 feet wide and 35 feet long. These are available for a supplement in selected parks.

The distinction between chalet and caravan is another key way to understand Haven Leisure's product range. The caravan-based accommodation is currently subject to 10 or 11 month site-use licences. Caravans account for about two-thirds of the accommodation stock, and since the quality of accommodation is the core service, they are constantly being upgraded, refurbished or replaced with improved versions on a four- to five-year cycle despite an anticipated life of ten years or more.

Distribution channel management

The agency distribution system is critical for Haven Leisure, as it is a volume player and with a million customers it cannot depend on direct sales. The use of high street agents as its distribution channel enables the company to maximize brochure tariff income, and the agents also contribute, together with advertising, to establishing the market. The *Travel Weekly* Corporate Profile reported that 50–60% of of its 1993 holidays were sold through the trade, but its strategy was to increase the proportion: Haven had 25 sales support staff servicing 2600 agents, scheduled to increase to 3000 by the following summer.

When negotiating with travel agents, Haven Leisure seeks two separate rackings in order to reach its two distinct audiences. In the typical agency, Haven Europe is usually found with Eurocamp and Eurosite brochures, while the Haven UK brochures are placed with those of its competitors such as Butlins and Center Parcs. The advantage for customers is that they can see at a glance the range of brochures offering the type of holiday which they are seeking, while for operators the choice of brands tends to heighten awareness of the holiday type through the greater prominence it gains on an agency's racks when compared to the visibility of a single brochure.

Traditionally, British holiday products have been under-represented on travel agency shelves. They are not seen as a major revenue opportunity and still account for only 10% of the total holidays sold by retailers. The sales price of a week's Haven Leisure UK holiday ranges between approximately £150 and £550 depending on site, size of accommodation and season, with an average of about £300. (This still approximates to Billy Butlin' prewar maxim of a week's holiday for a week's pay.) But this price purchases a holiday for a family of four, although it presents the agent with only one commission opportunity. In contrast, a family of four purchasing an overseas package holiday would yield four commissions to the agent.

Haven Leisure conducts annual negotiations with its agencies, when in August the agency sales team makes agreements with each key account. The details of the negotiation are concerned with the base commission rate, overrides, and the setting of target sales levels by the agency for the forthcoming year based on a review of the previous year's performance. Basic commission is standardized and reflects industry norms, while the override is seen as an incentive to agents to grow the business they do for Haven Leisure, and is the subject of debate with each agency. Another important discussion is about the effectiveness of agency sales performance: this is carried out by reference to relative positions in the 'sales league' without revealing actual sales figures since these are regarded as confidential between the company and each agent. This stance is typical of travel industry public companies which are nervous about revealing such details. In other industries, detailed sales performance by members are openly circulated in the trade and amongst researchers; however, tour operating is a relatively new and small sector on the listed Stock Exchange, and is not well understood by its investors, particularly the institutions.

Although the commission for a Haven Leisure sale is relatively low reflecting its average overall price, the company justifies its claim on agency rack space by pointing to the opportunity it offers agencies for an incremental commission gain. Increasingly, rather than being a substitute on their shelves for other products, Haven Leisure's UK Holiday Centres are bought as second holidays or short breaks, while for other clients who cannot afford to go abroad or are constrained by other considerations such as a young family, Haven represents a market extension which few other holiday products could serve.

Brochure policy

The primary cost of gaining business for Haven Leisure is the production and distribution of its brochures. Some 2.5 million are produced annually, an investment of about £1 million, and 1.8 million copies are distributed to the travel agencies where they represent Haven's products on the shelves. The remainder are used for direct marketing purposes.

Haven uses a grading system to determine brochure delivery to agencies throughout the year, providing the specialist company which holds its distribution contract with the parameters to apply when servicing each agency. In principle, even if the company does not have an agreement with a particular agent, any retailer can have brochures on request, although any new agent's performance is reviewed at the end of the year.

Haven Leisure tactically discounts its products according to demand. The key pricing problem arises for the shoulder season (particularly May and June) when couples with pre-school children are the target of all companies operating in the sector. In terms of meeting its financial targets, the trick for Haven Leisure is to obtain the maximum possible price for each booking throughout the season.

Agency support

Haven Leisure supports its retail agents in a variety of ways. It invests in educationals for agency staff, organizing three types of visit to inform them about the company's services and to encourage enthusiasm for selling them. It provides product training for retailers organized on a regional basis by the area sales teams. Haven's Holiday Centres provide ideal facilities for the annual staff conferences organized by the multiples, for example Lunn Poly's three hundred or more new recruits on an out-of-season weekend when they take over an entire Holiday Centre. This also provides Haven Leisure with the opportunity to introduce the young staff members to the range of features offered by a holiday centre. Product sampling opportunities are also provided in collaboration with, for example, Shearings and Stena, and these enable staff to visit three different European parks. The company also collaborates with its agents on joint promotions, usually contributing 50% of the costs for local advertising, and supplies window displays and late sales support to its retailers, for example through window cards.

Managing quality

A key indication of Haven Leisure's ability to provide clients with the holiday they want is the high level of repeat business which the company attracts. At about 40%, this has to be seen in the context of an industry in constant change, where many clients seek something different from each holiday.

All Haven's holiday parks are independently inspected annually, and must be rated at least 3 ticks (out of a possible 5) in the National Holiday Parks Grading Scheme. In contrast to the majority of tour operators, Haven Leisure owns its accommodation stock and sites in the UK and three of its European sites (but rents space from local site operators for its other Continental sites). This gives it a unique level of control over the standards of facilities and services provided to its clients. Haven has significantly less control over its European product, since it shares sites with its main competitors, and its point of differentiation on the European sites is limited to the accommodation provided, the skills of its site staff and the company's processes to get customers to the site.

Customer research is a fundamental management discipline for modern companies: focus group studies are conducted on competitors' and Haven's own clients to monitor their responses to developments in the holiday centre product and the way it is advertised. Every Haven Leisure client receives a questionnaire in their welcome pack on arrival at their holiday centre. Client satisfaction is also monitored through market research including focus groups held with clients on site in the holiday centres by the Group's market research teams, with the results being reported to the board. Haven Leisure has set itself as a target a very low ratio of complaints to bookings (and regularly achieves this goal). Customers are encouraged to report any problems immediately to site staff, and most difficulties are readily resolved. However, inevitably there are some complaints. All letters are analysed carefully as well as a response being made to the specific matters raised.

Haven also monitors its youngest guests: 'The Tiger Club Board' was set up from Rory Award winners who are encouraged to tell Haven's Directors what they want. One result was to split the Tiger Club so that entertainment is provided geared to 5 to 12 year olds, and a seperate programme is provided for 12- to 17-year-old guests.

Based on interviews with Peter Allport, Haven Leisure, and company documents.

MANAGING QUALITY

Garvin (1988) has shown how manufacturers have tackled the problems of managing quality: 'At the best plants audit problems triggered an educational process in which the line workers were brought to the audit area to review units and discuss ways of avoiding future problems ... despite the diversity (in their backgrounds, attitudes and so on) the common goal was to increase employees' sensitivity to quality and to avoid repeated mistakes.' A study of 101 successful service firms in America concluded that their managers had several features in common (Zemke and Schaafe, 1989):

- Listen, understand and respond to customers.
- Define superior service and establish a service strategy.
- Set standards and measure performance.
- Select, train and empower employees to work for the customer.
- Recognize and reward accomplishment.

Similarly, it has been shown that in the best service firm:

> ... a consistent pattern to the managerial process is evidenced. One sees a pronounced emphasis on controllable details, continuous investment in training, a concern with the customer's view and reward systems that place value on service quality. In poor service firms, however, one sees an internal rather than external orientation, a production orientation, a view of the customer as a transac-

tions generator, a lack of attention to details affecting the customer, and a low priority placed on 'soft' service quality values.

(Shostack, 1985)

Consumer satisfaction with a service is a function of the appropriateness of its design and the quality of delivery by every member of staff in the service system. Tourism's appeals to customers go beyond the physical aspects of the service. Rather than component parts assembled in a particular form, tourism marketing stresses the set of attributes offering the buyer satisfaction of his or her wants and needs. It then becomes the objective of all the supplying organization's management and staff, and the basis of the industry's survival and prosperity, to deliver the benefits which marketing has promised to its clients. Appropriate tour package design and administration and carefully researched destination development linked to successfully communicated travel brands can bring the advantage of an overall increase in tourist activity and spending.

INFLUENCING HOLIDAYMAKERS' EXPECTATIONS OF SERVICE QUALITY

Tour operators have three main ways of communicating the quality of their products to customers. Statements about quality are often contained in a tour operator's marketing communications and in its brochures. In both cases, this may be explicit, as for example when a tour operator's brochure states that hotels are of a certain category of star rating, or implicit, conveyed in the text and images used to position the product. Examples of the latter include photographs of stylish restaurant service or of well furnished rooms, and descriptions of the knowledge and skills of resort staff. Some long-established companies refer proudly to the length of their experience in their industry, others list travel industry awards which they have won. This latter features strongly in trade promotions, and the trade press also publicizes the presentation of awards at lavish annual dinner functions.

The acid test ultimately lies in their customers' judgement of the satisfaction which they experience during their holiday. These points are interconnected, since the theoretical approach to understanding service satisfaction is based on a comparison of expectations formed during the pre-consumption stages with the customers' subsequent experiences of the service he or she receives. The key influences on expectations, apart from any prior experience which the customer may have had, are the company's marketing communications. One further aspect of communicating quality which will be considered in a later section of this chapter is the tour operator's pricing policy.

It should be borne in mind that tour operators set out to attract different segments of the holiday market, and therefore the way in which these quality statements are phrased or placed in the brochure and the relative importance given to each varies from one company to another. Overall, the purpose of these and other references to the tour operator's quality in their brochures has been explained by Middleton (1988) as to 'promote confidence in buyers, and to reassure them at the point of sale'.

QUALITY AS A MANAGEMENT STRATEGY

An attractive competitive strategy for tourism companies which, rather than selling on the basis of low prices, places an emphasis on their clients' satisfaction is through quality programmes. 'There is no doubt that relative perceived quality and profitability are strongly related. Whether the profit measure is return on sales or return on investment, businesses with a superior product/service offering clearly outperform those with inferior quality' (Buzzell and Gale, 1987).

From the perspective of competitive marketing, an improved understanding of customers' perceptions of the service yields insights on how to manage those services to their greater satisfaction. This may have two beneficial effects – it is likely to promote customer loyalty by encouraging repeat purchases from satisfied customers, and secondly it is likely to result in more refined positioning through product adjustment, client awareness and advertising appeals.

Gummesson (1988) has suggested that there are two ways to improve profit through quality measures. Improved market performance leads to increased sales and increasing market share (or decreased price elasticity): increased quality ultimately enables the price to be raised. Secondly, a reduction in defects leads to lower unit costs of production and costs of servicing complainants is also lower.

SERVICE BLUEPRINTING

The customer's evaluation of his or her holiday experiences can be examined through a technique known as service blueprinting. This had its origins in hard applications, where the symbols in an ordered technical drawing represent instructions to technicians which they use as a template in constructing buildings or in wiring circuitry. Shostack (1985) demonstrated how the concept can be applied in the analysis of service delivery systems. The service blueprint presented later in this chapter illustrates how the technique enables attention to be focused on three key factors in the quality of a service: its design, the roles of staff, and the interaction between staff and customers.

The concept of a service blueprint has been described as '... the process of defining the range of resources required for the performance of services, and of coordinating the various components' (Laws, 1991). Gummesson (1990) also remarked on how blueprinting helps in understanding the systemic features of a service and noted that: 'The purpose of blueprinting [is] to make sure that all elements are there, and to find out their cost and contribution to revenue in the composition of the service.' Shostack herself considered that a service blueprint should have three main features. Firstly, it must incorporate within the design a time dimension, enabling the researcher to follow the progression of the service delivery system which the customer experiences. Secondly, it should show the main functions which together comprise the service and show their interconnectedness. A third feature of the blueprint is that it should incorporate performance standards and the deviance levels which are acceptable at each stage of the process. The various elements in a service blueprint are arranged with reference to a line of visibility. Above this, the customer is aware of and often involved in the service processes. Below the line of visibility, a range of resources and skills are deployed, which, although the customer is not directly involved in them, are fundamental to the customer's satisfaction. This introduces a further feature of service blueprints: they can be used to identify failpoints, 'the parts of a service which are most sensitive to errors' (Gummesson, 1990). George and Gibson (1988) defined failpoints as 'the parts of a service blueprint which identify those processes of the service which are most likely to go wrong, and to function other than intended.'

Any service blueprint is best regarded as a 'plan'. It may not be an accurate nor a full representation of the service provision because the method relies on the interpretation of data provided by a sample of the firm's customers, and it therefore includes their perceptions and feelings. However, the blueprinting technique entails several steps (Payne, 1993), and these limitations can be largely overcome in the ensuing, analytical phase of the service blueprinting methodology: it takes on some of the characteristics of iterative or action research, in which managers are interrogated about the operational meaning (and validity) of their clients' commentary on the existing service delivery system. A subsequent phase explores the setting of managerial priorities and the remedial action to be taken in redressing the failpoints identified earlier.

An introduction to service blueprinting methodology

A service blueprint is a diagram which shows all the elements that go to make up the service being studied. Its purpose is to enable the service to be analysed as objectively as possible. Table 3.6 shows the sequence of steps in drawing up a blueprint of a service, while Table 3.7 indicates the range of methodologies which underpin the procedures (although these are not discussed further in this chapter).

The blueprint is divided horizontally by a line of visibility. Above this, what the client 'sees' is shown in the form of a flowchart beginning when the customer decides to purchase the service and following his or her contact with the various elements of the core phase that constitute the service they expect to experience. Below the line of visibility, the blueprint shows the elements and the processes connecting them which are required to make the service available. Thus the blueprint traces all

Table 3.6 Steps in service blueprinting

1. Study the sequence of service elements experienced by a range of clients.
2. Present the clients' experience as a simplified flowchart.
3. Study the features of the service delivery system(s).
4. Flowchart the elements in the service delivery system.
5. Analyse customers' experience of the service delivery system to identify critical points.
6. Analyse the managerial rationales for the crisis points in the existing service delivery system.
7. Assess the costs of existing service delivery system weaknesses.
8. Evaluate the opportunities for improvements and assess the costs of implementing them.

Table 3.7 Methodologies in studying service delivery systems

- Observation
- Participant observation
- Interviews
- Focus groups
- Analysis of customer correspondence
- Study of company documents

the components of the service and identifies how they culminate in the various encounter points during which the customer interacts with the service, thereby providing a framework for service design analysis.

The starting point for analysis of the blueprint is to identify the points where an existing service delivery system may cause problems for clients or staff. Fail points can be identified while drawing up the blueprint, by adding specific questions to the instruments used to explore customers' and managers' experiences of a service delivery system, but additional methods are required to investigate their relative significance (primarily to customers, but also to staff and the firm) or to examine the methods and costs of remedying them. However, the blueprinting method provides managers with valuable insights into where their customers believe that service is failing.

CASE STUDY 3.3

Service blueprint of an inclusive holiday

Following the conventions outlined above, the blueprint is divided into sections. The top section can be understood as the customer's conceptual flowchart of the sequence of events he or she is likely to experience during the service episode. The bottom section is invisible to the customer, and consists of the range of activities and events which are required to create the service.

The blueprinting analysis of an inclusive holiday shown in Figure 3.1 is based on research conducted for a tour operator to help the company understand aspects of their holidays which clients had found unsatisfactory. A variety of methods were adopted, including observation by participating in holidays to understand the sequence of events and service elements, interviews conducted with the company's clients to explore particular issues, both as they arose during a holiday and through focus group techniques following customers' return from holiday. The points of difficulty were then discussed in depth with the managers responsible for various phases of the holiday, and a range of changes and improvements were evaluated both for cost and effectiveness: these points are not included in this case study.

The numbered top section, above the line of visibility, shows the sequence of events which a client typically experiences. This begins with the selection and purchase of a holiday (usually some months beforehand). The various activities which the tour operator has to put into effect to enable the client to purchase a holiday are shown below the line of visibility, and include contracting for flights and accommodation, setting up the brochure and reservations system, and briefing agency sales staff.

Below the blueprint diagram itself in Figure 3.1, a number of potential failpoints have been noted in the shaded portion of the diagram, numbered in sequence from left to right for each phase of the blueprint. Failpoint 1 indicates that clients sometimes purchase an inappropriate holiday, perhaps to a destination which they do not like or to stay in a hotel where they do not feel comfortable. The analysis of this failpoint summarizes the views of the holidaymakers interviewed for this research, which set out to answer the question of whether clients held the tour operator to blame for the various failpoints. In this case, the general view was that the travel agent was responsible for poor advice.

The majority of problems occur during the core phase of the holiday. The allocation of blame for unsatisfactory experiences during the core holiday phase was distributed between the tour operator and some, but not all, of the companies and organizations supplying elements of the holiday package. The discriminating factors appear to be that it is clear to holidaymakers that certain service elements are provided by other organizations, notably the flight and accommodation, while the tour operator is thought to provide or arrange their holiday activities. However, the scheduling of flight departure and arrival times is generally regarded as a decision taken by tour operators, while the responsibility for chaotic or lengthy check-in procedures is not clear to holidaymakers.

Failpoint 3 is a problem commonly experienced during journeys by air, when passengers are required to queue for each aspect of airport procedures, typically including the actual check-in, a security check, passport control and further queuing to board the plane.

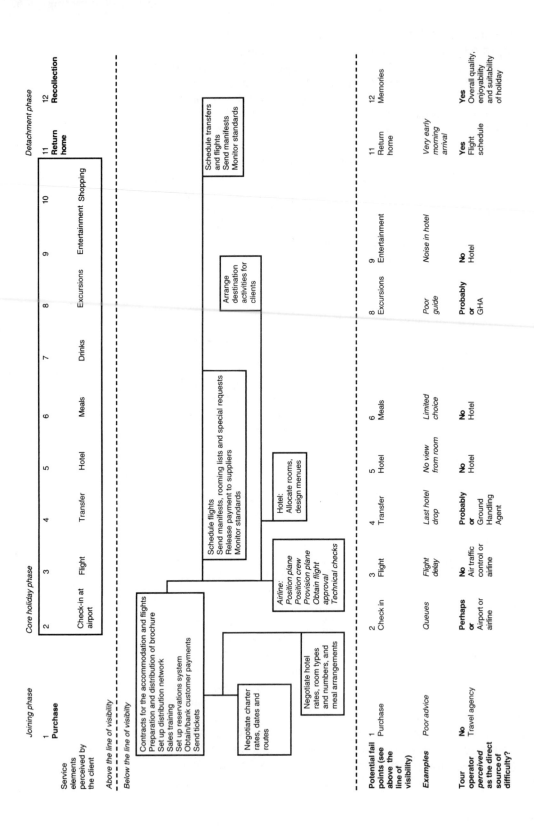

Figure 3.1 Blueprint of an inclusive holiday.

Extended queuing can be a source of stress, but it is generally evident to passengers that their tour operator is not responsible. However, some passengers do question why the tour operators cannot make better arrangements, particularly in overseas airports.

Failpoint 4 is another difficulty which can be experienced by any traveller. However, there is sometimes a suspicion on the part of passengers that charter airlines are not treated as favourably as scheduled carriers by air traffic controllers. Additionally, some clients fear that maintenance standards are lower on charter flights, especially those using older or foreign-registered equipment.

Failpoint 5, when a client's hotel is the last serviced by the transfer coach, can be very irritating at the end of a long day's journey.

Failpoints 6, 7 and 10, although not really the responsibility of the tour operator, can have consequences for the company if clients seek compensation, and for the resort representative who has to try to resolve this type of problem. It is sometimes caused by overstated brochure descriptions resulting in clients' raised expectations of an ambience or standard of service which the hotel cannot provide.

Failpoint 9 arises when the guide on a local excursion fails to adopt an appropriate style with his group, being for example either too jocular or too informative. This and failpoint 10 can be a significant disappointment to those holidaymakers who chose a particular destination because of the intrinsic appeal to them of either the local area and culture or the entertainment they hoped to enjoy. In the latter case, however, some clients are disturbed by the noise of a nightclub situated in their hotel or nearby.

The factors leading to failpoint 12 are discussed in Chapter 7.

Two points emerge from this analysis. The first is that although tour operators package the elements of an inclusive holiday, they often do not have direct control over the way in which the component services are delivered, leading to fragmented and varying experiences for their clients rather than the seamless consistency sought by the industry's managers. In part, this problem relates to the fragmented nature of the tourism industry itself. It is also the consequence of cultural differences between customers' expectations of service standards based both on the situations they are familiar with at home and on comparisons they make with holidays in other resort areas or organized by competing tour operators.

The second point is summed up by failpoint 13 in Figure 3.1. This indicates that, whatever the source of irritation and problems experienced during a holiday, when tourists reflect on their memories after returning home, it tends to be the tour operator which is held responsible for the overall quality and enjoyability of the holiday. This is significant because it has implications both for the probability that they will (or won't) purchase subsequent holidays from that tour operator, and because of the power of word-of-mouth recommendations to friends and relatives.

> Any of these elements has the potential to cause problems, but difficulties are more likely to occur with certain aspects of a given service operation. The potential failpoints discussed above have been identified by observation, interviews with holidaytakers and discussion with industry managers.

ISSUES IN MANAGING HOLIDAY QUALITY

This chapter has raised a series of issues relating to the provision of quality services by inclusive holiday industry managers. Table 3.8 summarizes these, which should also be considered in the context raised in the previous chapter – that of a fragmented industry in which coordination of service elements is the essential prerequisite for the industry's continuing success.

Table 3.8 Key issues in managing inclusive holidays

Service factors
- client cannot sample holiday before purchase;
- satisfaction partly dependent on interactions between staff and clients.

Leisure factors
- clients are at leisure, their time is unstructured.

Cultural factors
- clients are intent on hedonistic pleasures;
- they are away from their familiar environments.

Industry factors
- the inclusive holiday system depends on the quality of many organizations' contributions.

FURTHER READING

Carlzon, J. (1989) *Moments of Truth*, Harper & Row, New York.
Christopher, M., Payne, A. and Ballantyne, D. (1991) *Relationship Marketing: Bringing Quality, Customer Service and Marketing Together*, Butterworth-Heinemann, Oxford.
Laws, E. (1991) *Tourism Marketing: Service and Quality Management Perspectives*, Stanley Thornes, Cheltenham.
Ryan, C. (1995). *Researching Tourist Satisfaction*, Routledge, London.

Ryan (1995) and Laws (1991) provide reviews of the meanings and methods of researching satisfaction in tourism. Christopher, Payne and Ballantyne (1991) discuss the theory of relationship marketing, while and Carlzon (1989) provides a stimulating account of his experiences as its President in turning Scandinavian Airlines into a model of customer service in the tourism industry.

SUGGESTED EXERCISES	1. Taking a range of tour operators' brochures featuring a particular destination or type of holiday, contrast the ways in which they communicate their individual service styles.
	2. Write accounts of a particularly pleasing event which you experienced on a holiday and one which upset you. Explain your evaluation of them, and suggest what general lessons tourism managers may draw from your experiences.
	3. Draw up a service blueprint for a holiday you have experienced and discuss selected failpoints in its service design or delivery.

Marketing and distributing inclusive holidays

The growth in holidaytaking can be attributed, at least in part, to the success of the inclusive holiday industry's ability to market its products. This has stimulated interest in overseas recreational travel and has led to the development of a wide range of holiday products with strong appeals directed to customers with varied travel motivation. Chapter 4 considers some of the methods which tourism marketers have employed to achieve these results and analyses the problems which result from particular practices. The inclusive holiday industry depends on retail travel agencies for most of its sales, and Chapter 5 examines the relationships between tour operators and travel agents.

Creating the markets for inclusive holidays | 4

INTRODUCTION

There is an extensive theoretical and applied literature devoted to marketing and a growing number of textbooks have examined tourism marketing specifically, several of which are listed at the end of this chapter. The purposes here are to provide an overview of the significance of marketing in the development of the inclusive holiday industry, and to present a brief, critical review of some of the key techniques by which companies implement their marketing campaigns.

CUSTOMER PERSPECTIVES IN MARKETING INCLUSIVE HOLIDAYS

A clear understanding of who its customers are, what benefits they seek and how to present offers to them is crucial to the success of any company operating in a competitive environment. Chapter 1 pointed to the rapid growth of the industry, particularly during the 1970s and 1980s, but although some 12 million overseas inclusive holidays were sold in Britain in 1991, by 1995 sales had fallen to about 10 million, and some forecasts predicted a further decline in overseas inclusive holidaytaking. While noting the spectacular growth in holidaytaking, it should be stated that a large proportion of the British population do not take holidays away from home for a variety of reasons as indicated in Table 4.1, including relatively high cost and non-economic barriers to travel such as age or infirmity.

Furthermore, the pattern of holidaytaking appears to be shifting, with different preferences emerging for destinations and types of holiday, and a tendency to take more frequent but shorter breaks, as Table 4.2 indicates.

Inclusive holidays are only one form of leisure travel, providing clients with the key advantages of economy and convenience over making independent arrangements. However, the inclusive holiday industry, through its success in packaging travel arrangements, has also

Table 4.1 Reasons for not taking a holiday

Reason	%
Cost	48
Time	11
Personal disability	14
Illness	10
Infirm, elderly	5

Source: ETB, 1985

Table 4.2 The volatility of consumers' holiday preferences

Type of holiday	Summer 1996	Summer 1991
	% booked	
Lakes and mountains	3	3
City breaks	4	4
Long haul	3	14
Flight only	9	12
Other types	3	3
Beach holidays	77	66
Hotel	*61*	*37*
Self-catering	*16*	*29*

Source: Stats MR, cited in Beaver (1993).

made many places more accessible to individual travellers, and they now find a greater range of amenities there because of the developments associated with mass tourism.

Two linked aspects of consumers' holiday choices are significant to the argument in this book: the decision as to whether to make own's own arrangements or to purchase a packaged holiday, and the general and specific choice of destination to visit. The factors influencing choice of holiday mode and location preference can be understood from several perspectives, summarized in Table 4.3. These include the relative price advantages of buying a package as opposed to purchasing the elements separately; the ease of buying a holiday package, and their ready availability through high street and shopping centre outlets; and the prominence afforded to foreign travel in the media, both through specialist travel features and topics such as nature programmes which strikingly portray the attractions of distant peoples, places and ecologies.

PROMOTING HOLIDAYS AND DESTINATIONS

This general background to increased holiday and destination awareness, linked to individuals' varying needs for relaxation, change and

Table 4.3 A hierarchy of holiday buying decisions

To purchase a packaged holiday
- The desire to take an overseas holiday
- Price advantages of buying packaged holidays
- Ease of purchasing packaged holidays
- Advertising for holiday brands

To take a holiday in a type of destination
- Programmes portraying the culture or ecology of foreign places
- Advertising for other products set in exotic locations
- Media coverage of sports events held overseas

To go to a specific destination
- Previous knowledge of it
- Recommendation by friends who have enjoyed it
- Advertising by the destination
- Editorial features on travel destinations

participation in activities, has coincided with other trends which have de-emphasized the specific place-related objectives of travelling, stressing instead the price benefits and ease of holiday packages, wherever they may be located. Destination agencies, tour operators and travel retailers all contribute to the heightened awareness of holiday opportunities through their advertising, but their objectives differ somewhat. Consequently they tend to promote different aspects of the holiday experience, as Table 4.4 indicates.

Destinations have the most specific place objectives, focusing attention on the range of place benefits which they offer, and frequently alluding to their accessibility through tour operators' products. They also collaborate directly with tour operators to mount joint promotional campaigns, for example with the objective of stimulating interest in a newly developed resort area, or more generally by providing access to photo libraries and other technical services related to the production of brochures of advertising copy. The chief problems faced by destinations are their distance from origin markets, linked to their need to promote into many countries and the competition which their messages and images face in any marketplace from all other destinations trying to obtain business there.

Mass market tour operators' priorities are to attract customers to their holiday products and therefore they are less concerned about

Table 4.4 A typology of holiday industry marketing objectives and strengths

Holiday industry member	Marketing proposition	Market reach
Destination	Specific place	International
Tour operator	Holiday concept and brand	National, segmented
Travel retailer	Easy purchase of the components of travel	Local, general

selling any particular destination: their advertising literature and imagery is often rather generalized, promoting generic holiday benefits such as stylish living, exotic flora and fauna or the romantic, social or sporting opportunities offered by their holiday concepts. Although they offer a wide choice of destinations, most tour operators serve clients from only one origin market. They can therefore focus their market spend in spatial terms more closely than destinations, but their appeals also have to be directed accurately to the segments of the market for which their holiday products have been designed.

Travel agencies have the most general approach to tourism promotion, offering any destination and most tour operators' products, but because of their smaller scale they operate on relatively restricted promotional budgets. To overcome this, and to attract as many of the local population as possible to become their clients, they tend to take advantage of offers to stage collaborative promotional campaigns with any tour operator or destination which is willing to be a partner.

The cruise sector of tourism epitomizes the issues raised above, while also illustrating many of the practices common to the inclusive holiday industry, as Case study 4.1 shows.

CASE STUDY 4.1

The cruise holiday industry

Introduction

Cruising is one of the fastest growing sectors of the holiday industry, and its potential for development was confirmed when one of Britain's largest vertically integrated holiday companies entered the market in 1995 with the acquisition of its own cruise ships. This signalled a radical change to the way cruises had been marketed and to the product offered. At the same time, new ships were being commissioned by established cruise lines, the features of traditional cruising were being enhanced and extended, and new markets and new cruise areas were being developed.

At the close of the twentieth century it is sometimes difficult to recall the importance of passenger shipping which had dominated long-distance travel until the rise of air transport. However, as passenger jets were deployed during the 1950s and 1960s, their price and speed advantages undermined the traditional sea carriers' business, and some of the tonnage was switched from liner services to cruising. These cruise holidays were generally expensive and their emphasis on high standards of service attracted a rather exclusive clientele to areas such as the Caribbean or the Mediterranean. The security and comfort of a cruise ship also provided an excellent base for shore excursions to exotic and cultural locations which often lacked a developed tourist infrastructure, and cruise itineraries were planned to enable clients to visit several such ports of call.

Alternative cruise areas included the world's great rivers, especially the Rhine, Amazon and Yellow rivers, and scenic coastal voyages. Notable amongst these is the famed Norwegian Hurtigruten coastal voyage, operated since 1893 as a regular cargo and local passenger service for Norway's isolated communities, and accommodating passengers who join for all or part of the voyage. This was described by the TTG *Cruise News* (1995) in the following terms: 'A coastal steamer leaves every evening on an 11-day 2500 nautical mile journey calling at 34 ports, towns and fishing villages between Bergen, via the North Cape, to the Russian border.'

Since 1980, the cruise industry has grown at an average annual rate of 9.8%, and 161 passenger ships operated world-wide in 1994. Over 54% of all passengers cruise in the Caribbean, some 2.66 million passengers embark from Florida ports alone, and North America accounts for $5 billion of the $6 billion revenue generated (Showalter, 1994). An analysis of the spatial distribution of cruise ship capacity, calculated by counting the availability in each cruise area of lower berths, showed that 56% were located in the Caribbean and 20% in the Mediterranean, all other areas attracting less than 10% of capacity in the last quarter of 1994. A further distinction is made between category of ship, with five classes ranging from Super Deluxe to Economy. According to this study, the only cruise area with a significant trade in economy berths was the Mediterranean, while Super Deluxe and De Luxe + accommodation predominates in the Caribbean (Wild, 1994). Another report, by Price Waterhouse, valued the contribution of cruising to the Caribbean nations' economies at $984 million in 1992.

Elements of the modern cruise product

Cruising is a highly varied holiday product. Each ship has different characteristics of size, speed and ambience, offers several standards of accommodation, and most operate in a variety of cruise areas, moving between them according to season and market opportunity. The elements of a cruise therefore include the ship itself, the cabin's amenities, the quality of service, the range and types of entertainment, and the length, area and ports of embarkation and call for each cruise.

Features of cruise ships

The *ABC Cruise and Ferry Guide* regularly provides profiles of each cruise ship as a reference for travel agency staff and others involved in the cruising industry. It provides details of each ship's name, the cruise line which operates it, and features a photograph of the ship, followed by the following information:

- date the ship entered service;
- gross registered tonnage;
- number of passengers and crew;

- a passenger space ratio;
- the ship's summer and winter cruising areas;
- nationalities of the crew and staff;
- currency used on board.

There follows concise but detailed information on the range and quality of cabins, public rooms and deck areas, food and drink, and the style of service, described for example as 'quick and unobtrusive' or 'very helpful cabin stewards'. It then lists the ship's entertainment facilities and any special features.

On-board facilities

Ships built recently are designed to appeal to predetermined market niches, and while some are small luxury vessels – 'ultra-yachts' – the larger ships offer a full range of facilities. These typically include 'swimming pools, jacuzzis, work-out rooms, casinos, golf ranges and night clubs . . . [They may have] atrium-style architecture, glass-fronted lifts, and cabins with balconies and sitting areas and full bathrooms.' Some have helipads or a hydraulic marina which can be lowered when the ship is anchored to provide a sheltered environment for water sports (Hobson-Perry, 1993).

A key feature of cruising is that everything is included in the price, and entertainment is an increasingly important part of the package. 'Norwegian Cruise Line's SS *Norway* can put on full-scale Broadway musicals. The latest NCL ship, *Dreamward*, has a theatre capable of mounting Busby Berkeley style spectaculars, with 'rain' tumbling down during one routine and fireworks lighting up the stage in another' (*TTG Cruise News*, 1995).

Many operators now equip their ships with extensive shopping facilities, sometimes in the form of a mall. These provide passengers with a wide range of duty-free and lifestyle related items, both minimizing any need to go ashore to shop for souvenirs or bargains and maximizing the opportunities for revenue since they are typically rented by the vendors, often familiar international companies or their franchisees.

Catering

The logistics of providing consistently high-quality, varied catering to the clients while at sea is a particular challenge to cruise companies, while the high standards of catering are a traditional feature of cruising and all meals are included in the price: generally, only drinks are charged separately. For a typical client, the menu seems to change every day, but the rotation is actually managed on a weekly basis under the advice of a consultant chef. The presentation of each dish is carefully designed and tested with consumer panels before a demonstration plate is photographed. The ship's kitchen staff work to the photographs, a new set being displayed each day according to the rotation sequence: the result is very high-quality mass catering. Recently, in response to changing preferences, meals on cruises have emphasized a range of options including those with light food tastes or passengers following a variety of medical, belief or lifestyle diets.

In contrast, upmarket cruises work to an agreed framework, but the executive chef on each ship has more control. He or she radios headquarters with their purchasing requirements ahead of reaching each port of call. This list is relayed to the local agent who arranges for local suppliers such as fishmongers and fruiterers to be ready with a selection of high-quality produce for the executive chef to choose from for immediate delivery to the ship.

A closely associated feature of cruise companies' emphasis on style is the care taken to change the table flowers on a daily basis. In reality these are stored between meals in the ship's cool rooms and regularly trimmed and refreshed.

Managing the base port turnaround

A cruise ship's turnaround at its base port is carefully orchestrated to ensure that time at the quay is minimized (as there is no revenue potential during this period, but harbours levy a range of charges for their services and facilities). On arrival, customs board, the ship will be cleared of passengers, their luggage is taken ashore and any waste will be removed. The second set of tasks relate to ensuring that all the supplies needed for the ensuing period at sea are taken on board and properly stowed. A fleet of suppliers' trucks pull up at the quay side in a predetermined order to load the ship: once at sea, the ship must be entirely self-sufficient. The ship is fuelled, and new passengers are boarded and shown to their accommodation. A cruise ship accommodating 1000 passengers can be turned around in five hours, but is normally in port for eight to ten hours before departing on its next itinerary.

Minor maintenance is often scheduled for port stops along the itinerary when it is anticipated that most passengers will take shore excursions, for example a new dining room carpet might be loaded in Fort Lauderdale together with a team of fitters in order to change it on arrival in Jamaica a few days later when some of the air conditioning ducts to cabins might also be overhauled. The work has to be completed and calm restored to the ship before passengers return from their day trips.

Ports of call

Most cruises are less than a week's duration, although wealthy, upmarket clients might spend several weeks at sea. For a seven-day cruise, the average is about four ports of call, while the ratio is maintained with eight stops on a typical fortnight itinerary. Companies with a regular cruising pattern that includes several ports must find something for their passengers to do in each port, and the facilities offered there must match what is offered on board in terms of style, comfort and safety. The issue for the cruise company is to position their voyages to appeal to the broad market, and this depends on basing the ship at an appropriate port offering easy and frequent access to a wide market, and to provide ports of call which are attractive to clients. However, for many people taking a cruise holiday, cultural reasons for visiting particular ports are low on their agenda and constitute only a small part of their vacation experience.

The principle ports, especially in the Caribbean, become very crowded when cruise ships arrive (often more than one at a time). This puts overwhelming pressure on the infrastructure of the port and of the town itself as large numbers of visitors arrive within a brief interval. The impact of cruise visitors is further focused on particular areas and activities because of the limited time they can spend ashore, their unfamiliarity with the port and the organized, structured nature of the shore activities provided for them by the company's shore agent.

Private islands

Increasingly in cruising, the ship itself has become the destination. Many are floating resorts, and many passengers remain aboard in its secure and controlled environment throughout their cruise. One response, pioneered by Norwegian Cruise Line (NCL), is the private island concept. In 1977, they began to land cruise ship passengers by tender on Great Stirrup Cay in the Bahamas for a day's relaxation on an isolated and idyllic beach. This proved very popular, and the cruise line purchased it in 1986, investing $1 million to upgrade its facilities. RCCL had also introduced the concept of beach party shore excursions – its passengers were taken to Seven Mile Beach in Grand Cayman where they were provided with changing rooms, food and drink.

By the mid 1990s, almost all cruise lines operating in the Caribbean had private or 'out' islands. These are usually coves or peninsulas which are not easily accessible except by tender from the sea, although they are located on inhabited islands thus ensuring a supply of carefully recruited local labour. There is a high concentration of private islands in the Bahamas because of the number of suitable sites there, the frequency of ship calls and the proximity of the area to Miami, the major cruise base for the American market. Private islands are usually leased from governments, and are sometimes shared with competing cruise lines in order to minimize their costs of operation and to maximize their use. In one case (reported by Showalter, 1994) the signs are changed to feature the cruise line exclusively using it on that day.

It is often necessary to dredge channels and turning basins in order to protect the ship and to reduce the time spent tendering passengers ashore. Additionally, the shore site is usually improved by planting to obtain shade and atmosphere, and a range of facilities are built for the visitors' comfort and convenience. Local business interests, particularly handicraft markets, are encouraged, but are carefully controlled to ensure consistent quality of produce and service and to avoid conflict resulting from passengers being 'ripped off' as is known to happen in several community-based ports of call.

> There is always an attempt to provide an idyllic setting and some attempt to retain and even improve the natural environment . . . Overall, the cruise passengers' experience is highly controlled, well organized, and to some degree, even contrived. Cruise line surveys, however, consistently show this to be the highlight and most satisfactory shore feature on most cruises where it is offered.
>
> (Showalter, 1994)

Despite the evident attraction of the concept to cruise passengers, a number of problems have been identified (Showalter, 1994):

- ecosystems are disturbed by the numbers of visitors and frequency of calls;
- septic systems using salt water inhibit bacterial breakdown;
- there is a possibility of oil seepage;
- dredging disturbs reefs and other organisms;
- there is minimal contact with Caribbean citizens;
- it reduces time spent at established cruise ports where economic opportunities exist for local businessmen.

Fleet management

Cruise ships vary from vessels specially constructed for Antarctic journeys through large luxury yachts providing privacy to converted ocean liners and purpose-built holiday resorts accommodating 2000 or more holidaymakers travelling between ports. The industry has several segments including operators with a fleet of many vessels and niche players with only one ship: in the latter case, this single vessel is the only source of revenue, yet it has to bear all the administrative costs and does not enjoy the economies of large-scale purchasing for food, fuel and supplies.

Optimism by fleet managers and the sudden creation of capacity in the world's shipbuilding yards following the peace dividend of the early 1990s resulted in 22 new ships reported to be under construction in 1995, adding 35 000 beds to the 150 000 currently for sale by the cruise industry. Those completed in 1994 had averaged an investment per berth of $201 000, although the forecast was that the average cost would fall slightly over the following few years (Wild, 1994). However, with the large increase in capacity in the cruise industry, the problem will be to grow the market and to manage revenue yield.

Previously, the launch of a new ship was a rare event, and it could be expected to sell quickly, partly from its novelty factor and also because any new ship incorporates the latest technology in its construction, operation and passenger amenities. The latest ships have sophisticated engine management and navigation systems which improve fuel burn and minimize discomfort from bad weather, and they often feature very advanced naval architecture such as atriums and full air conditionning. Cabins now feature picture windows, direct dial telephones and many other amenities.

Most new ships are 90% or more financed by medium-term debt and after about ten years service it has usually paid off the mortgage raised to construct it. Subsequently the major expenses for its operation are food and fuel. Larger companies want the effeciency of operation and the customer appeal of new ships, and this creates a market for their older fleet which looks rather dated against modern marine architecture and is less fuel efficient to operate.

A feature of cruising is that ships have an operational life span of several decades, and typically undergo a number of major refits during their service in order to upgrade their engines, stabilizers and passenger amenities. However, it will be increasingly difficult to adapt older ships to meet the new safety regulations being introduced during the mid 1990s. For example, many will have to be replumbed for sprinkler systems, but it will be much more expensive to make radical changes to their internal layout to ensure that no corridor ends in a blank wall.

Hobson-Perry (1993) has pointed out that 'cruise ship owners have begun to turn to flags of convenience to avoid health and safety inspections, high fees and maritime unions from high wage countries.' As a result, most ships operating from the United States are registered in one of the following five countries – Panama, Liberia, Bermuda, Cyprus and the Bahamas.' Flags of convenience make it possible to crew a ship from any country, and this has led to the establishment of an international crewing agency in Monaco, while special schools have been set up in the Philippines and Korea to supply staff for cruise lines. Although passengers seldom show any concern about the nationality of a ship's staff , it is still a tradition that the captain, who represents the public face of the company, is a national of the owners' country.

Although 85% of cruise passengers originate in America, most cruise lines have been European owned until recently, but during the 1990s American companies including Hyatt are buying ownership of established cruise lines. Other cruise lines have been bought by investment companies. By mid 1992, 'three major cruise line operators accounted for a 47% market share, and the top six accounted for over 66% market share' (Hobson-Perry, 1993). Companies such as Radisson, although not owners, have taken a management interest in the *Radisson Diamond*. Many vessels have operating companies: one of Airtours' ships is managed by Kloster Lines, another by V Ships (based in Monaco), which is also involved with P&O and two Silver Seas ships. Three patterns are evident: some vessels are owner-operated, others are leased and, as is the case with Thomson, operated under an established brand name, while other vessels are managed.

Development of cruise products

Evidence of over-capacity in any industry is found in its heavily discounted products or upgrading as a common practice. In cruising, the efforts to differentiate products continue, with operators investing to improve the quality of their service, or developing themed cruises and offering new destinations to extend the market and to obtain the maximum revenue from each cruise in a more competitive environment with an increasing supply. On board, operators have experimented with creative selling opportunities, for example by selling cocktails in collectable glasses, or by offering superior dining facilities for a supplementary charge. By accepting credit card payments for on-board services (including tipping), cruise companies have overcome the difficulty of pricing in one currency for their international clientele.

New markets are being developed. In Europe particularly, shorter cruises based in the Mediterranean and reached by a flight included in the price have been found to have a wider market appeal, thus enabling a much greater number of people to buy this form of holiday. On board ships intended for this product, new facilities have been introduced to appeal to the new cruise clients, who tend to be less formal and younger than the industry's traditional clients. Ships now feature separate discos for adults and teenagers, a very relaxed dress code and special programmes to entertain children.

Another market with the potential for significant growth is the Far East. 'Currently 92% of passengers there originate in the US, and 5% in Europe, with only 3% of local traffic. However, there is evidence of demand from Japan, but for a Japanese cruise product' (*TTG Cruise News*, 1995). Adventure cruises to exotic locations which are otherwise difficult to reach, such as the Galapagos or the Antarctic, are another opportunity, and although this segment is quite small it attracts high-spending clients.

A shore stay of several days added to a cruise is an important part of the product, attracting many clients, especially to ships which move between cruise areas or on round-the-world itineraries. Passengers take part of the cruise and add on a stay at one or more ports to construct their own holiday according to their interests. This represents a significant additional source of commission to the travel agent, and if it is packaged by the cruise line, the shore stay is another source of revenue for them.

Another aspect of the search for new cruising regions is the opening up of ports which were not previously on cruise itineraries. For example, Dover hosted 25 cruise ships in 1994, a fivefold increase over 1991. This growth coincided with the expected decline of cross-Channel traffic and an associated reduction in employment opportunities in the area ensuing from the full operation of the Channel Tunnel, which began to accept revenue traffic in late 1994. As part of its strategy to diversify away from reliance on cross-Channel traffic, Dover announced plans for a £9 m cruise liner terminal there housed in the Western Dock's railway station, a Grade 2 Listed Building. This resulted in the Royal Cruise Line's decision to base *Crown Odessey* there in 1996, and both Costa and Fred Olsen announced their intention to move to Dover, at the expense of Tilbury and Southampton. In response, Tilbury is taking over the Port of London Authority's cruise berths further up the River Thames near HMS *Belfast* and at Butler's Warf.

Marketing and selling American cruises

It has been suggested that five strategic and tactical marketing factors were needed to support the growth of cruising during the 1970s and 1980s in America, including industry organization, collaboration with travel retailers and a clearer definition of the product and its market (Hobson-Perry, 1994):

- CLIA (Cruise Lines International Association) was 'formed in the early 1970s based on the need to develop an industry organization in order to build and promote the concept of cruising.'
- The industry began to work closely with travel agencies which sell 98% of American cruises. They are an attractive product for travel agencies to sell because of their high value and consequent high commission levels, their popularity and ease of booking.
- Thirdly, the changing 'perception of what cruises were all about. There was the entrance of Carnival Cruise Lines in 1974 along with their "fun ship" concept' reinforced by the successful TV series, 'Loveboat' which was set on P&O's Price Cruise liners.
- Cruises packaged with free airline tickets enabled ships to be based in the southern ports, whereas their market was mainly in the northern industrial cities. While embarcations from Seattle declined by 80% and New York by 19% between 1982 and 1990, cruise passengers increasingly used the southern ports. San Juan grew by 603%, Port Everglades by 436%. 'Today, Florida accounts for approximately 65% of all US embarcations.'

Five potential ways of segmenting the market have been identified (Marti, 1993):

- attracting patrons from a well defined geographic area;
- theme marketing catering for passengers' common interests such as bridge, sports personalities;
- itinerary marketing of distinctive areas such as the Caribbean;
- limited duration cruises;
- socioeconomic marketing directed towards an identifiable section of the population, for example newly affluent Americans.

The major selling tool of travel agents who sell the majority of cruises is the cruise brochure, and Marti (1993) has pointed out that if it is to be successful 'it must correctly reflect . . . the specific line's offering.' Each company's brochure competes with others, as well as describing many alternative offerings. Marti has carried out a detailed content analysis of the text and illustrations used in five cruise companies' brochures; his findings are summarized in Tables 4.5 and 4.6.

Table 4.5 Ordered word count, Caribbean cruise brochures

Word	Total occurrence in five brochures
you	628
our	94
Caribbean	61
cruise	59
we	47
more	38
island	34
most	34
ship	33
best	24
special	22
dining	20

Source: Marti (1993).

Table 4.6 Analysis of visual information in Caribbean cruise brochures

Variable	Total occurences in five brochures
Location of picture	
aboard	7
ashore	104
Cruise line identification	
yes	18
no	156
People	
passengers	78
crew	25
youths	5
18–35	67
middle aged	48
elderly	9
Attire	
formal	18
casual	60

Based on Marti (1993).

Marti concluded that:

> The hypothesis that generic messages prevail within the sales literature of the cruise industry has been tested and confirmed . . . brand character, exemplified by the potential for recognizing an individual line's product, is relatively absent . . . in a period of high competition caused by the addition of new cruise cpacity, [this] could hinder the effectiveness of cruise line marketing programmes . . .
>
> (Marti, 1993)

Summarizing studies of changes in the American market, Hobson-Perry (1993) noted that 'In 1985, the median age was 58, by 1992 it had dropped to just under 43.' More married couples bought cruises, and increasingly they brought their children, while the fastest growing sector in the early 1990s was between the ages of 25 and 40. With changing demographics and shorter cruises gaining in popularity (2–5 day voyages increasing from 24% in 1980 to 38% in 1990), the product attracted less affluent passengers. By 1990, 35% had a family income less than $40 000.

Cruising from Britain

The ex-UK market has a particular problem because Britain's weather makes it an unattractive cruise area, consequently clients have to travel considerable distances. However, this takes time and adds to the expense of a cruise. At a CIMTIG meeting in 1987, Bob Duffett, then with NCL, explained that the growth of cruising had led to a need to stimulate the market. For example, out of Miami in 1966, one 550-berth vessel departed twice weekly from Miami in 1966. This had risen to 13 or 14 departures on Saturdays or Sundays, with additional ships departing on Fridays and Mondays, making a total of about 40 cruises per week by 1986.

Subsidised airfares had been introduced enabling clients booked on a seven-day cruise to fly free from anywhere in the US to Miami, and a £99 transatlantic fare had been introduced in 1980 linked to cruises. This was cross subsidized, but was soon followed by a free air offer from Royal Caribbean. After a couple years of intense price competition, the industry reverted to marketing fully inclusive cruises. However, the first transatlantic cruise deal had been offered in 1971 on an all-inclusive basis.

Another difference is that capacity out of the UK is limited in contrast to the major cruise area, the Caribbean. Consequently the industry has a much greater variety of product there to sell, and awareness is higher, both amongst the public and travel retailers.

In 1995, P&O accepted delivery of the *Oriana*, the first cruise ship built mainly for the British market. This single ship, accommodating 1760 passengers on ten decks, represented a 50% increase to P&O's existing capacity, while the total cruise capacity was further increased by other new ships, including CTC Cruise Line's *Southern*

Cross. As a result, although it was fully occupied on its maiden voyage, it proved difficult to fill *Oriana* for the other 17 cruises of its first season, and discounting developed in the market. Brochure rates starting at about £1200 were reduced to about £600 on some one-week sailings, thus putting pressure on other operators' tarrifs.

Cruise line operators and specialist retailers interviewed by the trade press commented that they were optimistic that the publicity attendant on the new ships, the public announcements of upgrading to existing vessels, and improved marketing of cruise holidays would result in the growth of the ex-UK cruising sector to about 90 000 in 1995, an increase of almost 10 000 over 1994.

Selling cruising in Britain

A decade ago, Holloway remarked that 'In Britain, less than one in ten travel agencies are productive in terms of cruise sales; many counter staff lack the expertise or experience to sell cruises, and in spite of high levels of commission earned by such sales, more training is needed . . .' (Holloway, 1994). Shipping companies loose many potential cruise customers because agency staff lack the specialized knowledge to sell the product effectively."

Addressing a meeting of CIMTIG in 1994, a Royal Caribbean Cruises manager explained her view that more cruises could be sold in Britain. The problem was outdated perceptions compounded by nostalgia. Royal Caribbean had confronted the question of what they were selling: they offered stylish entertainment, interesting activities and year-round, mobile, full-board accommodation. Their advertising now carried these messages instead of using traditional 'ship shots'. They continuously monitored customers' views and responded to their interests by adding value, initiating fly-free cruising and opening up the UK regional market.

The role of the Passenger Shipping Association Retail Agent Scheme (PSARA)

While some cruise lines encourage direct sales, 85% of UK cruises are sold through travel agencies, but traditional cruise passengers prefer to deal with experienced staff. This has had two results: it has created an opportunity for about 20 retailers to specialize in the cruise sector, and it has led to the development of PSARA, described in its literature as 'The world's leading cruise lines and travel agents working together.' PSARA is jointly funded by 30 cruise lines, while over 1600 travel agents pay a fee (£125 in 1995) to join. They receive a package entitled *Tools for increasing your cruise sales*, as well as training, information services, manuals, ship visits and familiarization trips to help them sell cruising.

PSARA was cloned from the earlier American CLIA (Cruise Lines International Association) which has about 22 000 outlets, and enjoys a budget of several million dollars. Its purpose was also to provide training and information directed to the travel agents and uninitiated travellers. It publishes a range of leaflets, including *Choose to cruise . . . 101 reasons why!* These range from 1 'Be waited on hand and foot' to 80 'Down rum at a pirate ship party', and conclude with 21 cruise destinations.

PSARA's 300-page manual provides cruise company profiles, their sales policy and detailed information on all ships and ports. Some 40 training sessions are organized at locations around Britain annually, with courses ranging from basic product knowledge to selling skills for travel agency staff and marketing development for agency managers. Members are also provided with an exclusive a freephone help service and are encouraged to let their customers know of their membership by being provided with window stickers.

A quarterly magazine carries news items describing the latest developments in cruising, and provides other information which helps agents sell cruising holidays. For example, the November 1994 issue featured a double-page analysis of cruise lines' tipping policies. This indicates that some lines include gratuities in the selling price, and for those which do not it gives guidelines for cabin stewards, dining room waiters, the bus boy and the head waiter on a *per diem* basis.

Cruise lines often work with independent preferred travel agencies on joint marketing plans to develop cruise business locally. Methods include 50:50 advertising campaigns, direct mail using agency stationery, override commission and some discounting on selected departure dates. Independents generate about 60% of cruise sales. Advancing technology is not yet significant in the sales of cruising holidays, although this is changing with the use of Sabre, and RCCL's Cruise Match 2000 link to 20 000 US agencies. The problem is the wide range of accommodation offered, the individual style and features of each vessel, and the tendency for certain dates to sell well. The challenge is for agents to sell different categories of cruise according to clients' individual needs, and technological solutions are not yet persuasive.

Pricing is used to level the demand pattern for cruising, but retailers' involvement in price tactics has affected buying patterns and masks the underlying patterns of consumer demand. It is essential to regulate consumer demand through pricing since cruising is a highly perishable product. Early booking discounts give the advantage of ensuring some trade.

Tour operators' entry into the cruising market

Airtours, one of Britain's leading integrated holiday companies with tour operations, travel agencies and charter airline operations, saw an opportunity for product extension because of the lack of provision in the Mediterranean of cruise services which would appeal to its British and Scandinavian clients. The company's lack of previous cruise management experience was beneficial in developing new approaches to both the product and its marketing.

Airtours bought the Norwegian Cruise Line's 16 607 tonne ship *Southward* for £16 million in 1994, renaming it *Seawing*. The ship had carried 750 passengers for NCL, but has been converted to 1000 for the new owners, whose objective was to maximize revenue opportunities from the ship. It was reported that the cinema had been removed, the space being converted to add a further 16 cabins, while new bars, a casino, gym, teenage disco and children's play areas were added to compliment the normal entertainment found on cruise ships. *Seawing's* first summer programme of Mediterranean fly-cruise holidays was sold out within four months at fares from £399 for seven nights, inclusive of flights, on-board accommodation and food. The winter programme was priced from £239 for three nights. Airtours contracted NCL to continue to operate the ship and its on-board services and crewing.

By extending the portfolio of holidays it offered, Airtours had effectively created a new type of cruise product which would appeal to, and be affordable by, a sector of the holiday market new to cruising. They had been in a sound position to research the new market for cruise holidays, as the marketing director explained in an interview with TTG in 1995. Airtours had benefited from being parent to the retail chain, Going Places. All clients booking an Airtours cruise with the multiple had been asked what they expected in terms of food, entertainment and other services on board. A survey of 6000 customers have been used to mould Sun Cruises' product to the expectations of passengers. The Chief Executive of PSARA, Bob Duffet, commented:

> On one hand, they are telling customers there is no mystique about cruising, its just a package holiday in which the hotel floats. On the other hand, they must try not to take away the elegance of cruising because they would be selling themselves and the industry short.

Airtours claimed that it had achieved its aim of gaining around 60% of bookings from clients who have not cruised before. Its marketing director said:

> The ship has been fully refurbished and we have made the product affordable and less formal. We have applied the Airtours sales and marketing formula, so anyone who has enjoyed our other holidays will enjoy our cruises. We have a well thought out formula. The ship is the right size to give us the economies of scale we need to offer affordable fares, which is always the starting point for customers.
>
> (*Travel Weekly*, 1995)

Based on its initial success, and before Airtours could judge the ability of its cruising product to succeed year round, it bought another ship, Royal Caribbean Cruise Line's *Nordic Prince* with a capacity of 1100 passengers, for £35 million, and renamed it *Carousel*. Shortly afterwards, the trade press announced that one of its main competitors, Thomson, intended to re-enter the fly-cruise market, a sector it had briefly experimented with in the mid 1970s.

Seawing's summer base is Palma, to which Airtours operates a large number of charter flights from British airports, and from which it offers cruises to Corsica, Rome, Elba, Monte Carlo and Barcelona, and about a hundred cabins a week were allocated to Airtours' Scandinavian tour operator. However, the Mediterranean is less attractive as a winter cruising area, so it was planned to reposition the ship to a base in the Canaries, which was already well established as the primary centre for Airtours' winter programme. This reduced the risk because the flying programme supported a range of Airtours' existing products rather than being specially contracted for the cruising programmes. It also helped create economic conditions for the inter-season repositioning cruises, as passengers flying to Palma to join the ship returned by air to the UK on Airtours' charter series after the ship arrived in the Canaries.

Another advantage for Airtours and its clients arising from its integrated operations was the option for them to take a standard resort holiday as an add-on prior to, or after, the cruise. In logistical terms this feature was as easy to arrange as extending a normal holiday package by extra weeks, and it minimized the potential risk that clients might switch their holiday from hotel stays to cruising. Industry commentators considered that the type of cruising which Airtours has developed was unlikely to pose a significant threat to existing cruise operators, both because the product offer is rather different, and because there is a high degree of customer loyalty to particular lines and even to individual ships. Andy Stewart of Kloster Cruise commented: 'Attracting new cruise clients is good for established operators because it provides a wider base of passengers for them to try to attract, and it gives a better insight into what passengers cruising in the 1990s want.'

Sources: Hobson-Perry (1993); Marti (1993); Showalter (1994); Wild (1995); and interviews with Bob Duffet of PSARA.

HIGH AND LOW INVOLVEMENT BUYING BEHAVIOUR

In their marketing decisions, many tourism managers act as if they believe that everyone regards the purchase of a holiday as critically important. However, the importance of any category of product varies between one customer and another, and these variations can be understood by investigating their degrees of interest and 'involvement' in it. Cohen (1986) defined involvement as 'a state of arousal that a person

Table 4.7 High involvement feature of inclusive holiday purchases

- Holidays are expensive
- They are complex both to purchase and experience
- There is a risk they will not prove satisfying
- The choice of destination (or type of holiday) reflects the holidaymaker's personality

experiences in regard to consumption related activity'. Involvement is considered likely to be high when the purchase has functional and symbolic significance, and entails some risk (Asseal, 1987). Table 4.7 lists some of the features of vacations which make it likely that many tourists will experience a high degree of involvement in choosing their holiday.

The significance of regarding holidays as a high involvement purchase is the implication that considerable care will be invested in the choice of destination or type of holiday. The involved tourist often undertakes detailed and extended study of brochures, reading and watching holiday advertising, and visiting travel agencies for advice to identify suitable places to visit, given their individual interests and the time and budget available. This rationalist approach can also be seen in stimulus-response modelling of buyer behaviour (Middleton, 1988; Engel, Blackwell and Miniard, 1986) where information is transmitted by advertisers, received as an input by consumers, evaluated by them, and the process results in purchasing responses.

In contrast, the industry gains many sales by the low-priced offers often featured prominently in travel retailers' windows, holidaymakers choice of destination being heavily influenced by what is currently on offer. Thus the rationalist model of holiday destination selection has rather less validity in the conditions which have characterized much of the market for packaged holidays, when tour operators or travel retailers emphasize prices rather than destination attributes in their promotions. This shifts the customers' attention to a comparison of prices rather than of what each destination offers, potentially resulting in a reduced 'commitment' to the resort visited. Under these conditions, there is more likely to be a mismatch between the tourist's holiday expectations, and their destination experiences, resulting in dissatisfaction and complaint. This difficulty is exacerbated by two factors, one internal to the holiday industry, the other characteristic of contemporary society. Discounted, and particularly late offer holidays, often involve relatively low quality holiday components, including such features as inconvenient departure and arrival times, and unspecified hotel (or other) accommodation at the time of booking since it is allocated on arrival. While clients sometimes benefit under these trading conditions from accommodation better than they had anticipated, the reverse is often the case, mainly because those who booked early have opted for the superior accommodation and the better locations.

The industry has regularly experienced a high incidence of complaints about low standards of accommodation, poor resort location and associated difficulties particularly with respect to late booked holidays. At the same time, there is growing management emphasis, in tourism no less than other sectors of the economy, on product and service quality (Grönroos, 1990; Normann, 1991). This situation has to be considered in the context of growing consumer-rights awareness (Prus, 1989), and in the 'meta-context' of scepticism about the underlying values and institutions of western societies (Hughes, 1993).

The overall effect of price discounting by tour operators and travel retailers is to shift buyers' attention to the affordability of holidays, thereby widening the customer base but reducing the uniqueness of the appeals of specific alternative destinations. A further consequence is that consumers sometimes purchase holidays to inappropriate destinations. For example, young family groups or the elderly are tempted by reduced price offers to holiday in resorts where the range of entertainment is geared to youths, with resultant disappointment for each type of visitor. This has negative connotations during the vacation for the hotel, the resort and the tour operator, who have to respond to complaints. The travel retailer also becomes a target of complaint when the client returns, a situation which recent European legislation is likely to accentuate (Rogers, 1993; Grant and Mason, 1993), since legislation now requires retailers to accept responsibility for their clients' holiday satisfaction.

BRANDING INCLUSIVE HOLIDAYS

The visible manifestation of a competitive market where the need is to emphazise the benefits which distinguish one product from similar alternatives is a strong branding strategy aimed at establishing and maintaining a clear identity for the company so that customers will ask for their products by name. Bonn and Brand (1995) have emphasized the importance of the concept of brand equity, defined as 'added value that a brand name brings to a product beyond its functional qualities' (Guiltinan and Paul, 1994). The objective of investing in brand management is to make the brand the one which the consumer is most likely to purchase.

Branding is at the centre of much modern marketing effort. A strong identity is felt to give opportunities and benefits to the company. From a promotional point of view the task is to establish strong market awareness for the brand so that it becomes the first choice of the consumer. Branding builds on the core features of a product or service, offering additional benefits which distinguish one product from similar alternatives. The stronger the brand, the less readily will a consumer accept an alternative. Branding can be implemented through the consistent use of a corporate symbol or trade name.

The objective is to ensure that the brand is one of those which the consumer is most likely to purchase. However, it is also possible that a particular brand may have failed to satisfy a consumer in the past, in which case it is unlikely that he or she will repurchase it. These two groups of brands have been described as evoked and inept sets. Evoked sets have been described as 'the collection of brands the buyer actually considers in his decision process' (Howard, 1963). Inept brands are those which the consumer has rejected from the purchase consideration, either because he or she has had an unpleasant experience of that company's services, or because negative feedback has been received from other sources such as friends or media comment, and this category therefore represents a general failure in their management. Another category, inert brands, includes companies about which the consumer has so little knowledge that they are unlikely to be considered. Inert brands represent a failure on the part of marketing, in contrast to the successful marketing awareness gained for evoked brands.

As the case study of First Choice demonstrates, the larger integrated companies have the resources and marketing strength to develop recognizable brands for the retail outlets and charter airlines, but the trend is to maintain separate identities for each level of operation. This is not the practice with most acquisitions; smaller companies quickly loose their identity to the larger organization, although there have been several examples of an established company whose name has been reused after a period, but linked to its new proprietor's products.

CASE STUDY 4.2

The launch of First Choice

First Choice Holidays PLC is the third largest of Britain's vertically integrated holiday companies, carrying over 13% of summer and winter UK inclusive holiday clients in 1995/ 96. It is vertically integrated to the extent that it has both a tour operator and an airline. However, First Choice has not acquired a travel agency chain as it believes it can maximize retail distribution by remaining unaligned and building good relations with all retailers. The tour operator sold and operated some two million overseas inclusive holidays in 1995. Its charter airline, Air 2000, is the subject of a separate case study in this book, and carried 2.9 million passengers in 1994/95. The company is quoted on the Stock Exchange.

The tour operator's predecessor, Owners Abroad, was the subject of a failed hostile takeover bid from another of the triumvirate, Airtours. The successful defence was achieved in part by a 'strategic alliance' with Thomas Cook which took a supportive stake, but was followed by a profits warning and the removal of part of the board. Behind these events lay a business which lacked focus and was not reacting quickly to the fast-moving events in the travel market.

The restructuring plan

A study commissioned by Owners Abroad from Ernst & Young recommended restructuring, and a new chief executive was appointed in November 1993. During the implementation of this plan, a small team of top managers was fully briefed on the restructuring, and they were each required to sign letters of confidentiality due to the competitive nature of the industry.

A new team of marketing managers was set up and briefed about each brand, the volume and profit targets set for it, the brochure design and launch date: they had 13 weeks to set up the programmes, operating under dummy brand names in case the strategy leaked to competitors. Consequently, they had to contract hotels without revealing the branding strategy. A dozen working parties met weekly to coordinate the necessary activities across the company and, with the chief executive present, to speed up decision-taking. These groups covered, amongst other activities, advertising, brochure design, public relations and overseas holiday services. From the outset, the style of management at First Choice was action oriented.

Rationalising the product offers

First Choice's predecessor, Owners Abroad, had offered a range of programmes sold under several different brand names. However, there was considerable overlap and duplication of products and destinations in several of the company's 40 brochures, creating internal competition for its own customers and a degree of confusion amongst retailers.

First Choice began its first season with a simplified, rationalized and coherent range of only 16 brochures. The new approach was developed from a SWOT analysis conducted by the advertising agency, Ogilvy and Mather, which had identified four main markets. These were mainstream couples and families upmarket holidays, holidays for couples without families, and direct sell. The main programmes for families and couples were marketed under the name First Choice, while more select holidays offering, for example, cab rather than coach transfers and using higher grade hotels were sold under the established Sovereign brand name. Non-family holidays for couples were branded Free Spirit. Direct sell holidays continued to be sold under the name Eclipse Direct, but the brochures were endorsed by the new First Choice name. Thus three brands targeted at the travel agent were established with sufficient market volume in each to obtain a prominent position in the marketplace. Each brand featured the major destinations of Greece, Spain, Turkey and Portugal. The 16 brochures were all endorsed with First Choice's name and a consistent style, achieving a clearer racking policy and production cost savings.

The launch was supported by a carefully planned advertising campaign, designed to introduce the First Choice name to the public in a bright and powerful way and to achieve a high level of consumer awareness. For consumers, it was a fun, light-hearted campaign which began with teasers leading to a full release of the name. To First Choice, it was a serious, focused campaign rapidly building awareness and complimenting the style of the brochures which were designed to stand out on travel agents' racks through a prominent display of the First Choice logo and bright holiday colours. Whereas 4% of people asked by market researchers to name tour operator brands had mentioned the name of any Owners Abroad holiday brand while it was functioning, 40% recognized First Choice within a month of its launch. This rate of prompted awareness had risen to 57% by January 1995 and to nearly 70% by January 1996.

Innovations

For its first full season (1995) the objective was to make the holidays which First Choice offered a satisfying and different experience for clients. The innovations introduced included offering three types of children's clubs aimed at different age groups (a refinement previously confined to holiday centres), and all-inclusive holidays in Mediterranean resorts. This latter concept had previously been limited to exclusive Caribbean resorts and Club Med style operations. It offered the advantage of all-in pricing to attract bookings from families on a tight budget who were particularly concerned that they might not be able to afford entertainment or drinks while abroad. The concept appealed to hoteliers because more of holidaymakers' resort spending remained on their premises, although resort mayors and tourist board officials were less happy with this concept since it had the potential to reduce the cash flow for other local businesses. However, for summer 1996, the all-inclusive concept had been adopted by some of First Choice's competitors.

First Choice also set out to offer its customers a seamless service from the moment when they chose their holiday through to their experience of it, with the objective of providing a distinctive service which customers would seek out in future years and would be prepared to pay a premium for. Another challenge was to create differences between First Choice and its competitors which were clear to retailers: training was aimed at getting them familiar with the contents of the brochures, while a racking policy was developed to ensure that sufficient sales volume was generated. However, as one manager commented:

> The irony of the industry is that customers don't see anyone from the tour operator until their arrival in the resort . . . Another problem is that travel agents often fail to pass on to clients the tour operator's documentation, preferring to strengthen their brand by using their own orientation material.

Trading conditions

First Choice began its operations for summer 1995 at a time when the industry was faced with a series of difficulties which included excess capacity and high levels of discounting, and saw the return of the £99 holiday. These conditions led to low load factors and a general decline in optimism in the industry. At a meeting of the Chartered Institute of Marketing Travel Industry Group (CIMTIG) in January 1996, its Marketing Director, Kevin Ivie, presented a chronology of these problems:

June 1995

- The late booking rush anticipated by the trade did not materialize, but most tour operators had already paid second deposits on contracted rooms to hoteliers.
- Teletext was being used to move late sale holidays, but it was easy for competitors to monitor each other, resulting in sequential and rapid price reductions.
- Travel agents were constantly featuring 15% retailer discounts.

July 1995

- Exceptionally hot UK weather continued, and the rush to book high season overseas holidays did not materialize.
- There was real overcapacity, and a widespread recognition of downturn in the industry.
- The financial press began to speculate about holiday companies' profitability.
- Pressure began to mount to delay the launch of the 1996 summer season brochures (which traditionally began to appear from early August onwards).

August 1995

- The industry responded to low demand by heavy discounting and attempts to consolidate amongst all tour operators.
- Due to the continuing pressure to sell excess capacity for summer 1995, most operators decided to launch summer 1996 holidays after the end of August.

Monitoring standards

First Choice regards the satisfaction of its clients as the key to its success. Holiday service questionnaires are handed out to all clients on their return flights and their views are carefully analysed. It also takes their safety while away from home seriously. General standards are monitored by resort staff through a regular schedule of inspections, and the company uses independent experts to inspect its hotels' standards of hygiene and general safety.

First Choice (and Thomson) have, for example, removed all properties which use gas water heaters from their brochures after a number of incidents involving holidaymakers. However, German companies subsequently contracted these properties, arguing that gas heaters are more environmentally friendly!

Sources: Presentation to CIMTIG, January 1996, and interviews with Kevin Ivie, First Choice Marketing Director.

What is important in branding is the way in which clients perceive the service offered, so effective brand management depends on market research. The position of a brand can be determined by techniques which examine the perceptual space occupied by a product in its intended customers' minds, for example in terms of price compared to comfort or to convenience. Well established market research methodologies enable managers to assess clients' own understanding of the relative position of competing companies. For example, most motorists would ascribe rather different virtues to two-litre four-door cars sold under the brand names of Saab, Fiat or Alfa Romeo.

Figure 4.1 shows how a tour operator offering holidays in one destination can emphasize varying features of its holiday concepts to present its products differently. The features of holidays in the upper right quadrant are family oriented and expensive: the market for such holidays is likely to be quite small. However, many families are keen to purchase low-cost holidays, and the mass market packages offered by this company are positioned according to this understanding of demand characteristics, with a small proportion of expensive holidays (perhaps offering exclusive use of a villa with a private swimming pool) in contrast to the large number of three-star hotel or self-catering apartment-based holidays in the operator's programme.

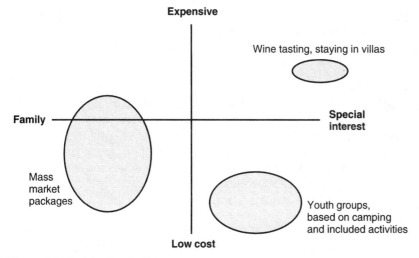

Figure 4.1 Positioning holiday concepts.

A problem arises at this point, because a brochure clearly depicting on its cover cheaper, mass market holidays is unlikely to attract the attention of more upmarket clients. Consequently, two brochures must be produced, distributed, promoted and racked in order to obtain this degree of market segmentation.

Yet another brochure, and a distinctive range of holiday products, will be needed to attract the youth segment of the market. These are positioned as low-cost, activity-based holidays. These are not compatible with the fourth market segment this company serves. A separate brochure will again be needed to convey the characteristics of the wine-tasting holidays using exclusive villas.

In addition to the position of each product in terms of its cost and orientation towards family or activity, two further points can be made from Figure 4.1. It conveys information about the relative size (or value) of each programme, and it indicates synergies in their operation. For example, both the more exclusive family holidays and the wine-tasting tours are based in villa accommodation. The tour operator gains flexibility by being able to substitute different types of client into the accommodation it has contracted. Additionally, any single destination area could cater to several of these holiday programmes, offering the advantage of enabling the tour operator to sell to different market segments to fill the seats it has chartered.

SEGMENTATION

Product development, differentiation and positioning techniques are linked to the technique of segmentation. This has been defined as: 'The process of dividing a potential market into distinct subsets of consumers, and selecting one or more segments as a target to be reached with a distinct marketing mix' (Wilkie, 1986). Segmentation is an effective marketing tool, but to be selected for management attention and action, as Kotler (1992) has pointed out, any market segment must have the following three characteristics, being:

- measurable;
- accessible;
- substantial.

Market segmentation can be performed on a number of criteria, such as customers' age, income or family characteristics, but the core of the approach is to identify the most relevant characteristics of visitors seeking particular sets of benefits from their tourism purchases. Desirable benefits may consist of such features as holiday price, exclusivity or distance travelled. Relevant client characteristics may include their age, holiday motivations, travelling companions, activity preferences and so on.

Several steps are required to gain an understanding of how consumers choose between similar services. Firstly a limited number of relevant and objective attributes are chosen by preliminary research as the basis for product profiles. A group of people are assembled who have characteristics of interest in the research. The list of product attributes previously developed is then ranked by each respondent before coding and analysis. The relative importance of different attributes for different contexts is determined in this way, and their managerial and marketing implications can be examined. One feature of interest in this approach to segmentation by product-related decisions is that any service has many attributes. It is often necessary to compromise in one area such as airline seat width against another service feature such as the width of aisles in the plane, or the type of catering trolley which can be used for meal or beverage distribution due to reduced width of the aisle with consequent detrimental effects on the style and quality of the service. If the process is repeated with several different study groups under controlled conditions, it will often be found by factor analysis that certain 'types' of people regard specific product attributes as most important while other 'types' have different priorities. This results in one of the more amusing outcomes of market research, the classification of consumers under evocative names such as 'grey foxes' or 'empty nesters'. Engel, Blackwell and Miniard (1986) have shown how a person-situation matrix can be developed to understand the different benefits which will appeal to each segment of the market (in this case for suntan lotion). Table 4.8 summarizes the segmentation characteristics of potential clients of one tour operator, and may be considered in the light of the preceding discussion of tour operator brand management.

The next logical step after product development and market segmentation is to develop a marketing communications strategy which reaches the chosen market segments successfully (and economically), attracts their interest and carries appropriate messages and images to them, stimulating them to purchase holidays which match their interests. The technical matters of selecting appropriate media and monitoring the success of an advertising campaign are not discussed here, but further reading is suggested later.

Table 4.8 Market segment preferences for features of holiday types

Holiday feature	Market segment preferences	
	Concept A rank	Concept B rank
Low price	1	5
Good quality accommodation	3	1
Facilities for children of various ages	2	7
Activities and excursions	5	4
Exclusive accommodation	n/a	1
Private airport transfers	n/a	3
Meals included	3	6
Holiday market segment and brochure type	Mass market family holidays	Upmarket villa holidays for older couples

Holidays are purchased when individuals perceive that the benefits they will obtain can satisfy their individual needs, but any decision to purchase is based on information about the service, and the way it is understood by each individual. The steps which a tourism supplier can take to attract potential consumers include the creation and placing of a desired image of the service (or the organization supplying it) with a target consumer audience. Ries and Trout (1986) have shown that the positioning should be regarded as a communications issue, and have discussed several examples of how the verbal and mental pictures which consumers have may be managed. The product or service is given and the objective is to manipulate consumers' perceptions of reality. The market position obtained for a service is of course also affected by each of the other marketing variables, pricing, distribution and the attributes of the service itself.

IMAGERY IN MARKETING HOLIDAYS

Image has a number of meanings. These include the artificial imitation of the form of an object through a picture, and an idea or conception. Echtner and Brent Ritchie (1993) have argued that destination images have two main components: some such as the climate, accommodation and other facilities are attribute based, while the mental pictures of them are holistic.

The effectiveness of image management techniques depends on an understanding of potential visitors' interests and attitudes towards the destination. A carefully selected image can be broadcast to establish a position for the destination in the public's mind, and if this image is sufficiently distinct from that of other, similar destinations, then people are likely to respond to the campaign by requesting further information and becoming more alert to the various commercial offerings of holiday principals and tour operators.

> From a practical standpoint, the more complete measurement of a destination image provides useful information for positioning and promotional strategies. For example, if a destination is found to be difficult to categorize or is not easily differentiated from other similar destinations, then its likelihood of being considered and chosen in the travel decision process is reduced.
>
> (Mayo and Jarvis, 1981)

Sometimes the imagery evoked is somewhat fragmented, negative or inaccurate. Embacher and Buttle, 1989) point out that 'since the goal of positioning strategy is to create clear, positive and realistic images' research is needed to identify issues which should be addressed in the marketing plan. As Grönroos (1990) has noted, 'the imagery may vary depending on which group of people is considered . . . or between individuals.' He discussed four roles which imagery performs. It communicates expectations and helps people to screen information; it acts as a filter, sheltering the organization from minor problems; it is reinforced when quality services are delivered; and it has an internal impact, influencing employees' attitudes.

Purchasing choices are influenced by marketing communications. The specific messages and images employed to stimulate consumption and to channel demand towards particular products or brands at once reflect society's current values and are a dynamic force in its development (McCracken, 1990). The images used in marketing holidays frequently emphasize the beauties of female and male human bodies, portraying them as vehicles of pleasure and self-expression in leisure settings associated with hedonism and display. While the use of these emotional appeals is not restricted to tourism (Rothschild, 1987), many travel brochures offer explicitly sexual images which emphasize the importance of appearance; furthermore, whatever the age of the target audience, brochures feature healthy and active clients engaged in enjoyable pursuits. At the same time, the appeal of holidaytaking is reinforced by advertising for a wide range of other consumer products in which physically attractive people are photographed posed against the exotic attractions of distant locations, thereby reinforcing the multiplex connections between healthiness and holidays.

Since one's health has a higher order of priority than most consumption decisions, and good health can be regarded as a form of personal capital (Heggenhougen, 1987), this provides a very potent basis for holiday marketing. Health-related tourism marketing exploits the desire to improve one's health while enjoying relaxation and pampering, fine and abundant food, or opportunities for participation in sports of many kinds and at all levels of expertise.

Figure 4.2 presents a conceptual business opportunity analysis of the links between health and tourism products and imagery. The vertical axis records the increasing size (market potential) of various health motivations in tourism purchases, travel for the purposes of cure being assumed to be a small segment compared to the large numbers of people interested in improving their health, undertaking physical activities, or improving their access to leisure facilities because of an infirmity. On the left of the horizontal axis, specialized facilities such as spa treatments represent the primary service of certain destinations (Israel being an example of a destination offering a range of curative spa holidays which several tour operators package for sale). The increasingly general appeal of exercise and diet facilities is emphasized by cruise lines, while destinations such as Hawaii emphasize their healthy environments. Improved access to leisure in Britain has been discussed briefly. The horizontal axis also shows that advertising based on health appeals can be targeted at all potential clients.

The archetypal inclusive holiday, a week in the sun, and the model for a large sector of the contemporary industry, was promoted by Vladimir Raitz in 1950 (see Chapter 1). Beach resorts located in hot, dry regions, particularly where alcohol is readily available, are still one of

Increasing market potential

Focus on health in tourism

Traveller's health motivation	Primary service	Service enhancement			Imagery
		Facilities	Environment	Improved access	
	Israeli spas	*Cruises*	*Hawaii*	*English Tourist Board*	*Attractive people and places*
Social access				√	√
Climate			√		√
Physical activities Improved fitness		√			√
Recuperation	√				√
Cure	√				√

Increasing general relevance of health focus

Figure 4.2 A business opportunity analysis of health imagery and tourism product development. Source: laws (1995).

the mainstays of the holiday industry. A significant part of their attraction for holidaytakers from northern industrial countries is the freedom to wear light and colourful clothing even when not on the beach, and to get a sun tan, perhaps wearing no clothes at all. (In fact, a number of tour operators specialize in arranging overseas holidays for naturists.)

The suntan was popularized by Douglas Fairbanks and Hollywood at a time when it had been regarded mainly as a form of treatment for tuberculosis. 'Going against the established wisdom which held that the fashionable body must avoid the effects of the sun, lest it be associated with the tanned labouring body, he allowed his darkened face to appear in films and the popular press' (Featherstone, 1982). The result was that beaches became transformed 'into a place where one gained a sun tan – the hall mark of a successful holiday. For the first time sunbathing on the beach brought together large numbers of people in varying degrees of undress, legitimating the public display of the body.'

BROCHURES

Brochures are one of the key marketing tools for tour operators. Rosemary Astles, then Thomson Holidays Marketing Director, stated: 'The brochure is still our single most important marketing tool. More than half our marketing budget goes on brochures. We have two products, one is the end product, the holiday. The other is [the brochure].'

Most of the early brochures were small in format, simply presented and listed only basic facts such as the resort name, price and travel schedule in bold type, with some basic information. Rather than enticing customers to choose a particular holiday, their main function was to provide basic details about what was offered in each place, and most tour operators expected that their clients would read about their chosen destination in one of the detailed guidebooks.

Although holiday organizers have always provided potential clients with brief descriptions of the itineraries and destinations to visit, it was in 1953 that Thomas Cook produced what is generally regarded as the forerunner of the modern brochure. 'Holidaymaking' was innovative, adopting the design values of a woman's magazine, emphasizing colourful places and romantic impressions. The text was enticing, too: 'Turn the pages of this magazine. What prospect will delight you most? The mountains and lakes of Switzerland, the sun soaked beaches of the Riviera, the placid beauty of the Italian lakes, the sultry glamour of Spain?'

By the 1960s, the presentation of brochures had evolved into their familiar form of glossy, sexy holiday catalogues, with a widespread use of superlatives and a clichéd descriptive style. Contemporary holiday brochures retain these stylish features, and incorporate a vast amount of information about alternative holiday choices in a highly structured format, illustrated in Figure 4.3.

Holloway and Robinson (1995) have calculated that a mainstrean brochure might well provide a quarter of a million holiday choices, taking into account the variety of departure airports, resorts, hotels,

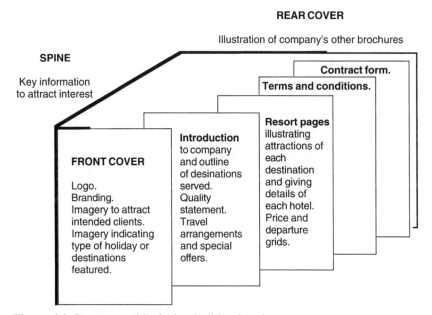

Figure 4.3 Structure of inclusive holiday brochures.

Table 4.9 Strategic objectives for tour operator's brochure management

---

Obtain sales
- Attract people to select brochure from rack
- Be easy to use
- Offer appealing holidays in an attractive way

Provide information for customer decision-making
- Destination
- Hotels
- Excursions and entertainment
- Journey
- Prices and supplements

Cost-effective distribution
- Cover designed to attract appropriate segments of the market
- Cover designed to impact on retailers' racks
- Brochures distributed to productive travel agents
- Monitoring and fine-tuning of distribution

Provide a selling tool for retail agents
- Detailed holiday information
- Booking codes for each holiday

Provide a contract between holidaytaker and tour operator
- Specify the commitment on each side
- Explain procedures in the event of a complaint
- Specify details of the holiday booked
- Provide details of the client(s)
- Record payment of deposit and insurance premium

---

duration of stay and season of departure. Thus the modern brochure is in effect a holiday catalogue. It has two target audiences – the ultimate client, and retail travel agency staff who use it as a detailed sales tool (usually in conjunction with the updated information available to them through the tour operator's CRS system).

Tour operators' brochures serve several objectives, presenting tour operators with a range of strategic decisions summarized in Table 4.9. The brochure represents a holiday company's primary selling tool. It is used as the response item to enquiries for customers visiting retail travel agencies or contacting the tour operator directly. Finally, the brochure has the additional important function of acting as the contract between tour operator and traveller, providing a form which must be completed with the details of the travelling party, identifying the lead person responsible for the booking, and referring to the detailed mutual responsibilities of client and company contained in the conditions of booking, another section of the brochure, before eliciting the client's signature.

Obtaining brochures

Most clients obtain their brochures from retail agents' shelves, more commonly known as racks. Racking presents a range of problems. The limited space in any retail agency leads to selectivity by the agency

manager in the brochures displayed. Several rationales can be identified. Some agencies specialize, for example, in cruising holidays, youth
tours or round-the-world itineraries, so their choice of brochures to
rack is relatively clear. Other agencies are part of a vertically integrated company which also includes a tour operator and their policy
(despite occasional denials) is to favour the display and sale of in-
house products, together with some niche tour operators' brochures
which do not provide any significant competition. Another approach is
to stock the full range of brochures which they know from experience
attracts their local clientele.

In each case, travel agencies typically hold backroom stocks of brochures which they do not display for lack of space, but may offer to
clients who express a specific interest or whose general enquiry matches what these companies offer. In addition, travel agencies often file
a master copy of the majority of tour operators' brochures. However,
unless a brochure is openly displayed on the racks, its potential as a
sales tool is undermined. Whether a client obtains a copy depends on
the agency staff's knowledge and enthusiasm, or on the client's prior
knowledge of the company and a direct request for the brochure. In
this event, most independent agencies can obtain a specific brochure
for their potential client, illustrating the pull feature of the distribution
system, since tour operators will typically take the opportunity to des-
patch a bundle of their brochures in the hope that the agency will
actively promote them.

The distribution of brochures

Brochures are generally distributed by specialist companies which
service all retailers in an area and act on behalf of many tour operators, although some larger tour operators undertake this function
themselves. Brochures represent a major cost to tour operators, consequently the actual number delivered to a particular agent is decided by
the tour operator according to previous year's sales results modified by
current trading conditions. Most tour operators evaluate the effectiveness of retailers by calculating the ratio of brochures they distribute (or
their cost) compared to the number (and value) of bookings received
from that retailer. This ratio is known as the conversion rate, and for
one tour operator it varies surprisingly between retailers. Apart from
the vertically integrated companies discussed above, medium sized and
small tour operators are also adopting a hard-nosed approach to selecting the retailers through whom they will trade. They expect evidence in
the form of sales results and restrict brochures and other forms of sales
support to productive retailers.

Once the stock of brochures is received, most travel agencies cus-
tomize them. This process used to consist merely of stamping each
booking form with the agent's name, address, phone number and

ABTA number. More recently, travel agents have adopted bright, large stickers which can often virtually obscure the cover of a brochure. These display the agency name and many feature the agency's own discount policy prominently. This exacerbates the problem for tour operators of ensuring that their brochures look distinctive in the agency racks. Brochures can be displayed in several ways, as a series of visits to different travel agencies will indicate. In some, perspex boxes allow the full front cover to be clearly seen; in other shops, the brochures are staggered in such a way that only a couple of inches of each cover can be seen. Another variant displays the spines of brochures. Given this variety, tour operators have to be very inventive in the design of their covers, which must also reflect their company's positioning and brand values and appeal directly and unequivocally to the intended segment of the market.

Achieving holiday sales from brochures

Gilbert and Houghton (1991) have listed several considerations in order to maximize consumer selection and use of brochures, including how they are displayed, how the consultant uses them in advising clients, and a number of 'consumer filters' such as the clarity with which they convey information, the brand names and the relevance of the images which they present to the personal needs of intended clients.

It is of course the contents of the brochure from which sales are achieved. Using text and photographs, the tour operator has to provide the detailed information which potential clients need in order to select a holiday which matches their interests. Furthermore – and critically – the brochure must be persuasive, since most intending holidaytakers browse through a variety of brochures before making their decision to purchase a specific holiday.

The way that different companies approach these objectives and the relative importance given to each can be assessed by a comparative contents analysis of selected brochures. It is illuminating to do this for several companies operating varied styles of holiday to a selected destination. The procedure involves at its simplest a count of the number of references to predetermined topics or a measurement of the column inches devoted to each.

It has been suggested that brochures function by providing essential information in an easily assimilated way. They may be subjected to critical appraisal on this ground and with regard to the impartiality and accuracy of the information they provide as a basis for clients' choice of destination. This is particularly significant in the case of activity holidays such as skiing. A study of skiing brochures' evaluations of the suitability of a set of resorts for skiers with differing levels of experience found little concurrence between competing brochures, at least some of which can therefore be criticized for providing inaccurate or misleading information with potentially harmful consequences (Goodall, 1990).

The significance of brochure design

Analysis of brochures and the organization of packaged holiday activities, as Selwyn (1992) has pointed out, helps in understanding the nature of contemporary tourism. His argument drew on doubts expressed by MacCannell (1976) about Levi-Strauss's rejection of a structuralist view of the modern world, regarding it rather as fragmented. Alienation from the modern world is held to arise from the 'mechanistic nature of work, the separation of work and home, [and] the anonymous rationality of modern bureaucracy.' However, leisure provides people with the opportunity to rediscover their sense of structure since the holiday experience enables them to 'recreate, frequently with the help of representations from the imagined pre-modern world, the structures which life in the post-modern world has appeared to demolish.'

Selwyn noted MacCannell's view that Parisian guides present tourists with museums, galleries, shopping, factories, building sites, the stock exchange, transport, markets, pissoirs and sewers, amongst many other facets of life in the city. 'The point of all this', MacCannell argued, 'is simply to "present society and its works" in a way that is fun.' The guides' style is to smooth over 'the rough edges of everyday concrete social relations' and this is facilitated by the holidaymakers' experience of being at leisure. On a global scale, tourists can now easily purchase souvenirs representing every kind of historical and modern society, but these cultural goods are presented as commodities.

Citing Eco, Selwyn suggested that the resultant 'blurring of boundaries has led to an apparent democratization of knowledge.' It is the tour operators' brochures which epitomize the easy but superficial access to history and culture, 'mixed with . . . a rich and spicy sauce of fiction'. He quoted from a Cosmos Distant Dreams brochure, stating that it adopted a consistent approach to the destinations offered. The descriptive text was structured under the headings shopping, activities, nightlife, eating out and sightseeing, as well as giving temperature charts. Thailand was described as ' "the land of smiles" where the people (many of whom today speak English) combine Buddhist charity and gentleness with a fun loving energy . . . Everywhere, you're surrounded by reminders of the country's serene cultural past. Like the spires of Bangkok's countless golden Wats or temples . . .'

Selwyn argued that 'contemporary tourism has developed its own promotional lexicon'. He distinguished between a structuralist text which emphasizes 'belonging to a group while sharing the histories of other people', and 'the language of the New World order'. This appeared to emphasize the pleasures sought by individuals, but in reality reflects the strengths and influence of the large companies which dominate the holiday industry. '... What they sell to contemporary tourists seems, from the post-structuralist view, to be not so much any real individual "freedom" ... in any recognizably real world, but more a sort of space in a world of "Peter Pans" ...'

ALTERNATIVE PRE-PURCHASE COMMUNICATIONS STRATEGIES

Specialist tour operators have somewhat different purposes than mass market tour operators in terms of the objectives for their brochures: these are generally seen by specialist operators as a relatively less important component of their marketing communications strategy. Typically, specialist tour operators are owned and staffed by enthusiasts who understand and accept that their clients will want to discuss the details of the itineraries they are considering at some length, booking direct after discussion with the tour operator's staff. A variant on this method of selling is the workshops or film evenings which tour operators organize to gain direct contact with old customers and with potential new ones. These are particularly helpful in the case of new destinations which present clients with a higher degree of risk in making their purchase of a holiday. The risk arises from lack of information about conditions in the destination, and may include an element of discomfort or physical risk on expedition-type holiday packages. These issues and clients' concerns can be more fully discussed at face-to-face sessions run by experts who have previously travelled in the area. However, once a destination such as China is well established, the need for such extensive pre-purchase briefing is reduced.

THE INFLUENCE OF TRAVEL JOURNALISM

So far, the discussion has focused on the deliberate efforts of tourism managers to promote their holiday products through selecting and disseminating positive aspects to potential visitors. However, a communications–influence analysis of the industry (Figure 4.4) has indicated that there are additional factors in the way in which people form their preferences for particular holidays and destinations, and their experiences during a visit. The model suggested that destinations have rather limited communications power to stimulate interest in their origin markets, both because of cost and cultural considerations, and because they rely heavily on others to influence potential visitors in their favour. In addition to the tour operators' promotions, the media articles featuring holidays are important sources of information for intending holidaymakers. While their visits are solicited and facilities are extended to many journalists, what they write is editorial rather than advertising copy. It may portray a tour operator, a destination, hotel or

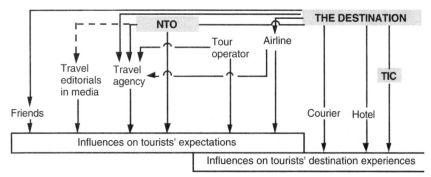

Figure 4.4 Destination communications channels and influences on tourists' expectations and experiences. Source: Laws (1995).

activity in a critical or unfavourable way, in particular emphasizing aspects of the journalist's experiences which may include negative as well as positive occurrences.

Just as the inclusive holiday product has developed a variety of styles, so also have the approaches and style of travel journalists evolved. One of the earliest travel programmes on British TV was Richard Dimbleby's series 'Passport', first broadcast in 1958. This featured him taking his children (one of whom in the mid 1990s is himself a senior broadcaster) on holiday to France. About the same time, popular and memorable wild-life films began to be screened, particularly those made by Hans and Lotti Haas and Jacques Cousteau, featuring exotic locations around the world.

The modern form of holiday documentary probably has its origins in 1969, when Cliff Michelmore began a programme which featured John Carter (still an influential commentator on the industry's affairs) as its roving reporter. This, and 'Wish You Were Here' (hosted on ITV by Judith Chalmers beginning in 1972), presented a critical view of the industry, adopting the medium's increasingly interrogative style of questioning familiar from interviews with politicians and trade leaders. These programmes also gave the tour operators' brand names and holiday prices after reviewing a particular destination or tour. With the widespread ownership of colour television and more creative editorial styles, a more recent innovation has been the Rough Guides more style conscious approach to evaluating the experience of visiting particular places (Carr, 1993). The broadcasting of nature programmes, notably David Attenborough's series, have also stimulated interest in travel to distant places through their vivid and evocative style.

This chapter has pointed to the achievements of tourism marketing in the rapid development of an extensive market for overseas inclusive holidays. It has also indicated that there are a number of issues which arise from the contrasting priorities and marketplace power of the various organizations involved in the industry. These points are further explored in ensuing chapters.

FURTHER READING

Grönroos, C. (1990) *Service Management and Marketing: Managing the Moments of Truth in Service Competition*, Lexington Books, Lexington, Mass.

Kotler, P., Haider, D.H. and Rein, I. (1993) *Marketing Places*, Free Press, New York.

Middleton, V.T.C. (1988) *Marketing in Travel and Tourism*, 2nd edn, Heinemann, London.

Payne, A. (1993) *The Essence of Services Marketing*, Prentice Hall, Hemel Hempstead.

Payne (1993) and Grönroos (1990) provide detailed theoretical analyses of issues and methods in service marketing. Middleton (1994) is a comprehensive discussion of marketing applied to the tourism industry, while Kotler, Haider and Rein (1993) analyse the ways that places market themsleves as centres for industry, commerce or tourism.

SUGGESTED EXERCISES

1. Carry out a detailed comparative analysis of the way in which several brochures intended for different market segments set out to attract clients to one resort with which you are familiar, and comment on the ways in which they portray the key features of the destination.
2. Interview the managers of a long-established local independent travel retailer and of a high street multiple in order to describe and contrast their brochure racking policies.
3. Describe and contrast the marketing methods used by two different industries, such as car manufacturing and home entertainments, and assess their relevance for the inclusive holiday industry.

Distributing inclusive holidays | 5

INTRODUCTION

The tour operators' role in creating package holidays is central to the inclusive holiday industry, but just as their success depends on suppliers such as hotels and charter airlines for the elements of which their holiday products are composed, most of them also rely heavily on retail travel agencies to sell holidays to the public. Taken together, tour operators and travel agencies provide the services of a distribution channel linking the great variety of tourism companies which supply tourists with destination services to their ultimate clients. The travel retailers make these services easily accessible to clients through the traditional full service travel agencies and the holiday shops which can now be found in the majority of shopping centres. These two forms of travel retailer provide contrasting approaches: whereas the traditional agency sells all travel, accommodation and related services such as travel insurance, enabling independent clients to create their own holiday (or business) travel arrangements, the holiday shops act as catalogue sales outlets for the tour operators who have already pre-selected and packaged a range of holidays, leaving the customer with the choice of which holiday package to purchase.

THE ROLES OF TRAVEL RETAILERS

In a typical case, tourists purchase their holiday from a local travel agent after selecting between the brochures of many alternative tour operators. The retailer is acting as an agent for the tour operator, earning a commission on the sales price of the holiday and being rewarded with higher commission rates by tour operators for whom he sells above a target volume or value of packages. The travel agent performs clerical functions for the operator but in addition advises clients on their holiday choice – a time-consuming, labour-intensive and skilled activity.

Organizations within the tourism industry trade with each other to provide a complete holiday service for their clients to purchase and are therefore mutually dependent. Various patterns of relationships are possible, as indicated previously in Figure 2.1, both to create and distribute tourism services. A number of functions are performed by the holiday industry distribution channel members, following the creation of packaged holidays by tour operators, the distribution of brochures to retail outlets by specialized organizations, the provision of reservations services by computer companies and the retailing services provided by travel agents.

In common with all retailers, travel agents combine two sets of skills: detailed knowledge of the products they sell, and an understanding of the processes of persuading their customers to purchase holidays (Davidson, Sweeney and Stampfl, 1988). As participants in the travel distribution channel their knowledge base is broad, comprising detailed and current information about the tour operators whose products they sell, and more specifically about the resorts, hotels and travel arrangements of which these products are composed. However, it is unrealistic to expect travel agents and their staff to have a detailed knowledge of the proliferating range of holiday destinations and holiday types. Their first-hand knowledge is usually limited to those resorts which the agent sells most frequently, while trade reference books and electronic data systems provide rapid access to impartial information about others.

Retailers succeed by understanding how their customers behave, by recognizing which travel services will appeal to them, and by making their sales offer more appealing than that of competing travel agencies. Effective travel retailers spend much of their time cultivating this awareness and stimulating their existing customer base to purchase travel services. One method is to mail an agency newsletter to all past and current clients which contains feature articles about new holiday opportunities likely to interest the clients, stories about travellers resident in the local community, or news of newly appointed or promoted staff. Another method is to organize film nights or to invite guest speakers from tour operators or destinations, at which events clients are able to discuss their travel interests in a more relaxed format than the retail outlet can provide. Successful retailers also invest in expanding their customer base by making presentations to youth groups, schools and similar organizations, often in partnership with a tour operator or NTO, sharing the cost and providing a video or a speaker. Others try to provide a customized holiday by chartering coaches for the local airport transfer to create a more seamless, integrated service after taking a large allocation of seats on a particular departure which they may try to sell in conjunction with a readers' offer linked to a local newspaper.

In order to achieve their objectives through selling holidays, retailers need to invest in staff training at three levels. Technical training is required to enable staff to read the manuals and cope with the requirements of the various principals' and tour operators' reservations sys-

Entice client into agency	Establish client's needs and budget	Offer appropriate range of holidays	Check availability and prices of customer's preferred choice	Assist client to complete booking form	Check whether client can be sold extras such as insurance or car rental	Take client's deposit

Figure 5.1 Steps to making a holiday booking.

tems; training in interpersonal skills can improve their techniques of dealing with individual customers; and product knowledge training is required so that staff can make relevant recommendations, appropriate for each client's needs.

Achieving a booking can be seen as a sequence of steps (Figure 5.1). The first entails persuading potential clients to enter (or to telephone) the agency. This can be achieved by siting the agency in a busy and attractive location, making its window display attractive and relevant, or by a range of promotional methods, including paid advertising or joint promotions with local (or national) newspapers or specialist magazines.

Once a potential client enters a travel agency, the objective of staff is to close a sale during the visit. This objective closely matches, but is not identical to, the client's purposes. The client's objective is to select a vacation offering the range of benefits he or she desires. The client may therefore require advice and a range of potential holidays to discuss at leisure with his or her travelling companions.

Most travel agencies display (and sell from) a predetermined selection of specialist and mass market brochures covering most popular destinations. Their staff tend to sell a holiday from brochure pages, supplemented by a check for availability and any detailed changes on the computerized reservations systems of major tour operators. Several surveys have found that agency staff are ill prepared to deal with travel enquiries other than core inclusive holiday packages. Evidence for this assertion was also found in the fact that, although tour operators provide retailers with marketing support in the form of staff familiarization trips, few travel agents are very active marketers. One study reported that 20% took no action, while most advertised irregularly in local papers or visited local groups.

Personal selling skills are at the heart of successful travel retailing. Two approaches have been distinguished in matching a client's needs to available services: referent and expertise bases. The salesperson acts in a referent capacity when offering his or her clients a source of friendship and shared identity: the consumers perceive that they have similar needs and characteristics, and so what is recommended or endorsed by a referent sales person is likely to have a direct influence on their decisions. It has also been shown that a sale is more likely to occur under these conditions. The second source of influence is the perceived expertise of the salesperson, that is his or her confidence in and knowledge of the services which are purveyed. The effectiveness of one style rather than the other seems to depend on the product or service being sold, expertise being regarded as more important when a complicated product or service is on offer. Weitz (1981) has argued that expertise is the most appropriate mode of selling when the salesperson is credible as an expert, has the required technical knowledge and in conditions where the customer regards the purchase as risky or complex and when the salesperson and client are strangers. In most cases, a combination of referent and expertise styles is likely to prove effective, and consequently the salesperson should adopt a flexible approach to customers, based on an accurate diagnosis of their needs. However, the approach adopted by many holiday catalogue shop staff tends to be based on personal knowledge or anecdotes related by their colleagues.

The travel trade newspapers regularly conduct unannounced visits to retailers, asking several for recommendations on the same set of holiday criteria, for example a quiet, comfortable hotel suitable for young children with a given departure date and budget range. The findings from these exercises indicate that few travel agency staff use many information sources, most limiting their search to the most obvious brochures (typically, those of the leading tour operators). An additional criticism is that staff often merely point to the agency's brochure racks, suggesting that their potential client 'takes some away to read'. This is unsatisfactory from the point of view of clients, since they are not obtaining full and impartial advice. Nor does it satisfy tour operators who expect to obtain a high proportion of their sales from the agency network in return for the commission paid on sales and the support they provide to retailers in the form of staff training, brochure supplies and window sales aids.

Traditionally, travel agents provided a full service of travel and holiday products, being able to book hotels, transport, insurance and many other services from the full range of principals, including tour operators. However, the typical modern form of travel retailer is a shop specializing in selling packaged holidays using their principals' descriptive brochures and their reservations systems. Many present a limited range of tour operators' products on their brochure racks, either because they are owned by a major group and therefore are unwilling to sell competitors' services, because they have an exclusive agreement with a particular operator in their locality, or because they are not licensed by a particular principal to sell its products. While this selectivity is rational for tour operators and travel retailers, it reduces the clients' probability of gaining impartial advice.

DISTRIBUTION CHANNEL THEORY

The term 'distribution channel' has differing definitions. It is generally used to connote the route by which manufactured products are moved from the producer to the consumer; another view emphasizes the concomitant changes in ownership of title to the goods as they pass from one organization to another. In a service industry such as inclusive holidays, ownership is not a factor, while the flows are movements of information and clients rather than the items sold.

> ... the idea of product flow, ownership flow, and title transfer are not always obvious or applicable where intangible services are marketed. In service marketing, consumers must come in contact with the firm to receive the service, but there is often little tangible evidence of ownership or title which removes much of the conventional concept of a 'channel of distribution' The vacation itself is the experience of the resort, cruise or tour.
>
> (Duke and Persia, 1993)

This characteristic of services underlines one of the key points put forward in this book, that the ability of the industry to function systemically is fundamental to its continuing success: travel agents have very little influence over their clients' holiday experiences, despite recent legislation which renders them liable (Grant and Mason, 1993; ABTA, 1994).

Managerially, the distribution or supply channel of any organization comprises the external organizations which are contracted to achieve management's distribution objectives, implying that the lead company recruits others which will provide specific distribution services in the way which will be least expensive for it.

A number of companies contribute to the success of a distribution channel. They each have specific functions, for example holiday creation and brochure production, brochure distribution, computerized reservations systems or high street retailing, and individual objectives of growth or profitability. This raises the question of how the overall efficiency of the channel is to be evaluated, and of how the costs and profits entailed in its operation are to be distributed amongst the members. Those organizations benefit from the greater sales value and volume which the lead company brings and are therefore willing to compromise on some aspects of their own operations, for example by not carrying competitors' stock or by keeping records and accounts in the form which the major company specifies.

The relative ability of members in a distribution chain to influence other members' actions can be understood in more than one way: it is partly a matter of the dependency of one organization on its partners in the chain of distribution, but it is also concerned with goal congruence and the limitation of conflict issues between them. In turn, the way in which such matters are made explicit and then managed has implications for the likelihood of long-lasting cooperation between channel partners.

The traditional tourism distribution channel consisted of small, independent retailers whose objectives are to maximize their own profits (or to satisfy a variety of other objectives they may have). During the last two decades, however, travel retailing has reflected the increased concentration of negotiating power or ownership of the system. Both vertical and horizontal integration has occurred in travel retailing to rationalize the ownership of outlets so that they are more effective in selling the services of the major tour operators. Some of the most familiar travel retailers are in fact owned by large tour operators (even though they operate under separate trading names), with the result that the organization is in effect an integrated business system. This provides several advantages, including the maximum retention of profits within the group, enhanced selling strength for the holiday brands which comes from in-house retailing, reduced outlets for competitors' brands, and opportunities for improvements in retail staff training in the tour operator's own brands, products and business systems. One further advantage is significant: the integrated tour operator and travel retailer has greater command of and more rapid access to information on constantly changing market conditions, and is therefore in a stronger position to make informed decisions about when, and how much, to adjust prices or which resorts or departures to promote at particular times.

A further factor distorting the operation of channels is that a dominant member, usually a major tour operator, can offer extra inducements beyond what is normal business practice to entice retailers (or their staff) to sell particular holiday brands. Such extra incentives are typically linked to volume performance targets. Thus, a distribution channel can be audited for efficiency. Other considerations revolve around understanding what customers want from the distribution system. This may differ according to each market and product segment as indicated in the discussion of tour operators' styles.

Taking a view of the holiday industry's distribution channel as a system invites examination of the allocation between members of the functions it entails, and of the ability of any of its members to increase their profit by shifting costs elsewhere in the channel. For example, a national tourist organization might benefit from tour operator or airline advertising which feature it as a destination. In another case, tour operators often require the travel retailers with which they trade to have staff trained in its systems and products so that the majority of client enquiries can be handled at the agency level rather than by the tour operator's staff. Table 5.1 considers the advantages and disadvantages of channel membership for two types of tour operator and for travel retailers.

For a tour operator, channel management tasks include the selection of dealers, setting up discount structures to reward and motivate channel members and the services required to distribute stock through the

Table 5.1 Distribution channel member outcomes

	Advantages of channel membership	*Disadvantages of channel membership*
Mass market tour operator	• Wider marketplace representation • Travel agent carries out selling and administrative functions	• Has to train and motivate agency staff • Depends on retailers for sales • Has to pay commission on sales
Specialist tour operator	• Wider marketplace representation • Agency staff unlikely to be familiar with detailed selling points	• Has to pay commission on sales • Has to provide training for retailers' staff • Limited control over brochure distribution
Travel retailer	• Obtains clients	• Dependent on tour operators for products to sell and for the quality of those products

Table 5.2 Factors constraining effective tourism communication and the roles of retailers

Factor	*Travel agents' functions*
Distance	Outlets located in customers' vicinity
Time	Provide facilities for advanced reservations
Information	Provide comprehensive information

system so that it is available to potential users. In tourism retailing, this primarily means the brochures on which clients base their decisions and which include the booking forms that function as a contract between clients and travel organizations. These tasks are continuous, the need to work with their retail partners beginning again for tour operators about the time when the coming season's brochures are finalized. Table 5.2 lists some of the factors constraining effective communication between destinations or tour operators and their customers, indicating the ways in which travel retailers help bridge these gaps.

This approach confers two advantages: it emphasizes the role which channel members perform in providing convenient information and booking links between distant destinations and potential clients, and secondly it calls attention to the systemic nature of the holiday industry, focusing attention on the collaborative aspects of the industry rather than the competitive features often considered.

RELATIONSHIPS BETWEEN TOUR OPERATORS AND TRAVEL AGENTS

Travel agents perform a number of important functions for tour operators after a holiday sale is made. They collect and pass on tourists' deposits and final payments to the tour operator, who normally retains most of the funds until the service has been provided when full payment is released to the principals. Consequently, during the interval before paying the principals, tour operators have substantial funds for a period and are able to place them on the money markets, thereby gaining a further contribution to their income and cash flow from the interest which may be earned. Against this advantage, many of their costs have to be paid in foreign currencies, and so another type of risk falls on the tour operator sector as the exchange values of currencies shift frequently under a variety of unpredictable influences. To counter this potential threat to their profitability, many tour operators purchase foreign exchange on the futures market, speculating against such fluctuations. The relationship between retail travel agents and tour operators is frequently raised in the trade press and at meetings of associations such as the Tourism Society and CIMTIG. From the perspective of travel retailers, a number of problems have been identified:

- the growing domination of the sector by a few multiple agency chains, each owned by one of the major tour operators;
- the low profit margins for travel agents;
- the smaller size and resources of travel agencies compared to tour operators;
- the impossibility of stocking and selling the full range of overseas inclusive holidays, let alone domestic products.

Case study 5.1 illustrates the type of situation which can arise in relations between operators and agencies.

CASE STUDY 5.1

Thomas Cook racking row

A year after the Office of Fair Trading (OFT) concluded that there was no evidence of consumers being disadvantaged by the growth of vertical integration, recommending that 'Customers must be made aware of any links between agents and operators . . . impartial advice should be given by agents in order to remove the risk of consumer choice being restricted by "directional" selling,' the Consumers' Association submitted a report indicating that the larger travel agency chains provided a restricted choice to their clients. In August 1994, Thomas Cook limited discounts on Thomson's summer 1995 holidays to 5%, although it discounted other operators' prices by 15%.

In November 1995, the trade press featured reports that Thomas Cook had sent a memo to all its branches listing all Thomson's exclusive properties in its main summer 1996 brochure, and identifying alternatives offered by Cook's affiliated companies, Sunworld, 1st Choice and Airtours. The report stated that the memo added, 'These alternatives should be offered to every customer who requires a Thomson exclusive property.'

Based on Skidmore (1995).

This brief case study illustrates some of the difficulties which can arise from the tour operators' practice of using their equity partner or owned outlet chains to promote their own products. Many customers are unaware of the connection between them and the consequent possibility that the agent's advice may be biased or incomplete. Related to this concern about the distortion of the industry's distribution practices, the number of holidays sold by each retail agency can easily be monitored by tour operators through management information systems using data from their CRS. This information is used as a basis for deciding on the following season's allocation of brochures to each retailer, and to modify a current a season's allocations. However, it is quite common for holidaytakers to visit several travel agencies, and to delay the purchase of their holiday for weeks after initially collecting brochures. Indeed, it has been suggested that brochures have a longer 'shelf life' in people's homes than almost any other printed medium. Consequently, the agency from which a tour operator ultimately receives a booking may not be the one which originally influenced the client's interest in that holiday, since the booking may have been placed at any convenient local retailer. To counter this, many agencies now place large stickers on all brochures when they are received (a task often allocated to junior and work placement staff) before the brochures are racked. However, by obscuring the front cover, this practice tends to reduce the potency of the tour operator's efforts to brand his brochures.

But the cumulative effect of all channel control methods adopted by the larger tour operators and the vertically integrated holiday companies is to reduce the ability of the small, independent travel retailers to trade successfully. Sixty per cent of the 10 million packages bought in 1995 were sold by the top three retail chains, each of which is part of an integrated inclusive holiday operation. The head of one, Inspirations, explained in an interview in the trade press that his group has the retail chain 'not to make profits but to give retailing clout.' Staff are 'incentivized' to sell their products, and their brochures are prominently displayed. Without this widespread presence in shopping centres, they would have to rely on sales by independent retailers, because those linked to other vertically integrated companies would give similar prominence to their in-house holidays. Overall, the effects of integration and channel leadership have been that the proportion of independent outlets has fallen, although a counter-argument can be advanced from the very low profit margins earned by travel retailers, implying that they cannot afford to invest in updating and upgrading their businesses. Colin Heal, Chairman of Artac Worldchoice representing 500 independent travel agents, reported that: 'At the end of September 1995, ABTA had 2280 member companies. It lost 150 agent members in the first eight months of this year.' He ascribed this reduction in independents to the expansion of multiple branch agencies. Table 5.3 charts some of the changes which have occurred in travel

Table 5.3 Changes in travel retailing

Period	Trading environment	Type of travel retailing
1950s	Limited demand for holidays or other travel Reconstruction of war damaged city centres	Full-service travel specialists located in major urban and business centres Limited competition
1960s	Gradual increase in city centre travel retailers with the development of demand for leisure travel	Coach and other domestic holidays sold by small coach companies and through newsagents
1970s	Rapid expansion in demand for holidays	Successful retailers expand the number of outlets – proliferation of high street retailers
1980s	Development of out-of-town shopping malls and large-scale town centres Many high streets suffer from shop closures and temporary tenants	First computerized reservations system for inclusive holidays Larger travel agency chains grow by acquiring smaller 'miniples', consolidating ownership and putting pressure on independents Development of specialized holiday shops, and decline of full-service travel agencies
1990s	Increasing financial pressure on travel retailers, increasing rate of acquisition and mergers	Increasingly selective racking policies Technological developments enable customers to create their own holiday packages by booking direct from home

retailing during the development of a mass market for overseas holiday taking.

THE EFFECTS OF COMPUTERIZED RESERVATIONS SYSTEMS

In addition to the growing dominance of holiday retailing by the large multiple companies, another factor constrains the ability of smaller independents to compete effectively. The industry is increasingly reliant on computerized networks but access to them depends upon the standardization and computability of computers and communications networks among suppliers and distributors. It is a costly investment and also requires staff training (McFarlan, 1994). Furthermore, the advantages of computerization accrue to all members of the channel, but unequally. Until the 1980s, making a holiday reservation for a client usually entailed at least one (and usually several) lengthy telephone calls between agency and tour operator. They were lengthy because telephone lines were expensive and in scarce supply resulting in frequently engaged lines, and because the reservations information was held manually with the need for reservations staff to check availability on a number of charts relating to departure and return flights and for rooms in each hotel.

Most travel agencies had to resort to counter-top telephone amplifiers, so that the staff could do other tasks while waiting for a tour operator to pick up their call or to service it. On answering, the tour operator's staff had to physically enter booking information on reservations charts which showed visually how many seats were available on each flight. Confirmation of hotel bed space often meant the further delay and expense of an international phone call or telex message. Most of this delay and uncertainty has now been obviated for the major tour operators by their investment in computerized reservations systems (CRSs).

The introduction by Thomson of the first UK videotext reservations system (TOPS in 1982) was followed four years later by the closing of the company's telephone reservations facility. The tour operator's reservations staff labour productivity increased threefold. TOPS, although it has now been superseded by more sophisticated systems, tripled the productivity of the company's reservations staff. It also increased the ability of travel agents to sell effectively since the availability of specific holidays could be confirmed to clients while they were in the shop, or they could observe the information on the screen as an agent sought alternatives for them.

It has been argued by some tourism experts that many of these functions can now be carried out by individuals in their own homes, thus reducing the future need for travel agents or tour operators. As Figure 5.2 shows, the way these are organized is changing with the increasing importance of computerized reservations systems and much wider public access to them which modern technology is bringing (Poon, 1993).

An alternative concern is that other types of retailer, for example the multiple grocery outlets, might extend their range of products to include the sale of holidays, merely adapting technology which is already installed throughout their branch network. With the recent

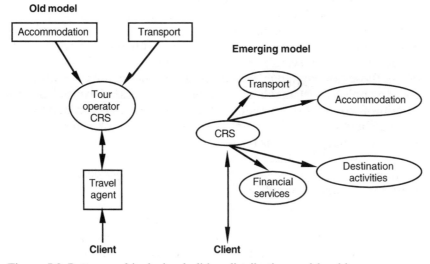

Figure 5.2 Patterns of inclusive holiday distribution and booking.

relaxation of ABTA's rule which for a long time restricted the sale of holidays produced by its tour operator members to retailers who were members of ABTA, this appears to be a possibility. It has occurred in other European countries, and some newsagents established in-store travel agencies during the 1980s, but this type of competition has yet to develop on a significant scale. In fact, a longer-term threat which might be posed to tour operators comes from combined information and communication systems such as the Internet. This has the potential to provide current information on all travel-related services. The range of information about destinations, hotels, activities and travel rivals what can be found in many brochures, and has the added advantage that potential clients can 'communicate' directly with the service providor at very low cost. It may also become secure enough to encourage people to make payments in the system using their credit cards or bank accounts. This could pose a challenge to the need for tour operators, both those offering highly specialized destinations and activities and the mass market operators whose packages consist of standardized flights and hotels.

PUSH–PULL DISTRIBUTION STRATEGIES

Two major strategies have been distinguished for marketing communication. In one case the service provider advertises to the client through public media such as newspapers, magazines, television and radio. The interest thus stimulated is felt by channel members as a pull through the distribution system when clients request specific brochures or information from travel agencies. This interest acts as a signal to the tour operator and principals, who respond by increasing the stocks of their brochures held by agents.

The alternative strategy is for tour operators to promote their service to channel members, through public relations campaigns, educational visits, trade seminars, discounts or free offer schemes in recognition of sales results achieved either by an agency or by individual staff members (see Figure 5.3). The expectation is that staff will be more enthusiastic about selling those holidays compared to those of other companies which do not provide similar benefits to their retail partners. However, the real criterion for selling one holiday rather than another is its match to a specific client's needs, thus there is an undercurrent of ethical concern about the widespread industry practice of providing educational visits for staff, even when these are well organized.

Typically in the tourism industry, the push strategy described above is used to enhance the pull strategy with which it is run in parallel. In either case, the specialist travel publications and mass media have important roles to play. They act as vehicles for paid advertising and they have a role through editorial judgement and comment in communicating opinions on travel products which they have elected to sample. Wilkie (1986) has distinguished between push and pull strategies:

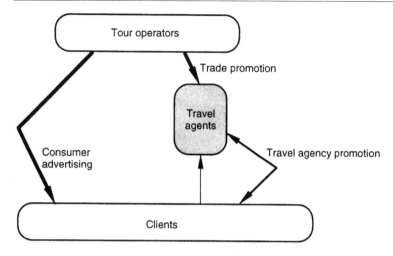

Figure 5.3 Push–pull strategies in channel management.

'Push strategies are aimed at gaining strong channel support for help-ing to sell the product to consumers ... they are used extensively for products ... which require sales persons to recommend brands while they assist consumers in buying, and by new brands ...' The goal of a pull strategy is to 'have consumers demand the product at their retail stores, thus setting off a chain reaction in which retailers then demand the product from their wholesalers, who respond by placing increased orders from the manufacturer.'

TRADE ASSOCIATIONS AND THE REGULATION OF THE HOLIDAY INDUSTRY

The complex structure of the inclusive holiday industry, its changing power relationships and the importance of its products to clients and destinations where it operates has led to the development of a number of organizations which aim either to improve its internal functioning such as ANTOR (Case study 5.2), or to regulate relationships between its members as Case study 5.3 on ABTA shows.

CASE STUDY 5.2

The Association of National Tourist Office Representatives in the United Kingdom

ANTOR (the Association of National Tourist Office Representatives in the United Kingdom) is believed to have begun in 1951 when the representatives of France, Norway, South Africa and Switzerland met mainly for social purposes. In 1954, they adopted the name ANTOR and established formally a voluntary and non-political organization. Its purposes are to provide a forum for the exchange of views of its members, and to communicate these views to other organizations within the British tourism industry such as ABTA.

ANTOR has published a brochure describing its role and services which states:

> . . . ANTOR is able to co-ordinate and improve, through mutual co-operation, the services that National Tourist Offices offer to the British travel industry. Similarly, ANTOR is able to help provide a better understanding, within the travel trade, of the roles and services its members provide, enabling all parties better to meet their different but often parallel objectives.

Writing in the newsletter of the Association of Women Travel Executives in 1995, Phyllis Chapman, ANTOR's recently retired Honorary Secretary, raised the question of why countries which can be considered as competitors can combine with a common purpose:

> . . . They have realized the advantages of an organization that can speak for them all when dealing with other trade bodies, and often have a representative on their committees. ABTA and ANTOR have had a successful joint committee for many years. One modest venture, the 'Factfinder', developed into the *ABTA/ ANTOR Factfinder and World Travel Guide*, now published by Columbus Press. Newly arrived tourist office directors who are ANTOR members are personally introduced to the ABTA President at a special meeting . . . Members with small budgets soon realized the advantages of joining forces to organize workshops for travel agents, and meetings for tour operators and press.

ANTOR also commissions occasional studies of matters concerning its members. One recent study examined the roles and organization of the National Tourist Offices in Britain. According to ANTOR data, the average UK-based NTO has only 7.5 staff, a quarter have three or less, and only a quarter employ more than ten staff.

In general terms, all NTOs share the common objective of wishing to improve the value of tourism to their respective countries. However, their approaches differ according to their resources and the specific characteristics of each destination's relationship to British tourism. For example, the proximity of France to Britain determines the demands placed on the French National Tourist Office in London. This has two consequences: France receives a much higher proportion of people travelling independently rather than on packaged holidays, and more British tourists visit France than any other destination. The result is a very high level of enquiries to the French NTO for specific information on local tourist services coming directly from members of the public, in the form of personal enquiries at its Piccadilly office and by mail and phone. In contrast, the NTOs of smaller and remoter destinations tend to concentrate their resources on servicing the travel industry to help tour operators to develop holiday packages and to improve retailers' awareness of their countries.

Each destination has its own set of objectives for its tourism sector, and the NTO's work has to be understood and evaluated in the context of its government's domestic and international tourism policies. These are examined in detail elsewhere, but examples of policy objectives include the wish to promote out of season tourism, to develop selected regions of the country, or to encourage the use of new infrastructure such as an airport or resort. Other countries set out to increase the average length of stay of their visitors, or seek to attract holidaymakers with specific characteristics which the government feels will benefit its tourism sector, such as those with greater affluence.

In addition to these long-term strategic roles in promoting a country's tourism, from time to time many NTOs have had to adopt crisis management measures to deal with an unexpected decline in arrivals resulting from one of the serious problems which occasionally disrupt tourist traffic, such as terrorism, floods and earthquakes or political upheavals.

The survey cited earlier suggested that ANTOR members' offices receive over 3 million phone calls annually from the public requesting information. The NTOs are able to respond by providing a range of maps, operator and hotel guides, and local information leaflets featuring attractions and activities. A further half a million people visit NTO offices to collect this type of information. This volume of requests for holiday information is significant because the survey indicated that over half of those enquiring had not yet booked a holiday. It is therefore likely that the quality of information provided and the style with which their enquiry was handled might well be a determining factor in their choice of holiday destination. Another way in which NTOs communicate with potential visitors is by participating in some 70 consumer exhibitions annually throughout Britain, providing additional opportunities for direct contact with the public in a holiday-purchasing environment.

A second sphere of influence for ANTOR members is the travel trade, which also relies heavily on NTOs for detailed destination information. A survey revealed that more than 45% of all UK retail agency staff contact an NTO at least once a week, and a majority of them believed that the provision of consumer information is the primary role of NTOs. However, NTOs also provide window posters and displays as well as more technical services such as shell brochures and viewdata pages, and participation in trade and incentive exhibitions.

Many NTOs regularly stage evening receptions for travel agency staff in a region or town. Typically, these events are based around a video of the destination, followed by a presentation by a tour operator featuring it, and a question and answer session. On many such occasions, the evening concludes with a meal which features typical destination dishes (or drinks). During such an event it is common to hold a raffle or ticket draw for a variety of small prizes such as bottles of the country's wine, with the main prize being a fully paid holiday for two to that destination. Such events are often organized by groups such as the Travel Trades Club and are sometimes opened by invitation to tourism students at local colleges. They are regarded both as enjoyable social evenings when people with common professional interests can meet, and as providing opportunities to learn more, in a relaxed environment, about aspects of the industry.

Tour operators also benefit from support by NTOs. The work done for travel agencies is also relevant for them, but in addition they require introductions to suitable destination partners providing accommodation, transport or other services, and many draw on the NTO's stock of photographs to illustrate their brochures, although other sources including photographic agencies are available.

Against this background of competing destinations, ANTOR's role is to communicate and represent their common interests to other travel industry associations such as ABTA, and with the government and the media. Membership of ANTOR provides small NTOs with an opportunity to keep in touch with developments and networking with colleagues from other countries enables them to gauge the quality of agencies, operators, printers and other suppliers on whom they depend for their business. It represents all members as their formal channel of communication to the travel industry's leading bodies and to government. It is not just the small NTOs which benefit – the nature of the job is such that many experience quite a fast turnover in their staff, so newly arrived NTO managers benefit from the introductions which ANTOR provides to relevant British businesses, the media and government agencies.

One crucial issue is how to select good travel journalists for destination visits. This is a common form of publicity in which journalists representing the media which potential visitors are likely to read (or view) are invited on an expenses-paid tour of specific areas of the destination. On their return, they are expected to file articles for publication within a reasonable time frame which it is hoped will attract visitors. This approach is seen as a complement to advertising, giving the reader the benefit of a detached report by an experienced journalist of his or her own impressions and experience. A simple formula is adopted by many destinations to evaluate the effectiveness of their spending on journalists' visits. This is based on a measurement of the column inches of text (or minutes of TV transmission time) achieved multiplied by the number of readers and viewers compared to the cost of buying that much advertising space in the same media. NTOs requirements are quite varied, but for each press visit they have specific objectives such as spreading aware-ness of a newly opened region. They will expect to see it featured in the write-up, together with practical information such as how to make a booking to get there and mention of the tour operators which feature the area. This represents one of the difficulties resulting from the differing priorities of business partners which have been high-lighted earlier in this book and elsewhere. In general terms tour operators prefer developed destination areas with thousands of bed spaces and a sophisticated tourist infrastructure. On the other hand, many destination countries are in the process of promoting new areas as destinations in the hope that an influx of visitors will stim-ulate tourism enterprise in relatively remote, small and undeveloped areas.

As part of the benefit it offers its members, ANTOR stages three workshops annually, one for the media, one for tour operators and one for the conferences and incentives sector. These are for invited guests only and take the form of a hotel-based meeting where each country exhibiting has a table for a series of short, small meetings, thereby enabling them to hold discussions with several potential cli-ents in one day, while clients have the opportunity of meeting several suppliers.

ANTOR has formed a standing joint committee with ABTA for the purposes of continuous liaison. In addition to routine business, it was consulted on the EU legislation on packaged holidays and deals with urgent issues which arise from time to time and affect several ANTOR members. One example is safety problems in resorts con-cerning matters such as the clear indication of a swimming pool's depth or standards for lift doors.

Another type of problem arises when members of the UK trade fail to honour their contractual commitments. Destination-based organi-zations such as small coach operators or independent hotels find it daunting and difficult to pursue their rights in Britain and may contact their country's NTO for assistance. In difficult cases, ANTOR will present the facts of the case to relevant trade bodies such as ABTA.

ANTOR has established a range of awards to stimulate the improvement of standards of service and knowledge in the tourism industry. The Eddo Marx award was established in memory of its Chairman from 1981 to 1983, and is presented by ABTA's National Training Board to a tourism student. The Silver Otter Award is pre-sented annually to a Guild of Travel Writers' member nominated for an initiative which is of value to tourism and to local residents. The Association also awards a Diplôme d'Honneur to people who have rendered it an outstanding service.

ANTOR's current Executive Secretary, Pierre Claus, took on the role after he retired from the Belgian Tourist Office in which he had worked since 1958. He explained that Britain is different from the rest of Europe, where the majority of tourists make their own holiday arrangements. In the UK, most people rely on packaged holidays for short breaks, and travel agents and tour operators dominate the rapidly growing long-haul market. He anticipates changes in booking patterns and points to the French based MINITEL as a model of how developments in information technology may improve access to information and thereby alter the future role of NTOs.

Based on Chapman (1995), interviews with Pierre Claus, and ANTOR documents.

CASE STUDY 5.3

The Association of British Travel Agents

In 1960 ABTA (the Association of British Travel Agents) introduced a code of conduct, in effect a statement of basic business ethics, but in 1972 the reconstituted ABTA required both its travel agent and its tour operator members to provide binding codes of conduct (once approved by the National Council). These were revised in 1975 after consultation with the Office of Fair Trading. Voluntary codes of practice (Table 5.4) have the advantage of being quickly revised as trading conditions change, but it is difficult to enforce them effectively, and to cover an entire industry.

In its 1994 Members' Handbook, ABTA discusses the unique and difficult position of retail travel agents. It notes their role in the fulfilment of clients' dreams, for which payment is required in advance.

> The financial failure of, or inadequate performance by, tour operators or travel agents causes unacceptable social problems and great damage to the reputation of the travel trade as a whole . . . This is why ABTA has developed into a trade association concerned – apart from its normal trade association functions – to solve such problems, or at least mitigate their consequences, by becoming an independent, self-regulatory body . . . One major factor . . . is the provision of financial protection for the holiday-maker. This . . . has been provided for over 20 years in the form of individual company bonds and funds contributed by the members (£140 m). In addition, a large number have held CAA ATOL bonds . . . The organization introduced a rule in 1965 that an ABTA member tour operator could only sell their foreign inclusive holidays through third partys who are ABTA member travel agents. . . . This practice was inevitably a restrictive one . . . and in 1976 the OFT referred Stabilizer to the Restrictive Practices Court.

In 1982, the court decided that Stabilizer was in the public interest and could continue to be enforced lawfully.

Table 5.4 Codes of conduct in trade between tour operators and travel agents (selected points)

Tour operators' code of conduct
- 'To ensure that the public receive the best possible service from tour operators.' Also, 'to maintain and enhance the good name of ABTA and its members, to encourage initiative and enterprise, to ensure that the public interest shall predominate in all considerations of the standards of competitive trading between tour operators, and to encourage growth and development of the travel industry.'

Conduct between tour operators and members of the public
- A variety of standards are given covering brochure standards, cancellation by the tour operator, alterations to the holiday, cancellation by clients, overbooking, building works, liability, complaints correspondence from clients, correspondence from the association, arbitration, advertising, surcharges, airport etc. taxes, misleading use of ABTA's symbol and resort representatives.

Conduct between tour operators and travel agents
- 'Members of the Tour Operators' Class must not sell their foreign inclusive travel arrangements through anyone who is not a Member of the Travel Agents Class.'
- 'Members of the Travel Agents' Class must not sell the foreign inclusive travel arrangements of anyone who is not either a Member of the Tour Operators' Class or another Member of the Travel Agents' Class.'

Source: ABTA Members Handbook, 1994.

In 1990, the EC issued a Directive on Package Travel to harmonize consumer protection across the whole community. Each member country had to put it into law by 31 December 1992, although each country could choose how to implement it. In the UK, the Directive is implemented within the Package Travel Regulations of 1992, with the responsibility for regulation resting with the Trading Standards Office and ultimately the DTI. The law now includes new liabilities and criminal offences in sales procedures, and financial protection for the consumer has been imposed upon the industry rather than by the choice of individual companies.

ABTA, in common with the bodies representing any industry, has a wider remit, which it summed up in its handbook in the following terms: 'ABTA's commercial role is to influence events, for instance at government and EC level . . . so as to create as favourable a business role as is possible consistent with its members' right to compete freely with other sectors of trade and industry and each other.'

DIRECT SALES

In addition to the pattern where clients purchase holiday services from travel agency intermediaries in the channel of distribution, most tour operators also sell some of their holidays directly to the public. Dealing direct with the customer means that the operator's cash flow is improved because payment is tendered to the operator rather than being routed through the agent, and of course the direct sale method also eliminates agents' commissions. Other tour operators rely mainly (or exclusively) on direct sales, citing as benefits either that their specialized form of inclusive holiday requires expert knowledge at the point of sale or that they have no need to maintain links with agents since they have an established clientele. A further saving results from tighter control of brochure distribution, thereby reducing wastage, and an allied improvement in the conversion-to-sales ratio. For many direct sell operators, another important gain is the more effective market segmentation which can be gained from analysis of detailed customer records. Thus it possible to have relatively low start-up costs for direct-sale tour operating, but market awareness of the new operation has to be generated and that is likely to require extensive advertising and public relations support.

Against these benefits, the direct-sale operator incurs a range of costs which are largely avoided by distribution through the channel system. These additional costs range from postage, phone and allied expenses to the extra staffing required to deal with enquiries from interested people who may or may not purchase services from the operator. Therefore, additional office space is also required to accommodate sales and reservations staff. Tour operators which choose not to distribute through retail networks at all therefore have limited opportunities to reach potential clients as they have no high street presence. Since many clients will not carry out extended search activities for services which are of only marginal importance to them they are more likely to select a holiday from an alternative brochure which is readily available in a local retail outlet. Table 5.5 summarizes the

Table 5.5 Features of agency and direct distribution

	Direct sales	*Agency sales*
Tour operator		
Advantages	Improved cash flow Fast monitoring of market conditions Own customer database	Many outlets Potential for agencies to 'convert' clients by skilful selling
Disadvantages	Extra staff cost Extra communications costs Need for extra staff accommodation Need to promote energetically	Need to pay commission on sales Inability to control brochure use Cost of staff training and product familiarization Slower cash flow
Client		
Advantages	Expert advice	Impartial advice
Disadvantages	Phone contact	Personal contact with sales staff Convenient location

advantages and disadvantages of direct and agency distribution for tour operators and their clients.

Parkinson (1989) has suggested that direct selling is the most effective form of distribution for small companies, but points out that it depends on either sufficient promotional effort or on building a database of customers. A key benefit is 'the ability to monitor and control all aspects of the selling process and simultaneously to establish and maintain contact with customers. This enables the business to obtain constant feedback on their marketing efforts and also to monitor changes in the market place.'

THE CONTRIBUTION OF RETAIL TRAVEL AGENTS TO THE INCLUSIVE HOLIDAY INDUSTRY

Travel retailers face a number of difficulties resulting from the competitive trading environment in which they operate and potential developments in technology which might undermine their essential role in the distribution of travel services. They have been a key element in the development of the inclusive holiday industry, contributing to its rapid growth through their knowledge and enthusiasm of the products and places featured in tour operators' brochures and by the easy availability of these products which the network of travel distribution has created for literally millions of clients.

Porter (1987) has emphasized the analytical need to understand what each member organization contributes to an industry's activities. The significance of travel agents' roles is indicated in Table 5.6.

Table 5.6 The contribution of travel agents to the inclusive holiday industry's value chain

- Client advice
- Distribution of brochures
- Reservations
- Ticketing
- Acquire and provide unbiased information efficiently
- Additional services such as insurance
- Advice in the event of dissatisfaction

Based on Poon (1993) (modified).

FURTHER READING

Beaver, A. (1993) *Mind Your Own Travel Business*, 3 vols, 3rd edn, Allan Beaver, Radlett.

Davidson, W.R., Sweeney, D.J. and Stampfl, R.W. (1988) *Retailing Management*, 6th edn, John Wiley & Sons, New York.

Moutinho, L., Rita, P. and Curry, B. (1996) *Expert Systems in Tourism Marketing*, Routledge, London.

Poon, A. (1993) *Tourism, Technology and Competitive Strategies*, CAB International, Wallingford.

Poon (1993) and Moutinho, Rita and Curry (1996) provide technical and challenging accounts of how information technology is contributing to changing relationships in the tourism industry. Davidson, Sweeney and Stampfl (1988) present a general analysis of modern retailing practices while Beaver (1993) provides a highly detailed account of how to set up and operate a travel agency.

SUGGESTED EXERCISES

1. Study several consecutive editions of one of the travel industry's newspapers (*Travel Trade Gazette* and *Travel Weekly*), analyse feature articles and letters to the editor regarding relationships between tour operators and travel retailers.
2. Restricting yourself to the resources available to any member of the public, such as guidebooks, telephone directories, newspaper advertisements and the reference books in public libraries, assess the difficulty of arranging all the elements for a family's foreign holiday without using the services of travel retailers or tour operators.
3. Contrast the distribution systems and methods used for inclusive holidays with those of the financial services (insurance or savings) industry.

Creating and operating inclusive holidays

This part provides an account of how the remarkable achievements of the holiday industry have enabled large numbers of people to visit distant destinations. From the simple and very small-scale beginnings described earlier, the holiday industry has increased in sophistication to a point where, by the beginning of the 1990s, British tour operators were able to produce some 12 million overseas package tours annually. Chapter 6 examines some of the ways in which tour operators develop holiday products. The success of overseas inclusive holidays is inextricably linked with the development of a charter section in the airline industry, as Chapter 7 shows.

Tour operating $\boxed{6}$

INTRODUCTION

Tour operators are the key organizations in the inclusive holiday industry, providing the logistical skills to package travel, accommodation
and destination activities in ways which appeal to the travelling public.
However, they are dependent for their own products on those supplied
by a range of organizations, notably charter airlines and destination-
based businesses such as hotels and ground handlers, which supply the
elements of which holiday packages are composed, while the tour
operators' success in selling holidays depends largely on the network of
travel retailers.

The tour operator's business revolves around booking blocks of
travel space and hotel beds from other companies specializing in these
activities, and delivering large numbers of clients for them on a regular
basis. The tour company bears the risks of researching and organizing
a programme many months ahead of its sale, and it incurs the costs of
brochure design, production and distribution, and of the installation
and staffing of a reservations system. It also has to invest in a marketing communications programme to gain public and trade awareness for
its holiday programme in order to stimulate tourists' buying decisions.
The tour operator can create interest in its holiday programme through
media communications campaigns directed at the public, and by edu-
cating the travel retailers it deals with about the special characteristics
and advantages of its holiday offers.

PACKAGING HOLIDAYS

Tour operators deal in holiday concepts consisting of certain basic elements, particularly hotel or other accommodation, travel between
home and resort and various activities at the destination, as indicated
in Table 6.1. The skills of successful tour operating lie in selecting an
appealing combination of these elements, marketing the packages
effectively so that a sufficient number of holidays can be sold at prices
which enable the industry's participating companies to earn realistic

Table 6.1 Elements of inclusive holiday concepts

Basic elements
- Return flight between origin and destination

plus

Accommodation
- Standard hotel accommodation in resort
- Superior hotel accommodation
- Budget hotel accommodation
- Self-catering accommodation
- Hosted chalet accommodation
- Camping

Transfers
- Coach
- Taxi
- Limousine
- Self-drive car

Form of holiday
- Resort based
- Two centre, including transfer
- Touring with guide
- Cruising
- Cruise combined with resort stay
- Self-drive, no structured itinerary

Activities
- Day and evening group excursions
- Adventure tour
- Themed activities
- Skills-bsaed programmes
- Non prearranged

levels of profit, and operating the holidays in a manner which pleases the clients.

Increasing spending power, increased awareness of holiday opportunities and the falling (relative) cost of holidays has enabled more people to exercise choice between an increasing number of holiday options. As more people travel the range of destinations and the types of holiday offered have become more varied, reflecting the tour operators' increasingly sophisticated differentiation of their holiday products, as Table 6.2 indicates. This variety of holiday types also helps the tour operator to fill capacity on the flights between origin and destination by targeting a variety of segments in the market for holidays with different products.

MARKETING INCLUSIVE HOLIDAYS

Marketing theorists have pointed out that all purchases are made to satisfy needs. Any item purchased must be able to perform the function claimed of it, and for which it was primarily acquired; this is the core of the product. However, it seems that consumers often have in

Table 6.2 Differentiating inclusive holidays

Holiday element	Market sector		
	Mass volume	*Exclusive*	*Specialist*
Accommodation	Large, member of group	High star rating	Small, local style
Airline	Charter	Business class	Scheduled
Transfers	Coach, multi drop	Limo	Group coach
Departure airport	Many, local	Regional	Regional
Journey schedule	'Market days'	Any day	Ad hoc
Duration	7-day multiples	As requested	Determined by activity
Excursions	Coach, general interest	Chauffer driven	Key element, design for each group
Cost	Low price	Premium	Varies
Ethos	Fun, relaxation, informal, group activities	Stylish, exclusive, personal recognition of individual clients	High degree of contact with local culture or ecology. Focus on individual interest and involvement in activities

mind a more complex concept, one which includes a wider range of benefits. As Kotler and Armstrong (1987) put it: 'to best satisfy customers, the producer has to offer an augmented product.' These additional features of products have been identified as the locus of new competition: 'The new competition is not between what companies produce in their factories, but between what they add ... in the form of packaging, services, customer advice, financing ... and other things that people value' (Levitt, 1969).

Tour operators market their holiday packages in the fullest sense: they develop their products, take pricing decisions which they feel will attract the greatest volume of travellers or yield the best profit, promote their holidays to customers and travel retailers through appropriate media, produce and distribute detailed information in the form of holiday brochures by which clients can take buying decisions, set up reservations systems to handle bookings and administrative systems to deal with suppliers and distributors, and develop new holiday concepts for forthcoming seasons and work towards business goals of growth, market share and profit just as any other business does. In addition to the four fundamental marketing tasks (often referred to as the '4 Ps'), marketing is also the function of management which bridges the gaps between companies and their customers, as Chapter 4 showed. The key to tour operators' success is to understand what their customers want, and to provide it in convincing, enticing ways. The prosperity of destination areas, and of the other businesses contributing elements to the inclusive holiday system, is dependent on their ability to attract large numbers of holidaymakers. The very simplest inclusive holiday package, consisting of only two service elements – return travel with accommodation at the destination – is a useful starting point for more detailed analysis. As Figure 6.1 shows, this basic or core holiday product can be enhanced with other features making it more attractive to

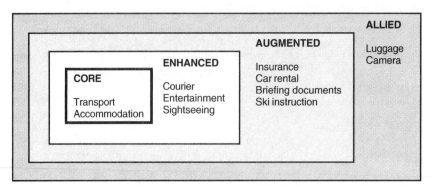

Figure 6.1 Core, enhanced, augmented and allied holiday product concepts.

clients in the context of a competitive marketplace. Most tour operators improve on the basic holiday package by including features such as transfers between airport and hotel at the destination, and the services of resort representatives who provide clients with further opportunities for a variety of leisure, cultural, sporting or entertainment activities during their destination stay.

The precise mix of additional service elements and the style with which they are presented helps the tour operator to establish a unique position in clients' minds, contrasting with that of its competitors. These additional service elements are a managerial tool by which managers can distinguishing their organization's style from that of competitors along dimensions such as completeness of holiday experience and its cost, quality or convenience. More significantly, all these aspects are included in the client's perception of the overall holiday experience. Marketing experience indicates that clients' views of a tour package are widening to include in their expectations of the overall holiday experience a range of additional benefits. These additional facilities can provide a basis for marketing the programmes, and can be added to the holiday itself or developed for clients before or after their tour. On tour, extra benefits include better flight scheduling, more comfort or uprated service standards, welcoming drinks or other tokens and full service at the destination. After the holiday, a satisfaction questionnaire, with any follow-up needed, may be offered. Some companies also organize reunions for their clients which evoke memories of the holiday, renew old acquaintances and may result in further bookings for the coming season. Bathurst (1995) has vividly described the 'fumes of lager, leching and cheap aftershave' which she encountered when attending a Club 18–30 'Zoo Ibiza' reunion held in Skegness.

The way in which tour operators achieve their business objectives also has profound effects for their partners in the holiday industry system; for example, by introducing a 'new' destination area they may be putting an established competitor at risk, or at least force it to invest in infrastructure improvements and facilities upgrading. Similarly, new types of holiday concept can undermine the basis of established busi-

Table 6.3 Inclusive holidays – features and advantages

To consumers
- Convenient purchase of all tourism elements
- Quality guarantees
- Protection through branding
- Convenient arrangements

To hotels and airlines
- Tourists 'bundled' into economic groups for transport and accommodation
- Reduced marketing expenses
- Simplified booking and payment arrangements

To destination-based organizations
- Regular arrival of groups
- Predictable requirements
- Reduced marketing expenses

To retail travel agencies
- Easy to provide a full holiday for clients
- Pre-existing market demand
- Low capital and staffing costs

To tour operators
- Widespread awareness and interest
- Easy to expand or change programme
- Standardized products offered
- Little capital investment required

nesses, so the tour operators' development decisions have a wide significance. Packaged holidays are also important to the other organizations in the tourism industry system, their main significance arising from the large numbers of holidaymakers which tour operators are able to organize on a regular basis, creating a level of demand for specialized services and infrastructure. Taking the foregoing points together, inclusive holidays therefore provide different features and advantages compared to independent travel arrangements, as Table 6.3 indicates.

PORTFOLIO MANAGEMENT

One of the key decisions for tour operators' managers is about the nature and composition of their portfolio of holidays – the range of destinations, modes of travel, quality of hotels, variety and style of activities offered and the markets to which the products are to be targeted. Case study 6.1 discusses how Kestours develops its holiday packages.

CASE STUDY 6.1

The development of Kestours group business

Kestours was established in 1956 as a specialist in bespoke group travel, its clients ranging from sports groups to conference organizers. Now its portfolio includes package tours to Dublin, Lourdes and Barbados, and a wide variety of specialist group tours. Examples of the company's recent clients and tours include the National Baton Twirling Association tour by 130 participants to Milan in 1992, followed by all arrangements for the European Twirling Championships in Edinburgh in 1994; the National Association of Master Tile Fixers' annual conferences; British Judo Association competitions in Athens, Geneva, Salzburg, Nice and Paris; charters for up to 2500 supporters to watch overseas matches by the Welsh Rugby team; the South Wales Police Choir tour to Barbados; newspaper readers' travel offers, including *Woman's Own* and *Woman* to Barbados and the South Pacific; a fashion shoot in Barbados for Freeman's mail order catalogue; and many school and university sports tours. Kestours carried a total of 4900 clients in 1994.

A general brochure entitled *Sports Tours 1995* offers club programmes arranged by coach or air with local departures, and accommodation determined by the nature of the resort and the composition of each party. Prices include one tournament; others are charged extra. The brochure contains a note of warning:

> We look to party leaders to take charge of their group – and that includes behaviour. It is a sad fact that a small minority of people consider that once they have left Britain, the rules of good conduct cease to apply. Please be aware that Kestours are not interested in carrying such individuals and will fully support any action taken by transport operators or hoteliers to safeguard the interests of the majority of sportsmen for whom these tours are intended.

The founder of Kestours, Eric Huggins, had been a school sportsmaster and part-time courier for George Wenger (founder of International Summer Schools, an early tour operator) on holidays to the Alps in the 1940s when he had been paid £5.00 per trip. His headteacher, noting that the local girls' school visited France, suggested that Eric organize a tour. He approached Wenger, asking for the empty return seats from Basle on an Eagle Air flight at the start of the season. These were obtained at £3.00 returning to Blackbushe airport. Eric was able to put together a ten-day holiday for £21.00 in 1953, including the outward journey by rail, full board in Interlaken and a full programme of excursions including the cog railway trip up the Jungfrau Joch.

Eric Huggins also played for his local football club (Beckenham). Its manager was a friend of Lorri Scott, manager of Hitchin, whose attempt to organize a Belgian match for his club in 1953 had run into difficulties. After some thought, Eric arranged a five day tour to Ostende for £13 2s 6d by coach staying at the Cardiff Hotel and including two games in Ghent. He was asked to repeat the arrangements the following year, and soon most clubs in the Isthian League became his clients.

Tour operating was becoming more organized, and in 1969 the European Union of Football Associations first required the companies providing travel for its members to deposit a bond of £2000. This money was invested in Swiss government bonds, eventually providing Kestours with substantial growth in capital value. In 1971, Eric opened a retail travel agency using one of the rooms as an office for the tour operation, and in 1972 he obtained an ABTA licence. His hobby had steadily built into a business, and in 1972 Eric decided to give up teaching and became a full-time tour operator. Many of the sports groups travelled by coach or rail and crossed the Channel by ferry but he also gained experience of chartering small airlines, including the first DC8 operation into Luxembourg. In Easter 1975, Kestours organized European tours for 120 football teams using back-to-back air charters.

The present Managing Director, Glynn Huggins, explained that the early Kestours experience illustrates the effectiveness of niche marketing in building a business. They had had no established programmes to compete with, and the opportunities were their own creation. The advantage for Kestours of having a unique selling proposition was that it conferred the opportunity to set operating margins, secure exclusive contracts for accommodation and in some cases for flights, and to create a name as a major player in their chosen market. Further development was taken seriously, with money and time invested in research such as visiting potential sites. This had the characteristic of undercover work because of the risk of competitors pursuing the same opportunities if they noticed what you were doing.

An example of how Kestours developed their philosophy of niche marketing is provided by their programme of tours to Lourdes. As an official travel agent to the British Volleyball Association, they needed to obtain the cheapest rate to European destinations where matches were played. At that time (1974) this involved producing an inclusive tour brochure to secure ITX seat rates. Toulouse was one destination which they needed to serve, and therefore they decided to feature it in a brochure. They explored the potential of the surrounding area and saw the possibility of developing the market for pilgrimages to Lourdes, at that time served by one other operator using coach and ferry travel arrangements. However, Kestours had only sold its programmes direct to sports clubs and groups, so in order to attract business from retail travel agents for its new brochure, Kestours decided to obtain listings in the various 'who goes where' guides used by travel agents, enabling them to assess the demand for their Lourdes tours at minimal expense.

Twenty years on, Kestours has a special Lourdes brochure which is well known in the travel trade and supported by the French Government Tourist Office (who also recommend it through their Manila office to Philippine tourists visiting Europe). This has been achieved without widespread promotion or advertising and the programme returns gross margins of around 27%. Furthermore, the programme does not involve much financial risk as it is operated without commitment to allocations.

In 1995, the Lourdes brochure featured the new Eurostar service through the Channel Tunnel. This journey takes 10 hours 20 minutes from Waterloo, changing in Paris to the TGV service which has only one stop before reaching Lourdes. Kestours managers regard this as a strong selling point because of the speed and comfort of the new service, which they are the first to offer. The unique service has proved very attractive to their Philippine clients.

Kestours has traditionally been a family business, owned and operated by the founder and his relatives. However, in 1992 a Welsh sports tour operator failed and they rapidly decided to buy the goodwill. This consisted mainly of the mailing list, and Kestours worked through the night of the purchase to fax and mail all clients of their new acquisition, thereby retaining 98% of the booked business. This was for the Five Nations Rugby International Supporters and took place on just one weekend of the year when Wales played abroad. This extremely peaked business profile had caused their predecessor severe financial and administrative problems. Kestours again applied their niche marketing skills to find destinations which were not well featured, and particularly those which could be served from the local airport, Cardiff. They recruited a member of staff (their first employee) to develop ideas and produce a business plan. In June 1994, they decided to develop tours to Dublin. The airline flying the route, Manx, was interested in building up traffic in order to put on larger and more economic aircraft. Kestours and Manx had thus identified synergistic advantages in developing business on the route. The Irish Tourist Board was approached and agreed to assist with funds for marketing the project. Hoteliers were keen to build on the existing one weekend per year business, and the first programme featured five hotels with prices from a low of £129 per person for two nights. Kestours accept that the programme has been keenly priced in the initial years. The plan is to increase margins to a more realistic level once the programme is established and good working relationships have been formed with suppliers.

Even before the brochure had been printed and circulated to its target South Wales agents, over 100 people had booked. By the end of 1994, marketing included sending a journalist from the South Wales daily, the *Western Mail and Echo* to Dublin, receiving in return a page of editorial featuring Dublin, and running a competition for a weekend in Dublin in conjunction with the paper.

To coincide with the Five Nations Rugby International in Edinburgh in March 1995, Kestours developed a programme of coach- or flight-based holidays in Edinburgh from Cardiff for the Wales v. Scotland match, offering a choice of 24 hotels from £97 to £549.

The Rugby World Cup in 1995 provided the opportunity for spectator tours to South Africa in May and June, less than a year after South Africa's first free democratic elections. A special brochure was produced offering a range of complete itineraries for supporters including entrance to the opening match (South Africa v. Australia) and all the matches of either England, Scotland or Wales, plus a choice of various excursions to National Parks, Sun City or the winelands, and an end-of-tour gala dinner. Prices ranged from £1570 to £3790. For this programme, Kestours acted as agent for Specialized Travel, itself one of a few companies appointed by the South African Rugby authorities for the World Cup series. The brochure offered additional departures for Russian, Czech, Romanian, Hungarian and Western European fans. The project was promoted from mailing lists built up over the years, and particularly from personal contact with the rugby world and local travel agents who had been productive with rugby bookings to other destinations. The total booked for the series was 50.

Kestours' other specialized sports programmes include club tours for netball groups to Wales, Jersey, Malta, Grand Cayman and Barbados for adult and youth groups. Brochure prices include travel, accommodation and arrangements for fixtures organized in conjunction with local netball associations.

Sports groups account for approximately 90% of Kestours clients, including supporters for the various Five Nations Rugby Internationals, and is mainly sold direct, but the company's business portfolio also includes package holidays sold through the travel trade to Dublin, Lourdes and Barbados as well as specialized tours such as the Lewis Carroll journey. This was presented and accompanied by Edward Wakeling, a writer and expert on Lewis Carroll. Two tours were operated, each costing £1329.00 for 12 days including accommodation in specially selected hotels such as Gogarth Abbey, formerly the country home of Alice's family, a cocktail party on the first day and dinner in the Great Hall of Christ Church College, Oxford, where the author had been a mathematics don, admissions to all the main places in Lewis Carroll's life, and talks. The party size was limited to 20 in order to give personal attention to all participants and enable entry to places not normally accessible to visitors.

Increasing regulation of the holiday industry and competition from larger companies has altered the market environment for companies such as Kestours, which places greater emphasis than previously on direct selling. Across the country, multiple retail agencies are unable, or unwilling, to work with more than a few tour operators, from whom they expect override commissions, training and advertising support. Small tour operators are not able to offer them this and are not interested in building volume at the expense of profit margins.

A concern to small tour operators is that pressure on independant retailers' finances puts the tour operator at risk, and causes problems through their late release of clients' money when it is due. In 1994, Kestours worked with approximately 30 independant travel agencies, but this was reduced in 1995 to ten. Kestours has therefore cut back on travel agents' support and launched a concerted effort to raise its profile in order to attract direct bookings. Recent examples of its approach include:

- Taking a travel programme from 'Red Dragon' radio in Cardiff to Ireland, and receiving in return two half-hour programmes about their products to Ireland.
- Running holiday competitions in the glossy magazines to promote the Barbados product (September 1995 in *OK* magazine, and January 1996 in *Chic*).
- Using mailing lists and the medium of direct mail more intensively.
- Upgrading the company's sports brochure to widen its appeal.

The inside front cover of the 1996 brochure highlights what Kestours can offer sports fans, stressing Experience (the company is in its 40th year), Security (Kestours is bonded with ABTA, the CAA and IATA) and Variety. This is explained by references to their experience in taking diverse groups to a variety of locations – 'No problem!' The next page features a map of Britain explaining the supplements to brochure prices for regional departures, and outlining the company's policy on accommodation based on value-for-money budget accommodation with the option of upgrading to a higher standard. Four bold coloured bands focus attention on Football, Rugby, Cricket and Other sports. The body of the brochure is colour-keyed to these four products, with two or more pages devoted to a brief description of the destinations available for each sport. To take one example, cricket tours are offered to Kenya, with a choice of charter or scheduled flights; to South Africa, Sri Lanka, Cyprus, Spain, Holland and Barbados. Prices to Barbados in early December start at £435 for four people sharing a self-catering villa. Kestours has a resident manager in Barbados, who arranges fixtures for both school and seniors matches for touring parties. The brochure advises: 'The pitches on the Island are always very fast and true, but don't be surprised to find the outfields a little bumpy!' The brochure provides a page of easily read booking conditions (although these are printed in a somewhat reduced typeface compared to the text in the body of the brochure). The booking form provides in the normal way for details of the lead client and his or her travelling companions, but also has a section for the group's sports requirements. This asks for details of the sport, the number of fixtures required, the standard of the team and the average age of its members, and the league, division and position at which it played last season. This also asks for details of the team's colours. The booking form insists that insurance must be taken out, and that it must include cover for the risks of the team's chosen sport. However, clients are free to chose an alternative to Kestours' insurers, but must provide the tour operator with details, including the policy number and the 24-hour emergency contact number of the insurer. The rear cover of the brochure emphasizes some of the benefits which Kestours offers, including a free place offer, an early booking bonus and a discount voucher on next year's bookings for clubs which introduce a new client. Long-haul clients also receive complimentary sports bags and baseball caps in Kestours housestyle. This sports bag is the only illustration on the front cover, which states in a clear type face, 'KESTOURS 1996 SPORTS TOURS'. In smaller, vertical lettering, the front cover also proclaims, 'EUROPE AND BEYOND'.

Table 6.4 provides a breakdown of Kestours business in 1994.

Table 6.4 A profile of Kestour business (1994)

Programme	Number of clients
Travel only (mainly rugby supporters booking travel to the Five Nations Internationals	1619
Dublin	966
Barbados	711
Edin burgh	398
Amsterdam	367
Lourdes	141
Scheveeningen	67
Jersey	54
Bray (Dublin)	52
Lloret de Mar	50
Trinidad	41
Ostend	33
Paris	32
Hannover	32
Rotterdam	19
Antigua	15
Tobago	2

RISK IN PORTFOLIO DEVELOPMENT

Hooper (1995) has identified several factors which are affecting the way in which holidays are packaged: competition, which is driving price and quality down, the potential for further expansion based on

Table 6.5 Degrees of risk in portfolio development

Destination, or holiday concept	Market being served	
	Established	*New*
Established		Uncertain about how to reach clients and about which products they will respond to
	Low risk	
New	Need for new managerial skills to organize new types of holiday, or to work with new destination-based organizations	**High risk**

the needs of elderly travellers, and the threat arising from experienced travellers who may prefer to make their own ground arrangements. For an established company, any major changes to its portfolio represent a business risk, the risk increasing with the extent to which the new holiday, or the new market being served, differs from that in which it has experience, as Table 6.5 indicates.

Research for the next year's programme may simply entail checking and updating the existing arrangements with the hotels, ground handlers and charter airlines it already uses. Over a period of time public interest in some established holiday products will decline and ultimately they will be removed from the tour operator's brochure, while conversely most tour operators will also expect to add new hotel properties or extend the range of their operations by including new destinations each season. Thus, year on year, an established tour operator's programme is likely to change, and most expect to increase their volume of sales in an expanding market. Figure 6.2 shows how the resultant differential development of products may reshape a tour operator's portfolio of holidays over a period of years, drawing on Ansoff (1968). While one type of holiday, for example long-haul twin centre holidays, has increased in importance, another (Mediterranean beach three-star

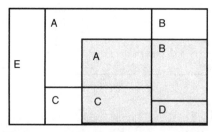

Figure 6.2 Differential product portfolio development: shaded area = volume of sales and share of four products – A, B, C, D – in 1988; unshaded area = relative volumes of four products sold in 2003 (note that D is no longer featured in the portfolio while E represents a new product).

hotel holidays) has declined both in volume and importance to the operator. The factors leading to policy decisions to change the range of holidays offered include both product- and market-related judgements by the company's managers, and the resultant brochure(s) reflect their forecast of what business activities will be most profitable for their company in the coming season, and will indicate how they anticipate that consumer preferences will evolve over the next few years since it is too expensive to develop a holiday series just for one season's operation.

For small companies, product development research is usually undertaken by the owner, while the larger tour operators have a group of staff (usually with resort management experience), who travel extensively to contract new destinations and hotels. Following the choice of destinations and hotels to offer for a coming season, the tour operator is faced with a series of tasks including costing all the holiday options, preparing the brochures, getting them printed, and launching the new holiday programme both to the trade and to the consumer. Figure 6.3 summarizes this discussion, and identifies the sequence of tasks which a tour operator performs in creating and operating their holiday programme.

However, the real test for the coming year's programme is how successfully it sells, and this can only be gauged after the programme has been fully planned and is presented to the trade and the public as a brochure. While small companies rely on their experience and past knowledge of customers' preferences, the larger organizations also conduct extensive market research, or more commonly they commission studies from specialist organizations. As the season progresses, many of the larger tour operators reprint their brochures, deleting holidays which are not selling well, adding other hotels in popular resorts, and adjusting prices in order to maximize their revenue or volume targets.

In addition to product development and enhancements, tour operators must also be able to recognize and respond to the differing (and changing) interests of their clients. Some, especially the larger companies, aim to provide a range of holiday types which, although they may be branded as separate programmes, cumulatively aim to appeal

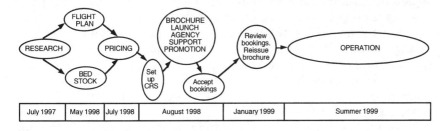

Figure 6.3 Schedule of activities to prepare an inclusive holiday programme.

to the broadest market. These larger companies also have the financial and management resources to set up contracts for large volumes of beds and seats, and through their scale advantages can usually produce a particular holiday package for less than the smaller companies.

MASS MARKET PACKAGE HOLIDAYS

Tour operators providing mass market holidays base their business on regular programmes of flights to well known and developed resorts. Success comes from maximizing load factors on the travel portion, as will be shown in Chapter 7, and through volume buying to negotiate very low rates with the accommodation suppliers they use. This enables them to sell their holidays at low prices, thereby stimulating demand. The design of mass market holidays reflects research into market trends and the power of mass tour operators' volume buying. The holidays which mass market tour operators offer must have a wide public appeal, and they must be readily available for purchase through the network of retail travel agencies. The history of the industry illustrates their belief that they could expand the market, although some recent trends appear to indicate that the demand for inclusive overseas holidays is finite.

A high degree of organizational and managerial skill is required, with attention paid to product specifications, promotion, sales and channel member management. They undertake detailed analysis of booking trends and cash flow as sales build up after the brochure launch, so that prices can be adjusted throughout the season, more accommodation secured at popular resorts or allocations released from those which have not sold as well as anticipated. This flexibility is one of the key trading strengths of the tour operators, enabling them to overcome a variety of unforeseen situations such as civil unrest, earthquake or major storm damage which sometimes deter visitors from specific areas.

However, this flexibility also suggests that the mass market tour operators regard the available destinations and hotels as substitutes, and it also explains their concern that each resort in their brochures should be presented in equivalent terms and offer equivalent service standards. Rather undiscriminating, if appealing, text and place imagery is often used in their brochures so that clients are more attracted by the general idea of taking a holiday, and the specific concept of taking a holiday with that company, rather than by the attractions of a specific hotel or resort area. For a typical client, all salient information will be contained in the brochure or on the central reservations computer which retail agents can readily access from their high-street office locations for speedy confirmation.

Mass market tour operators tend to regard their clients as providing continuing revenue opportunities once they have reached a destination area, and develop the opportunities for further revenue through the provision of organized excursions, entertainment and activities. They, or their resort offices and staff, generally earn commission on these sales. This is paid in local currency, and therefore provides a useful way of offsetting the costs entailed in maintaining the resort office, hiring both local and expatriot staff, and arranging airport transfers for clients, particularly in countries where the exchange rate is unfavourable.

A result of the large tour operators' tendency to organize destination-based activities is that their clients are buffered from experiencing the authentic way of living in the locality where they take their holidays. Figure 6.4 shows the varied ways in which tour operators mediate the destination experiences of their clients, through selecting the activities which they will undertake during their holiday and by organizing excursions, meals and entertainment to a common standard which is consistent with what that tour operator provides in other resorts. Although there is inevitable some local flavour, it is generally bland and often rather artificial, as exemplified in the 'traditional' local dances which form an attractive feature of many evening events. Two caveats should be noted to the foregoing analysis: in the first place, these criticisms can also be levelled at many of the smaller tour operators, and secondly, many independent travellers also do not establish a deep contact with local culture, either because of language and similar barriers, or because either they, or the residents, are cautious about approaching each other. These issues are discussed more fully in Laws (1995).

SPECIALIST TOUR OPERATORS

Tour operators which specialize in a particular destination or type of holiday are providing services for one, or a few, distinct segments or

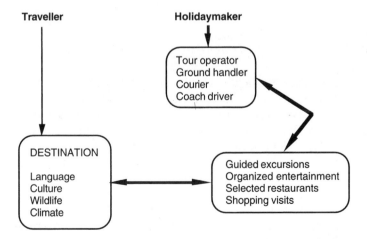

Figure 6.4 Buffering holidaymakers from destination culture.

niches in the market, and they are therefore relatively small. Smaller tour operators have more varied approaches to their businesses. Many offer selected opportunities for individuals or groups to visit destinations of particular interest to them. Their brochures may feature a limited selection of hotels and resorts, in one or a few countries. Another approach, discussed in Case study 6.1 on Kestours, provides a range of holiday packages and itineraries intended for groups of clients with specialized interests, such as sports, while other companies have expertise in activities such as bird watching. Others specialize in adventure holidays throughout the world, perhaps offering a selection of four-wheel drive desert crossings, mountain trekking or guided tours of remote areas. Another approach is to exploit the opportunities offered by clients' special interests, whether for naturist, naturalist or wine-tasting holidays. The length and timing of each tour will reflect conditions at the destination: climate, festivals and so on, and each tour will be designed to maximize particular interests. Smaller companies tend to specialize, offering a limited range of destinations or holiday types, but their advantage is that they can respond quickly, producing new types of holidays for quite small numbers of clients. Their speed of response results largely from the direct involvement of the proprietor in the operation as well as the planning of their business activities.

Although specialist tour operators often accept bookings placed through the retail agency network, few retailers have the detailed knowledge to advise their clients, and many others do not rack this type of brochure, either because they anticipate only a low volume of sales or because they are part of a vertically integrated group which places the emphasis on the sale of in-house products. Furthermore, the small tour operators are unable or unwilling to offer higher than standard commission, thus further decreasing the rationale for most other travel agencies to deal with them. For these and other reasons specialists tend to prefer their clients to book direct with them.

COMPETITION BETWEEN MASS MARKET AND SPECIALIST TOUR OPERATORS

The market philosophy of small and specialist tour operators is to identify and service small sections, or niches, in the general inclusive holiday market. However, this must be considered in the context that the major tour operators can easily erode any market niche once it is established by independent tour operators and has grown to a size which it makes it a profitable business for them. The major companies now routinely offer long-haul, villa, youth and other focused holidays which had been the preserve of specialized tour operators. As is noted in a subsequent chapter, the major tour operators, through vertical integration with retail agencies, also dominate the channel of distribution from which customers purchase their holidays. In response to these pressures, and exacerbated by dissatisfaction with the influence of the large companies on ABTA's policy-making, an association was established for specialist tour operators. AITO (the Association of Independent Tour Operators) had 150 member companies by the end of 1995, and publishes a directory of 'real holidays', listing 350 different brochures. Some tour operators specialize in holidays in their own country, either for domestic consumers, as illustrated by Case study 3.2 on Haven Leisure, or for incoming tourists, as in the case of Frames Rickards discussed in Case study 6.2.

CASE STUDY 6.2

Frames Rickards Ltd

Frames Rickards operates UK sightseeing and coach tours, mainly for inbound tourists visiting Britain, and a coach charter service. Frames Rickards is unique in that it operates its own fleet of coaches (16 in 1995, and 40 staff) from its own combined coach garage and terminal premises in Central London.

Origins of Frames Rickards

The company traces its origins to two roots. It dates back to 1850, when Charles Rickard started a business which gained the transport contract for Royal Mail in 1894, when, as the present Chairman pointed out, 'coaches were horse drawn.' The modern fleet of coaches, painted in a distinctive burgundy with gold lettering, carry the livery granted by Queen Victoria to Charles Rickard, and the company is still the Queen's Appointed Road Transport Contractor.

John Frames began to transport temperance groups on excursions from Preston in 1881, became a rail and shipping agent, and eventually moved to London where he established a charabanc company. In 1967 Frames acquired Rickards, and in 1991, after the Gulf War depressed holiday business worldwide, the company was restructured. Three partners bought it out, and continued to trade under its well established name, retaining most of the staff.

Sightseeing excursions

The day excursions and coach tours mirror each other in marketing and operational aspects. A whole-day tour of London is featured at £49.50 with lunch included, and reductions for children under 16 and for April departures. This departs daily from Frames Rickards coach station at 08.45, visiting Westminster Abbey, the Changing of the Guards, the Tower of London and the Crown Jewels, and St Paul's Cathedral. Lunch is taken aboard a cruising river boat chartered exclusively by Frames Rickards. The brochure points out that Westminster Abbey is sometimes closed to the public, in which event the drive route is extended and the tour visits the Tate Gallery.

Another daily tour also departs from Frames Rickards coach station at 08.45, visiting Canterbury, Leeds Castle and the White Cliffs of Dover for £38.00, with similar reductions for children and April departures. Lunch is not included in this tour, but the brochure states: 'There is time for lunch and shopping in the interesting area close to Canterbury Cathedral.'

Coach tours

Coach tours include four days visiting York, Durham, Edinburgh and Chester for £275 staying in four-star or equivalent hotels on a dinner, bed and breakfast basis. Another tour visits the English Lakes and Brontë Country, the four-day itinerary costing £270. Some of the four-day tours are featured in other inbound operators' brochures, for example British Airways Holidays, but most are sold from Frames Rickards' own brochures.

Frames Rickards produce two brochures, one for sightseeing and one for coach tours. These mirror each other in several respects.

Sightseeing brochure

Sightseeing Tours and Excursions: London and Britain is a small format brochure which is distributed mainly through London hotels. The cover features traditional touristic images of Britain: Stonehenge, thatched cottages, Tower Bridge and the Changing of the Guards ceremony, the flags of Britain and the company's five most important non-English speaking markets, the Grey Line logo and a very cheerful Beefeater. As an added incentive to take the brochure from distribution racks offering a selection of excursion brochures, the cover states clearly that it includes a free tourist map, this also encourages tourists to retain it, thus increasing the likelihood of gaining a sale. There is no index as such. Instead, a colourful display draws attention to a range of Frames Rickards services including half-day, day, evening and three- or four-day tours and their special features. These are Frames Rickards', coach station facilities, its unequalled experience, the convenience of hotel courtesy pick-up, air conditioned coaches and friendly, skilled drivers, with entrance fees included in the tour price.

Coach tours brochure

An A4 brochure features the coach tours of Britain, Ireland and France, and other products of interest to overseas visitors. It is distributed by Frames Rickards' agents in North America, Australia and other markets. The cover features three photographs: a young couple relaxing on the terrace of a hotel, enjoying extensive views over a tranquil wooded lake; a close-up of a mounted guardsman; and the facade of Hampton Court Palace. The majority of tours are about four days in duration, although two, A Taste of Britain, and The Best of Britain, are eight-day tours. The latter is priced at £595.00

using four- and five-star hotels and extends as far north as Ullapool, with weekly departures from May to October. It is also possible for clients to join the four Scottish part of this tour in Edinburgh at a cost of £250.

Each page features a simple, clear itinerary map, the location, name and star (or crowne) rating of each hotel used, and a boxed statement of what is included, such as sightseeing and number of meals. General information, including the conditions of booking, are set out on the inside rear cover in the same typeface and size as the rest of the brochure. Clients are advised that 'passengers will be asked to change their coach seats once or twice a day. This has proved to be a fair system of seat allocation.' There is also detailed information about payment, surcharging, gratuities and cancellation penalties.

The brochure provides a choice of hotels in London for overseas visitors including chauffeur-driven transfers from Heathrow. The rear cover invites clients to 'mix 'n' match'. 'Our tours and packages are ideal when you want variety and a timetable that suits you. Use them like building blocks and create your ideal vacation when you put together two or more of our programmes. What is more, you can save money.' This is a reference to a reduction if two or more escorted tours of three days or longer are booked. Other reductions include special deals for those aged over 55, departures between November and March or for groups.

Bookings

The *Sightseeing* brochure distributed in the UK has traditionally been booked late, generally a day or two before departure, through the hotel concierge service or directly by telephone. The coach tours programme, distributed in Frames Rickards, overseas markets by its agents, has traditionally attracted advanced bookings but in recent years the trend for both products has been towards later bookings. The tour bookings are scrutinized about five weeks before departure, and where bookings are low, a judgement is taken resulting in cancellation or a firm commitment to operate a specific departure. Despite the reduced revenue compared to a fully sold tour, Frames Rickards feel confident about operating a tour with 20 or so seats empty, because clients gain from the comfort of extra space, but if there are only half a dozen clients aboard, the size of the coach can be intimidating to them, and so, if it seems unlikely that more bookings will be taken, a tour may be cancelled. Clients are then offered an alternative departure date or itinerary, or a refund. However, clients have a contractual right to cancel with a 50% penalty up to the day prior to departure.

Reservations system

In 1995, Frames Rickards was not using a computerized reservations system. It had experimented with a link to National Holidays, and it is a member of Grey Line. Its American partner uses CRS, but faxes the reservations it has taken for Frames Rickards tours on a daily basis. It is anticipated that a CRS will be adopted within a few years, but the present manual system is effective and flexible. In particular, it is responsive to direct customers' queries, and as a component of staff training is to familiarize them with the tours, they are able to offer best advice to clients on a personal basis.

Pricing

Frames Rickards' policy is to price its tours at a realistic level, and it aims never to be the cheapest with a particular product, reflecting its emphasis on reliability and quality. The brochures offer discounts for early season and group bookings, and to the elderly and for accompanying children. Supplements are charged for single accommodation. The company pays commission to its agents (including hotels) for selling its products, and also offers overrides for those which achieve high levels of business.

Foreign exchange

Many clients use Frames Rickards products as building blocks in a customized itinerary, buying their transatlantic ticket from their travel agent, together with a few days in a London hotel, a day excursion, car hire to visit friends or relatives, and ending with a four-day coach tour. This type of business indicates another trading difficulty for Frames Rickards: it has to price its brochure for the following April in September, and since half its business is from North America and, much of its revenue comes from its American agents, it also has to decide on forward selling rates for the dollar. If the price is too high, its programme will not sell, but conversely, underestimating the future foreign exchange rate would result in a large loss, irrespective of the success of the programme itself.

Operating the tours and sightseeing

Business can be attracted in two ways: by offering discounts or through establishing good working relationships with the agents who distribute services. For sightseeing, this is mainly hotels. Guests often ask their hotel concierge for advice, and in addition to providing supplies of the excursion brochure for display in the hotel, Frames Rickards also builds a working relationship by providing free hotel pick-up services for clients on its tours and sightseeing trips. Its ability to do so is enhanced by its ownership of a passenger terminal in a convenient central location.

It operates a fleet of feeder coaches calling at larger hotels, as well as using taxis to collect individual clients. Everyone joining a day trip is brought to the terminal where all the sightseeing coaches are scheduled to leave at around the same time, 08.45, with the tours leaving somewhat earlier. Thus the pick-up from each hotel connects with all departures. This has proved an efficient way of getting up to 11 tours under way promptly, although the departures are sometimes delayed by London's congested traffic conditions.

Drivers and guides

Sightseeing tours are staffed with a driver and a qualified London guide. In addition to English, most are offered in five different languages (German, French, Spanish, Portuguese and Japanese) on selected days of the week during summer. Clients on day tours expect a concentrated commentary, but their preference during extended tours is for periods of quiet, and a brief introduction to the sites and attractions along their itinerary but with detail provided by local guides in important cities such as Chester or Edinburgh and on visits to historic castles and palaces. It is the quality of personal relationships, both with other clients and with the courier driver which are important during a tour of several days' duration. The mixing on each tour of clients from many countries adds an additional dimension of interest.

The courier drivers are often praised by clients, some of whose comments are quoted in the tour brochure. Furthermore, many of the agents who have experienced Frames Rickards tours remember their driver courier as a distinguishing feature.

Coaches

Frames Rickards operated a fleet of 16 Volvo and Scania coaches in 1995, including capacities of 29 or 53 seats. All are air conditioned, with double glazed, tinted windows and sun blinds. Air suspension and individual reclining seats provide passengers with high standards of ride comfort, and the coaches are fitted with speed limiters and a retarding system for extra safety.

Interruptions to the schedule

The traffic conditions, particularly in London, cause some operational difficulties. The morning transfers are sometimes delayed waiting for courtesy coaches and taxis to arrive in time for the scheduled 08.45 departures. Some day tours feature lunch during a cruise on the River Thames, either in London or in the country near Windsor, but if the water is too high, the vessel sometimes cannot sail because of reduced clearance under bridges and lunch has to be served while it is moored followed by a coach trip.

When they occur, these difficulties are sometimes the subject of clients' complaints, and big state events, such as the arrival of a foreign head of state or the opening of Parliament and the consequent Royal processions, can dislocate central London, but most clients find this interesting in itself.

Regulation and representation

There are a number of industry committees which represent the interests of Britain's coach operators, dealing with issues such as parking for coaches in central London, or legislation on seat belts and speed or motorway lane restrictions. A technical problem is the security of anchorage for seat belts on coaches, and as it is not involved in the schools contract market (unlike most of its competitors) Frames Rickards has decided not to fit seat belts until the manufacturers have developed a secure anchoring system.

Another regulatory constraint placed on coach operators is a speed governor limited to 65 mph. Frames Rickards was concerned about the potential impact of this on the schedules for its longer tours, and a year before its introduction it fitted one coach with the system to determine if its future programmes would have to be modified. Experience proved that this would not be necessary.

Another concern, which had not been resolved at the time of writing, is the probability that coaches will be restricted to the inner two lanes of multi-lane motorways. The problem with this is that a coach could become sandwiched between two heavy lorries, and most operators feel that passengers' safety is enhanced if drivers have the right to use all lanes of the motorway at their discretion.

Consumer protection legislation embodied in the Package Holiday Regulations also affects the sightseeing and coach tours sector. In particular, Frames Rickards had to modify their brochures to meet the requirements for detailed explanations of the terms of their contract, although the initial three pages of text required (in a 26-page brochure) were reduced to one page. The Chairman commented that none of his customers had asked about these terms, although some had expressed concern earlier when a brochure stated that the terms were 'subject to change'. The company also had to open a trust account to hold clients' money until a tour was completed, in accordance with the requirements of the new legislation.

Management philosophy

Experience and reliability are at the core of Frames Rickards' management values. The company's third brochure, for its coach charter business, features a photograph of Queen Victoria's carriage, as well as one of a modern fleet coach, to emphasize its long tradition of high-quality coach operation. Frames Rickards is never the cheapest operator; instead the philosophy is to set a fair price and offer clients good value.

Frames Rickards sees its reputation as a strength, the tangible element being its long experience as a high-quality operator. Another aspect of this is the long family tradition: the present chairman's grandfather originally promoted the company in America, and the distribution of annual brochures reminds agents of the length of their relationships.

The company encourages agents to join its tours on their visits to London, and regards this as an important factor in gaining their confidence to recommend Frames Rickards tours.

Frames Rickards takes care to listen to its customers, although it does not undertake formal market research. Most comments are positive, and in particular clients appreciate the skills and personalities of the drivers. Its drivers are permanent staff in contrast to the contract staff hired by most competitors.

Sometimes, as happened in the early 1990s, a long-established tour such as the three-day Devon and Cornwall programme drops out of favour for indeterminate reasons, although it attracted a viable number of passengers the following year. Equally, new tours are introduced from time to time, and while some have proved popular, it has not been possible to predict their success: each is a business risk based on the managers' experience, but the acid test is clients' response.

Based on interviews with Brian Coupland, Chairman, Frames Rickards.

TOUR OPERATORS' RELIANCE ON OTHER ORGANIZATIONS

Tour operators can be visualized as being at the centre of a web of business relationships, depending on travel agencies to sell the holidays which they have created by bringing together the facilities of a variety of service providers, notably the airlines and hotels. A crucial role for tour operators is therefore to arrange contracts for quite large numbers of seats and beds (usually on a recurrent basis), an activity referred to in the theoretical literature as organizational buying. The characteristics of organizational buying behaviour differ in important ways from that of final consumers. Organizational buyers are more expert than private purchasers and take a significant proportion of the supplier's capacity, generally on a continuing basis. Organizational purchasing is often undertaken by teams consisting of several people from both the supplier and purchasing organization; this means that their role relationships and the structures of their respective organizations become factors in the final decisions taken. For example, a particular negotiator may feel that a promotion depends on his or her ability to arrange terms which are favourable to the employer, whereas another may be required to refer all details to head office for approval. As Case study 1.2 on the Holiday Club of Upminster indicated, many tour operators' managers have long-standing relations with individual hotel proprietors, and may therefore be reluctant to force rates as low as the larger companies, thus reducing the competitiveness of their own pricing.

Negotiating for, say, two hundred aircraft seats and an equivalent number of hotel beds for each week throughout the season represents a different order of buying power and complexity than the situation confronting an individual buying several tickets to take his family on their annual holiday. The organizational buying process embodies elements of role and boundary crossing behaviour for the individuals who conduct the negotiation on behalf of their organizations, while the relative strength and the differing priorities of the two companies are other contexts to the dynamic relationship between them. Furthermore, the outcome of organizational buying negotiations has lasting significance: many companies prefer to conduct business negotiations with companies they have previously dealt with, since long-term relationships provide a firmer basis for the day-to-day conduct of detailed negotiations which may be required as the season progresses. In another sense, although one of the business partners may be dominant in respect of a particular agreement, the relationship between them is one of mutual dependency. For example, any hotelier is generally the less powerful negotiator (since the tour operator can open talks with alternative hotels or even switch to a different resort or country) if the terms it requires cannot be agreed. However, the tour operator is dependant on the skills of the hotelier to ensure that the experiences of the clients staying there are pleasing. When this is the case, the hotel is highly likely to be featured in the next season's brochure, but if they are dissatisfied, the tour operator (and the travel retailer from whom the clients bought their holiday) will have to have to expend time and effort investigating their complaints, and may have to offer compensation. In extreme cases, the tour operator will also be faced with the need to devote time to finding a substitute hotel, conducting negotiations with it and monitoring the standard of service it provides.

Trading with organizational clients therefore entails an understanding of the factors within each buying and selling organization that determine its decisions so that effective strategies can be developed. The organizational buying process also involves detailed considerations by teams of managers of the cost and payment terms, and after the negotiations formal approval by senior officers of both organizations is needed to seal the agreement. Since each partner has unique organizational characteristics which dictate the way it conducts business, but each is also an important supplier (or purchaser), different strategic approaches may have to be adopted for each organizational partner. Additionally, the buyer and seller are dependent on each other for services and flows of funds from the ultimate clients.

Just as the large tour operators have greater market power than the smaller specialists who require fewer beds, so the large hotels (particularly when part of a chain) have greater bargaining power compared to the independent, family-owned hotels. Table 6.6 summarizes these power relationships.

Table 6.6 Power relationships in contracting hotel bed space

| | Type of hotel | |
Type of tour operator	Member of major chain	Independent
Mass market	Favours tour operator	Favours tour operator
Small, specialist	Favours hotel	Balanced

FURTHER DESTINATION PERSPECTIVES ON TOUR OPERATING

The orientation and responsibilities of tour operators have been contrasted with those of national tourist offices (NTOs). The NTO's role is to promote the country for which it is responsible, whereas 'a tour operator's allegiance to any destination is tenuous' (Ashworth and Goodall, 1990). Nevertheless, inclusive holidays represent solutions to complex sets of problems for both their clients and the destinations. While the familiar tour operators' brochures make it easy for clients to book all the components of a holiday in a remote place, destinations also obtain two key advantages from hosting packaged holidays:

- tour operators bring a regular flow of visitors to destinations;
- they overcome the difficulty destinations face of reaching out into the varied and diffuse markets from which their clients come.

CASE STUDY 6.3

Making the market for Dubai as a destination

In the early 1990s, the government of Dubai commissioned a study into its position and potential as a European winter sun destination. The winter sun market is one of the main segments of European tour operators' business, attracting nearly 5 million clients. Almost all European holidaymakers to Dubai purchase inclusive tours, Kuoni being the leading operator to Dubai from Europe. The report included a competitive analysis of the 1992/93 Kuoni brochure. This offered a total of 68 000 rooms, 75% of which were costed within 10% of Dubai's price range. Table 6.7 presents an analysis of the spatial distribution of Kuoni's winter product.

In 1992, 15 000 Western European tourists visited Dubai during the winter, mainly on tour operators' packages. On the basis of its

Table 6.7 Geographical distribution of
Kuoni's rooms (winter 1992/93)

29 820 in Far East
10 766 in Caribbean
 2 900 in Kenya Coast
 4 969 in Egypt
16 000 elsewhere
 1 020 in Dubai

Source: DCTPB (1993).

cost, distance and range of attractions, the Dubai Commerce and Tourism Promotion Board (DCTPB) estimated that almost one million Europeans could be considered potential visitors to Dubai. The Deputy Chief Executive of DCTPB remarked that 'our promotional efforts aimed at those one million will be more effective than if we try to reach all 233 million Europeans!'

Ian Raitt, Director of the London office, explained how this was achieved.

We disseminate Dubai's messages to key audiences in several ways. Dubai does not undertake consumer advertising. Instead we provide facilities for influential journalists to visit the state . . . from titles as diverse as *Horse and Hound, Meeting and Incentive Travel, Business Traveller* and the BBC *Top Gear* and *Travel Show* programmes.

Another strand to our service is a monthly *Dubai Update*. This is a compilation of articles culled from media sources in the Gulf. The demand for this has built up from about twenty to nearly 2000. One reason for its success is that we get it to our readers just before the beginning of each month, so it is very up to date. It features short articles of general interest and others of concern to investors, politicians, the business community, journalists and travel retailers and tour operators.

A key factor in the development of the UK holiday market to Dubai is the excellent air connections between them. In January 1994, seven airlines provided direct flights, including a double daily service from Heathrow by Emirates and a daily British Airways flight. Several consolidators provided fares ranging from £375 return, and lower fares were available on connecting services through European or Middle Eastern centres.

We arrange presentations for travel professionals to inform them of Dubai's facilities and attractions. Often, these are staged jointly with one of the airlines which feature Dubai as a destination. We also organize Dubai's representation at major events such as the World Travel Market (WTM). In 1992, Dubai was awarded the prize for the best stand. The 1993 show featured 5500 organizations from 137 countries, and Dubai was represented by the DCTPB, Department of Civil Aviation, Dubai Duty Free, Emirates, three golf clubs, three tour operators and 13 leading hotels. Dubai's stand was again highly visible in trade and consumer media coverage. During WTM, Dubai was featured in ten trade journals, and the editorial coverage we obtained in these alone would have cost about £24 000 if we had bought the space. This is significant because our strategy is to create travel industry awareness.

As well as informing travel retailers about Dubai, we encourage tour operators to develop packages to Dubai. We highlight the success of Dubai as a destination, emphasizing that its unique combination of features has resulted in good business for all operators who feature it. We can help them by setting up links with Arabian Adventures or other GHAs (ground handling agents).

In 1990, only Kuoni, Jasmin and Swan Hellenic had tours from the UK to Dubai. By January 1994 19 tour operators featured Dubai as a single destination, a stopover or in multiple destination combination tours. Prices ranged from £369 for a three-night package up to £2700 for a special interest 15-day tour of the Emirates. A typical price for a seven-night beach hotel package was about £700.

Since then, Dubai has twice been rated the world's number one tourist destination in an annual survey (1994 and 1995) of 12 000 industry professionals conducted by Lawson International.

Based on Laws (1995) which presents a much wider analysis of the role of tourism in Dubai's development.

PRICING INCLUSIVE HOLIDAYS

The purchase of a holiday represents a deliberate decision in which the individual (or a group such as a family) invests part of their limited resources. The price paid for a holiday is constrained by the customer's budgetary considerations, but is often treated as a priority in planning personal or family expenditure. This implies both that the tourist has chosen not to spend money or time on alternative products, and that he or she cannot visit alternative destinations during that vacation. However, the exception is that some holidays such as cruising, multi-stop itineraries and coach tours are designed to include a selection of destinations in one holiday.

The pricing policies adopted by the inclusive holiday industry have been subjected to increasingly critical comment, although for different reasons, by consumer interest groups, experienced managers and by academic commentators. A number of apparently conflicting factors are involved in understanding the issues. The starting point for this section is an examination of how holiday prices are calculated. Beyond that, it considers the effects of a competitive pricing strategy for the industry.

The price at which a service is offered has two functions for the consumer, and of course it is critical to the service provider. Firstly, price acts as a primary signal of quality and accessibility for consumers. When compared with similar purchases, their relative prices act as an indicator of what to expect from each, the more expensive service being presumed to offer more or specialized benefits. Secondly, the price set for any good or service is a filter – too high a price excludes the service from consideration by many people.

Any company's main source of income for profits and to cover costs of production is revenue from sales. Since revenue is a function of both price charged and the volume of sales achieved, management has a set of related decisions to take. Economic theory indicates the strong likelihood that sales volume will decrease as price is raised. The rate of change in volume purchased as prices are raised (or lowered) is known as the price elasticity of demand. Elastic demand is indicated by a shallow slope to the demand curve, and highly elastic demand means that there will be a significant change in the number of clients for a given adjustment in price. In addition to an understanding of consumers' reactions to price changes, managers also need a detailed knowledge of the changing costs as they adjust the volume of service which the organization offers.

Calculating the price of an inclusive holiday

Until 1971, government regulations set a floor price to inclusive holidays: they could not be sold for less than the standard airfare plus a nominal supplement. The relaxation of that rule stimulated a major increase in package holidaytaking, clearly signalling the price sensitivity of the product. This was reinforced by another expansion of the market by some 20% during the mid to late 1980s, thought to be largely a direct result of the price wars between major tour operators at that time. Bywater (1992), has pointed out that the ceiling price for inclusive holidays is limited by the cost to a client of buying the components separately, although most mass market holidays are sold for rather less than this notional maximum price. Underlying the price charged to purchasers is the costs to the tour operator of buying the constituent elements of the inclusive holiday, the marketing, promotional and distribution efforts, and the administration needed to organize these activities. Table 6.8 indicates the main elements which have to be calculated in costing an inclusive holiday. Some of these have to be paid in the local currency of the destination, adding an element of uncertainty to the calculation of the price to charge since currency rates are subject to many influences. Tour operators can buy protection against this risk by purchasing currency ahead of having to make payments, but although they gain by being sure of the sterling cost of the

Table 6.8 Cost elements in pricing an inclusive holiday

- Research to establish programme
- Brochure production and distribution
- Marketing
- Agency training
- CRS and telecommunications
- Commission to retailers
- Air transport
- Hotel transfers
- Hotel accommodation and meals
- Resort representation
- Administrative overheads
- Banking and currency conversion
- Contingency
- Profit margin

overseas elements, they may also lose any advantage from a strengthening of the exchange value of sterling.

Pricing and the supply characteristics of tourism sectors

Another consideration results from the characteristics of the two main sectors supplying elements to the inclusive holiday system: both transport and the accommodation sector are fixed-capital fixed-capacity enterprises. A vehicle can carry only the number of passengers for which it has seats, typically 200 or so for a charter aircraft. Similarly, hotels have a given number of rooms, with rather more bed spaces. Of course, an aircraft can operate with some of its seats empty, although the fewer its revenue passengers, the higher must be its ticket prices to cover direct operating costs and to ensure that each journey makes a reasonable contribution to the operation's overheads and investment. The significance of this for the holiday industry is the need to ensure that clients are recruited in economic group sizes and on a regular basis.

When demand is insufficient to take up all the holidays offered on the market, tour operators are confronted with two alternatives: price discounting to fill spare capacity, or flight cancellation and consolidation to ensure economically viable group sizes for the remaining flights and the 'release' of contracted rooms. Both measures may attract financial penalties. In contrast, tour operators seldom own the facilities which their clients use during the holiday, and are therefore able to buy extra space in the more popular destinations without the risk of long-term investment.

Variances from standard price may reflect the relative power of market intermediaries such as group organizers who generate significant volumes of repeat business on a regular basis, or it may be a response to seasonal (or weekly) patterns of demand. At periods of known low demand discounted business can still bring in sufficient revenue to make a contribution to the company's running expenses over the costs of providing the service. At the other end of the price spectrum, premium rates can be charged when demand outstrips supply, hence the high cost for peak season holiday departures.

Another supply characteristic of tourism is the inability to store services. Once a plane door has been closed, a seat on that flight can never be sold again, and so there is a temptation to accept any reasonable fare for extra passengers after the costs of the flight operation have been met. A low fare sold at the last moment before departure would be reasonable in this sense if it were set high enough to recover the actual costs involved in ticketing, the relatively small additional fuel costs incurred by the extra weight carried, and the baggage handling and catering expenses. In addition, a contribution to the company's cash position would be sought. Price reductions are an attractive revenue-enhancing tactic, as it is impossible to store tourism services for sale at a later date in the way in which goods can be kept in inventory. Reducing the price of travel just ahead of departure encourages passengers who would not otherwise have travelled. However, against this, it seems that people have learned the rules of late booking and have changed their buying behaviour to take advantage of reduced price late offers.

The objective of pricing tactics is to match demand to supply, generating revenue to cover costs and to ensure profit over a time period. Other objectives of pricing decisions include the nurturing of new routes, expansion and so on. This suggests that a large tour operator may apply different pricing principles across its portfolio of holidays at any one time.

Holiday industry pricing policies

Companies tend to hold one of two mutually exclusive views of their position in the industry: some large companies set out to dominate it by gaining and holding market share, even at the expense of short-term profits, while other, usually small companies feel that they have established a scale of operation which suits their philosophy and ambitions. These companies often become the target of hostile takeover bids by the larger organizations. Other, smaller companies, lacking the capital resources to upgrade their reservations systems or for other reasons such as the impending retirement of a founding partner, may approach larger companies seeking a buyout.

The share of a market between existing firms will be changed as a consequence of successful marketing campaigns initiated by one of them. Successful companies attract customers from their competitors, and so will gain a larger share of the market. The increased business may be a larger proportion of customers newly attracted to the market, or there may be no overall increase in demand, just people switching away from other firms. This increasing concentration in the industry will probably tend to speed up as the successful firm benefits from economies of scale, and as managers continue to gain in experience. However, their profitability is being undermined by price-based competition: the CAA recorded a fall for the top 30 ATOL holders from 5.1% net profit (and £1120 million revenue) in 1981, to 1.7% net profit in 1986 when their combined turnover was £2132 million.

Companies can adopt a variety of approaches to pricing, but any policy should be evaluated in the context of its overall aims, as McCarthy and Perreault (1988) have pointed out: 'Managers develop a set of pricing objectives and policies in the context of the company's objectives. The policy explains how flexible prices are to be, the level at which they will be set over the lifecycle of the service, and to whom and when discounts will be allowed.'

The complexity of pricing decisions for a tour operator has been highlighted by Holloway and Robinson (1995). Robinson, the Group Marketing Manager of First Choice, one of Britain's leading tour operators (this company is also the subject of Case study 4.2), and his co-author noted that the company 'produced some 2,300 brochure pages for the summer 1995 season. Most featured a price panel with perhaps 100 separate prices, making a total of almost a quarter of a million prices.' First Choice's pricing is based on a straightforward cost-plus approach, but also reflects specific objectives such as to regain market share in specific resorts or to achieve an overall price advantage. They conclude that '. . . the brochure price is determined, but so too is the proposed policy on early booking discounts, child discounts, late sales reductions, travel agent commission incentives and the like. This is because the overall profitability target of the programme must be set against the actual sales price likely to be achieved' (Holloway and Robinson, 1995).

Price setting for yield management is therefore based on setting various price thresholds, reflecting assumptions about price-related differences in buying behaviour, particularly in respect of seasonal and departure airport preferences and responses to late or early booking reductions. This can be assessed from analysis of the company's (or industry's) historic data (Relihan, 1989). More serious adjustments to the level of a company's business are achieved by varying contracted capacities. The terms of most holiday industry contracts enable tour operators to release seats or bed spaces at agreed intervals before departure if holidays have not been sold, although they usually incur a financial penalty. This facility is generally used to 'fine tune' programmes, and adjustments are based on a comparison of current sales levels for each holiday departure with those achieved historically. During the mid 1990s it was being used to dump quite large numbers of holidays of most types: the *TTG* reported (13 December 1995) that Airtours had reduced its summer 1996 capacity from 2.2 million to 1.85 million in the face of predictions that the UK inclusive holiday market would fall by between 1.25 million and 2.5 million.

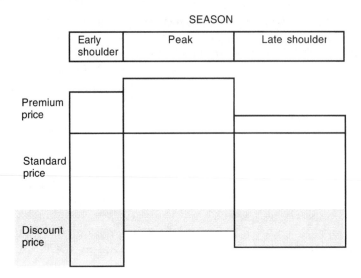

Figure 6.5 Seasonal price banding for inclusive holidays.

Seasonal pricing

One of the most common ways of setting holiday price differentials is the seasonal banding, typical of tour operators' brochures and familiar to all who purchase inclusive holidays, in the form of price and departure date matrices. This is represented schematically in Figure 6.5. The peak season, when little discounting is offered and many holidaymakers are willing to pay premium prices, is shown as a broad vertical column, flanked by two shoulders of unequal width representing the early and late seasons. The more restricted nature of demand during the shoulder seasons limits opportunities to charge premium prices, but offers scope to stimulate market demand through a variety of discounting practices.

Departure supplements

One of the crucial factors for the success of an area as a destination is the ease of access to it from origin points, particular by direct flights. Charter airlines incur a range of costs when positioning their aircraft away from the main base for these flights, and it might be expected that this will be reflected in the supplements charged by tour operators for regional departures. Other technical considerations, such as the use of smaller aircraft, are also factors (Laws, 1996). However, as Table 6.9 indicates, price differentials for regional departures represent another opportunity for price engineering rather than directly reflecting any extra costs incurred. Table 6.9 also shows that the regional pricing structure further distorts the basic holiday price by the differential application of seasonal price banding to each departure airport.

Table 6.9 Supplements to fly to Majorca by season and UK airport of departure

Departure airport	Low season supplement	High season supplement
London Gatwick	0	£41
Luton	0	£41
Edinburgh	£9	£114
Glasgow	0	£118
Aberdeen	£3	£89

Source: Trend (1994).

Late booking

Price reductions for late booking are a widespread holiday industry response to its unsold capacity and are typically offered shortly before departure. This has proved an effective way to tackle one of the problems characteristic of the services sector, the inability to store inventory (Cowell, 1986). Tour operators consider it better to obtain some revenue for a particular holiday (which can be defined by departure date and airport, duration and resort of stay) which they have not been able to sell at the price offered in the brochure. One common approach is to invite clients to pay a stated price, for example £100 per week, for a known departure and duration, but leaving the hotel and even the resort to the tour operator's discretion. From the customer's perspective, this introduces a higher than normal element of uncertainty (or risk) into the holiday purchase transaction.

Another response to weak sales is to relaunch a holiday programme in the form of a revised edition of the brochure. This enables the tour operator to consolidate flights, to delist hotels (and even resorts which are not selling well), to include other, cheaper hotels in popular resorts and to reprice their entire programme. Conversely, when business is bouyant, some companies relaunch with increased capacity and higher prices. Noakes (1995) reported that Unijet had launched the second edition of its summer 1996 brochure and interviewed a senior manager who was optimistic about the coming season:

> Unijet today releases second-edition summer brochures with an average price increase of £10 a head ... 'Our early business was very good ... if it continues well, we may add extra capacity ... To keep the momentum is going to be incredibly difficult – customers are becoming so cynical, especially about differential discounting ... We would be naive to expect a pre Christmas rush ... Sales were 15 to 20% ahead of last year.' Noakes reported that the company declind to disclose figures.

Each of the three price boundary approaches discussed above has contributed to the expansion of the market base of clients for inclusive holidays by the combination of low prices and the high visibility of travel agency windows featuring price discounted holidays. However, the benefits for tour operators of increased numbers of clients through the late booking discount mechanism has to be set against difficulties which have resulted. These include customers who did not obtain the quality of holiday which they had hoped for, an apparent shift away from the traditional early booking of holidays in favour of waiting for these late offers to be made, and approaches to managing both the supply and distribution channels which have tended to favour the major tour operators and the vertically integrated holiday companies strongly.

It was suggested earlier that price-led marketing has expanded the overall demand for holidays and it is often asserted that this has brought 'less desirable' clients into the market. The meaning of this is generally left unspecified, but two features are apparent. Less desirable clients include low spenders, such as youths, the elderly or people with low incomes. Although their presence imposes demands on the resort's infrastructure, tour operators and the resort-based businesses cannot sell low-spending clients the lucrative extras such as souvenirs, excursions and entertainment in the quantities which better-off clients regard as essential elements of their augmented holiday. The second suspicion is that many people buying the cheapest holiday packages are more likely to indulge in undesirable behaviour on arrival, including heavy drinking and noisy late-night carousing. The concern often has another dimension as it reflects an unproved general assumption that there is a direct link between detrimental client behaviour in a resort and low-priced access to it through the medium of cheap inclusive holidays.

Some destination managers have indicated that they do not wish to host such groups, and are actively trying to attract clients who will spend more and are assumed to be more sensitive to the destination's culture while less likely to offend local people (or other visitors) by their behaviour. A newspaper report entitled Tourists? We only want the cream on Jersey, thank you' illustrates these concerns. Following an attempt to open the Channel Islands to package tourists, hoteliers refused to reduce their room rates to the level which the tour operator had offered, between £13 and £23 a day, and the island airport declined to offer a 25% reduction on landing charges. Explaining the resistance, an executive of the Jersey Hotel and Guest House Association said: 'Airtours wanted to offer holidays so cheap that you have to wonder whether the people they brought over here would have any money to spend when they arrived . . . we don't want to downgrade the island as a cut-price destination' (Leith, 1995). Supplier resistance such as this is becoming more common, and overall it implies a limit to the ability of tour operators to price their holidays very cheaply. Some relatively new destinations, such as Dubai, take the view that setting high prices will minimize any social disruption through the undesirable behaviour of visitors (Laws, 1995), while some traditional mass market destina-tions, as Case study 2.1 on Majorca indicates, have adopted a policy of moving upmarket.

TOUR OPERATORS' COMMERCIAL OBJECTIVES

The divergent approaches of the mass market and specialist tour operators can be accounted for, at least in part, by their forms of organization and ownership. Tour operators are commercial organizations, and like all enterprises they have a variety of performance targets to meet. Their proprietors expect returns from their investment in the business which are broadly comparable to the profits available from placing similar amounts of capital in other business ventures. Although most began on a small scale, many entrepreneurs had growth as an objective, but face increasing calls for changes in the structure and organization of the business. This often results in a reduction in the direct involvement of the original entrepreneurial team which had established the company, and creates a need for management specialists, some of whom may be recruited from outside the tourism sector. Additional staff have to be recruited, trained and rewarded. Formal marketing and product management programmes have to be developed and financed, often using funds raised from external sources and bringing the need to service debt. As the business grows, control systems have to be established to enable managers to monitor results and more stakeholders now have an interest in the detailed management of the organization. At the same time, as the initial market becomes more fully developed, new client groups have to be identified and served, suggesting the likelihood of a further shift away from the original business base or philosophy.

An alternative objective which many small organizations pursue is to maintain a given level of business which their current level of resources and staffing can service effectively, forsaking future growth as Case study 6.1 on Kestours shows. However, this goal is difficult to sustain in the face of changing technologies, competition and consumer tastes. All of the companies operating similar types of service can experience development, consolidation or decline under the pressures of competition from new services, the introduction of new technologies or changes in legislation, political and economic conditions and consumer preferences.

THE TOUR OPERATORS' CONTRIBUTION TO THE INCLUSIVE HOLIDAY VALUE CHAIN

Tour operating is a dynamic and exciting business, innovative and imaginative in its ability to create and sell new concepts of what holidays are, effective in its ability to move large numbers of people on a regular basis across great distances for recreational purposes, and significant in the effects which result for destination communities and environments. Table 6.10 summarizes the discussion in this chapter.

Throughout this book, the interdependency of the various companies contributing elements to the tourism system has been stressed.

Table 6.10 Tour operators' contribution to the tourism value chain

- Selecting and packaging holiday elements
- Promoting and distributing them
- Providing information about destinations
- Ensuring affordable access to them
- Setting and monitoring quality standards in resorts
- Organizing excursions and entertainments
- Managing relations with suppliers and distributors

Although there are many examples of good practice in the relationships between tour operators and resorts, travel retailers and customers, too often some of these wider factors are not taken into consideration in tour operators' planning. The focus of concern for managers is often on the internal efficiency of their operations, with gaining or protecting market share or in earning profits for the tour operators' proprietors.

In the next chapter, attention turns to the interdependence of tour operators and charter airlines.

FURTHER READING

Bywater, M. (1992) *The European Tour Operator Industry*, EIU Special Report 2141, London.

Hodgson, A. (ed.) (1987) *The Travel and Tourism Industries, Strategies for the Future*, Pergamon, Oxford.

Holloway, J.C. and Robinson, C. (1995) *Marketing For Tourism*, 3rd edn, Longman, Harlow.

Vellas, F. and Becherel, L. (1995) *International Tourism*, Macmillan, London.

Vellas and Becherel (1995) and Hodgson (1987) provide accounts of many aspects of international tourism management, while Holloway and Robinson (1995) and Bywater (1992) discuss in detail operational aspects of tourism with an emphasis on contemporary inclusive holidays and travel retailing.

SUGGESTED EXERCISES

1. Analyse the range of price differentials charged by selected tour operators for comparable holidays and explain your findings.
2. What are the main points which a tour operator might put to a hotelier when negotiating lower rates for the forthcoming season and how might the hotelier counter these?
3. Examine one tour operator's brochures for three consecutive years to establish the full range of holidays offered. Analyse the changes and account for them in terms of marketing and strategic theory.

Air charters in the inclusive holiday industry system

7

INTRODUCTION

Transport is one of the key components of tourism, and consequently an efficient transport system is fundamental to the success of the modern holiday industry. The history of modern tourism can be traced in an ever widening network of flights from an increasing number of local departure airports direct to airports in the resort area. In 1993, charter flights from Britain served 40 countries in Europe and 80 worldwide. Air transport ties together the other elements of any holiday, enabling tourists to have speedy, convenient, comfortable and affordable access from their homes to the range of destinations throughout the world offered by tour operators. No mass-market destination can attract sufficient visitors to sustain a fully developed tourism industry without this regular access, as case studies of Tonga and Western Samoa (Laws, 1995) have shown. Medlik (1993) has expressed the view that 'chartering has assumed a particular significance in connection with inclusive tours by air, which were responsible for the growth of international travel/tourism following World War 2.'

TRANSPORT SYSTEMS

Transport is a subject of study in its own right, with analytical approaches developed from various backgrounds including technology, economics, sociology, marketing and other managerial disciplines, and can be examined in the contexts of its roles in areas, cities, trade or tourism. Economists, contemplating the logical linkages between observed events, are given to speculate on the direction of their causation, which they express in general terms as 'Is A the result of B?' or 'Is the shape and form of B the outcome of the characteristics of A?' The underlying question of whether holiday transport has been the driving force in creating holiday travel or whether the increasing demand for exotic vacations has stimulated the holiday travel industry is discussed in other chapters of this book. The concern here is to explain the nature of charter airlines' business, and to consider its contribution to the holiday industry.

Transport systems are organized around the elements of terminals, ways and vehicles, all journeys requiring the coordination of varying combinations of each element to achieve a smooth transit from origin to destination for both passengers and their luggage. A typical package holiday, for example, entails the travel stages for the outward journey from home to resort illustrated in Figure 7.1. On their return home after an interval of days or weeks, the tourists repeat these stages, but in the reverse order. Figure 7.1 can also be understood as a flow chart illustrating the steps which passengers experience in their journey, and it distinguishes the contributions which a variety of organizations make to their overall experience of the journey.

The journey is a major element in any holiday, and transport is itself a subsystem within the overall inclusive holiday systems model (as Figure 2.2 in Chapter 2 indicated). Charter airlines are essential features of the holiday industry network, while the style of their service is a significant factor in the overall quality of tourists' holiday experiences. This perspective is useful in emphasizing the mutual dependency of these elements in the holiday system, and can be extended to include consideration of allied issues such as the development of airports near both resort areas and tourists' origins. A commonly held view is that charters form one part of the supply chain needed to create inclusive holidays and that their business is derived from the demand created (or nurtured) by tour operators. However, once they have invested in their fleets, the combined capacity of the charter airlines, particularly those owned by the vertically integrated holiday companies, drives the number of holidays offered by tour operators and is a major factor in determining the optimum volume of business which the industry sets as its business target.

AIR TRANSPORT AND THE DEVELOPMENT OF HOLIDAY DESTINATIONS

Access is recognized as one of the key determinants in any destination's success (Murphy, 1986). The impact of air transport on the long-distance holiday industry is so fundamental that it is difficult to appreciate. The first recorded powered and piloted flight took place in 1903, when the Wright brothers' plane, *The Kittyhawk*, flew a distance which was actually less than the internal cabin length of a modern Boeing 747!

The significance of flight for tourism and for tourist destinations was not at first recognized, even by those which soon came to depend on air services – a plaque in Honolulu Airport commemorating the first flight to take place in Hawaii notes that it attracted very little public attention. Given its isolated position (Hawaii is the archipelago most

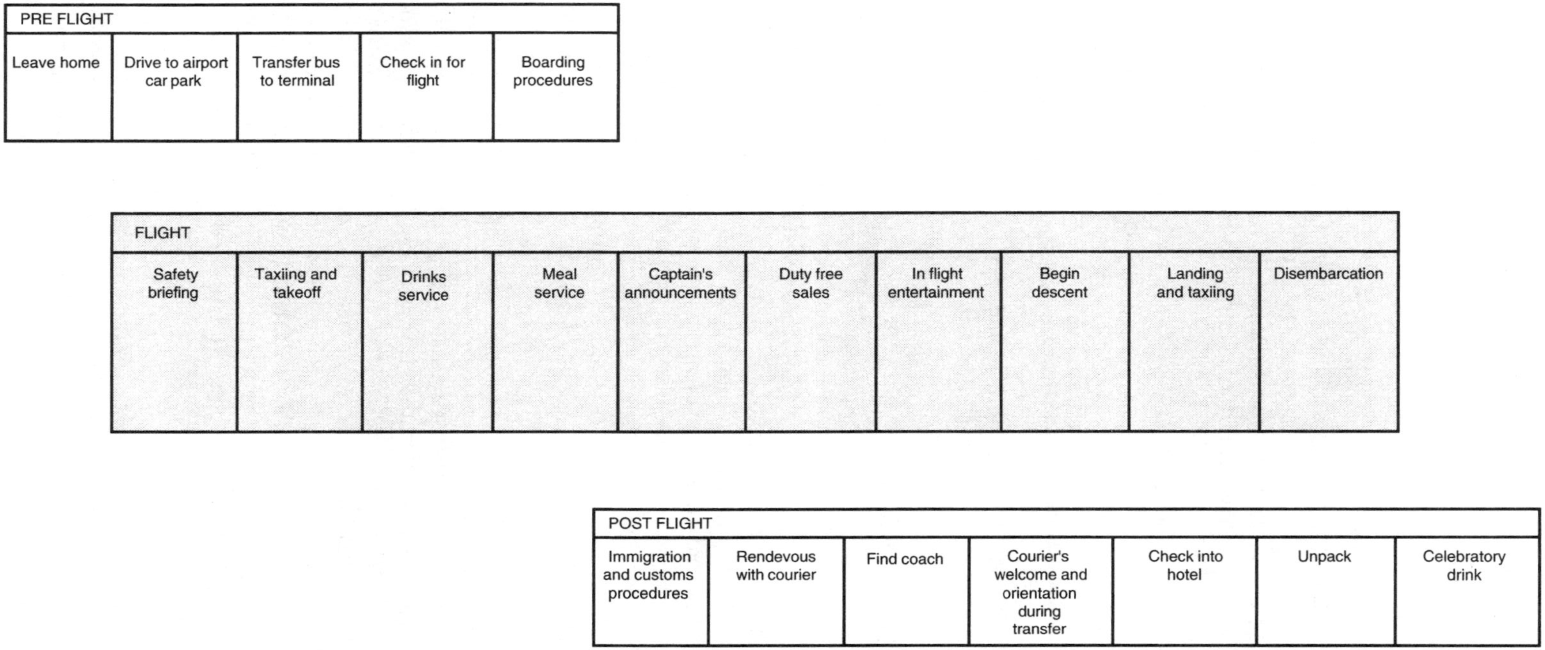

PRE FLIGHT

Leave home	Drive to airport car park	Transfer bus to terminal	Check in for flight	Boarding procedures

FLIGHT

Safety briefing	Taxiing and takeoff	Drinks service	Meal service	Captain's announcements	Duty free sales	In flight entertainment	Begin descent	Landing and taxiing	Disembarcation

POST FLIGHT

Immigration and customs procedures	Rendevous with courier	Find coach	Courier's welcome and orientation during transfer	Check into hotel	Unpack	Celebratory drink

Figure 7.1 Flow chart of stages in a holiday journey.

distant from a continental land mass) and its political, trading and social links to America, as well as the appeal of its climate and image, Hawaii rapidly became a major tourist destination once jet flights (the majority by scheduled carriers) made it more readily accessible and affordable to a wider market.

> The airlines were the single major force in Hawaii's tourism. They were the magic ingredient that converted the Hawaiian market from a limited market for the wealthy to a mass market of middle income and low income families ... A 1970 cost benefit analysis done by a Princeton University group found that for every ten percent reduction in airfares [at that time] there was a 13% increase in the number of visitors to Hawaii, a 9% increase in the [hotel occupancy] count, and a 3% rise in the average length of stay.
>
> (Stern, 1989)

He commented further: 'The precise relationship may have changed since 1970, but the extreme sensitivity of tourism to changes in the airline industry remains a constant fact of life.'

SCHEDULED AND CHARTER FLIGHT MARKETS

There are many similarities and some key differences between the two main forms of air travel available to passengers – scheduled and charter flights. From the airlines' points of view, the scheduled carrier's market is individual travellers, to whom they sell seats either through their appointed retail travel agency networks or direct. Increasingly, sales are made through electronic databases (CRSs, which major scheduled airlines increasingly see as important tools for the domination of their markets) and communications systems which people can access from their homes or from work. In contrast, the charter carriers' business is mainly concerned with selling blocks of seats or whole aircraft to tour operators for a season of regular journeys (or rotations). Another difference is that charters tend to operate from smaller regional airports, and furthermore they are more adept at deploying aircraft for seasonal demand, for example by relocating some of their fleet to a market such as Canada which has a strong winter business. These two factors result in their need for medium-sized aircraft rather than the variety of planes which a large scheduled carrier such as BA needs to cater for its range of routes. However, the scheduled airlines are increasingly entering the leisure market as their cost structures and their productivity approaches that of charter airlines.

Worldwide, charter traffic accounts for only about 10% of air passengers, but within the European Civil Aviation Conference area, almost half of all journeys by air are on charter flights, thus underlining their significance in the holiday industry and the scale of the industry within Europe. Table 7.1 provides a basis for contrasting the markets for charter and scheduled air services, emphasizing that holiday travel

Table 7.1 Distinctions between scheduled and charter passenger markets

Factor	Scheduled	Charter
Purpose of travel	Business, family, leisure	Leisure, VFR
Key advantage to passenger	Frequent, pre-booking not required	Low cost, sold as part of package, weekly
Key disadvantage	Expense	Pre-booking, limited departures
Who pays fare	Company, passenger	Passenger
Motivation for purchase	Need to travel	Desire to travel
Travel party	Individual or family	Couples, family, groups of friends
Season of travel	According to need	School holidays, summer, winter, weekends

is much more a discretionary purchase than business or family-related journeys, it is less frequent, most people travel with companions or family when taking their holidays, and the charters' business is more highly seasonal.

Although most air inclusive holidays are based on the various types of charter arrangement shown in Table 7.2, many tour operators take advantage of the greater range of routes and departure times available on scheduled flights. A further advantage of basing tours on scheduled flights is that small allocations of seats can be bought, and linked with this, it is not necessary to cancel departures when only a few passengers book. This is an important advantage for long-haul tour operators since their holidays tend to be higher priced and to represent to the client a greater degree of risk when booking because the destinations are relatively less well known to them. Secondly, charters are flown on the basis of payment regardless of whether all the seats are sold or not. Long-haul scheduled services tend to be on a use or return basis, which is critical when the seat cost is very high. Thirdly, with longer journey times, and at higher prices, people tend to want the highest affordable quality of service, and although standards are

Table 7.2 Types of charter flight arrangement

Type of charter	Key features
Whole character	A contract to hire the entire capacity of an aircraft
Part (or split) charter	A contract in which several tour operators share one flight individually contracted to the airline
Ad hoc charter	An arrangement for a single rotation
Series charter	A contract for a regular sequence of flights
Time charter	A contract for the exclusive use of an aircraft throughout a season

Based on Medlik (1993); Wheatcroft (1994).

improving significantly on charter flights, scheduled services are widely considered to offer superior standards. The key point is that only a few long-haul destinations can support the level of regular business needed for charter operations.

Long-haul charter flights only became feasible when licences were granted to the most modern twin-engined jets such as 767s to operate transoceanic routes. After this became possible, a study by the Australian Department of Trade and Commerce (cited in Frew, 1994) reported that most passengers on Britannia's flights there from the UK were very satisfied with their journeys, many having had previous experience as passengers on scheduled services to Australia.

THE ORIGIN OF CHARTER HOLIDAY FLIGHTS

During the last three decades of the twentieth century, the predominant form of international leisure tourism in Europe (other than transborder day trips for shopping) has been the inclusive holiday based on air charter flights. This concept had its origin in the conditions in Europe following the Second World War. During the war, many servicemen had fought or otherwise been engaged in foreign military campaigns in Europe or further afield, and many had developed an appetite to return in peaceful times. After the war, specialized equipment developed for the purposes of war, notably aircraft, became surplus to requirements and could be purchased relatively cheaply. In addition, the war had provided training and experience in logistical skills for pilots. As indicated in Chapter 1, the first air inclusive tour is widely thought to have been operated in 1950 by Vladimir Raitz when 17 people flew to Corsica in a war surplus Dakota and stayed in old army tents.

Shaw (1987) has pointed out that leisure travellers are sensitive to prices (an earlier chapter in this book discusses other issues related to holiday industry pricing practices). However, the steady reduction of the real cost of travel has been a significant factor in the development of the industry. Until the 1970s journeys by air were extremely costly because the smaller, slower aircraft then operated were dedicated to business routes and provided the highest possible standards of service and comfort. More importantly, most airlines were government owned and inefficient. Furthermore, their pricing and standards of service were set by the International Air Transport Association (IATA). IATA was initially formed in 1919 and recreated in 1945, its aims being to 'promote safe, regular and economic air transport for the benefit of the peoples of the world . . . and to provide means for collaboration among air transport enterprises . . .' This latter point resulted in IATA functioning as a cartel, and for these reasons airlines were exclusive, both in their ambience and their pricing, until the development of charter services.

As aircraft technology developed, planes became larger and faster. In combination these two factors resulted in a major increase in the number of passengers who could be accommodated, and this feature drove airfares down somewhat. With the introduction of jets, many major airlines sold their suddenly uncompetitive fleets of propeller and turbo-prop aircraft, thus opening a low-cost market of aircraft in good condition. This provided the opportunity for an expansion of charter operations causing the inclusive holiday market to develop radically. The early charters were typically operated with older-generation air-craft that had been purchased cheaply. The planes were reconfigured from the exclusive, low density passenger set-up favoured by scheduled airlines at that time to carry the maximum payload of passengers. However, charter airlines soon proliferated, and their marketplace become very competitive. They tended to regard passengers as sources of revenue, and service to them was kept to a minimum in order to win contracts from the airlines' clients, the tour operators. These too were generally engaged in a price-based approach to their business, in which the objective was to grow the size of the company rather than to prom-ote and enhance the quality of their service to the enjoyment of their clients, the holidaymakers.

The charter airlines' early achievement was significant in reducing the costs of air travel, and by doing so they broadened the market base for overseas holidays. But their emphasis on cost control, together with the rapid growth of the sector, limited the sustainability of this type of service. As holidaytaking overseas became a more established feature of many people's lifestyle, they became less tolerant of poor conditions (whether on the journey or at their hotel), opening opportunities for new strategies in charter airline management.

It has been suggested that this low quality type of service was the background to the success of Britannia in the 1980s: 'It began its plan-ning by asking the vitally important question of the type of airline it wished to be, and the markets in which it would participate.'

CHARTER FLIGHT QUALITY AND PASSENGER SATISFACTION

People setting out on vacation tend to adopt one of two polarized attitudes to the travel element of their package. For some, it is a bar-rier with potential problems to be overcome. These may include a fundamental fear of flying (which some airlines attempt to counter by offering short introductory flights, often accompanied by psychologists, and during which an experienced captain takes pains to explain the various sounds, sensations and events which occur on all flights). Other concerns are the possibility of delays, lost luggage, congested airports and the expense and risk of leaving the family car in a long-stay car park or the reliability of coach or rail connections needed to ensure they reach the airport on time.

In contrast, many tourists look forward to the journey itself, anticipating with pleasure the time they will spend both at airports and on board the flight. Modern airports offer the opportunity for shopping in an extensive range of stores familiar from the high street or in outlets selling exclusive and branded luxury items, while there is also the opportunity to observe some of the technical features of aircraft turnarounds or landing and takeoff. On board, many tourists want to know the technical details of their flight, its height and speed, the aircraft's takeoff weight or fuel load and the route they will follow. They wish to visit the flight deck, or at least for their children to be invited forward by the captain, and to have a souvenir photograph of the family on the aircraft steps with the plane's nose or its high tail silhouetted against a blue sky. Table 7.3 indicates the main factors affecting passenger satisfaction and identifies the organizations with most influence on each aspect.

The outbound journey is one of the key elements of the holiday, and as it is the first encountered any disappointing incidents (whether these occur at the terminal or during the flight) are likely to prejudice passengers against the rest of their holiday even before they arrive at their hotel. An unsatisfactory flight can therefore undermine the quality of the entire holiday system. A senior tourism manager, addressing a CIMTIG meeting in October 1995, castigated the charter industry for its obsession with product and technical issues. He argued that they had three customers: the in-house tour operator, third-party companies and their passengers. People discussed their good experiences with

Table 7.3 Factors affecting the quality of charter services

Factor	Examples	Organization with key influence
Aircraft type and specifications	Size, comfort, range	Aircraft manufacturer and airline
Cabin layout	Seat pitch and width, cabin stowage, toilets, galleys	Airline
Schedule	Departure and arrival airports and times	Airline
Punctuality		Air traffic control, airline, airports
In-flight service	Seat comfort, ratio of cabin staff to passengers, 'style' of service, in-flight catering and entertainment, on-board sales	Airline, caterer
Airport	Check-in, luggage handling, lounges	Airport, ground handler

several others, but a bad first flight turned people away from that carrier. He urged the airlines to concentrate more effort on a passenger focus, on giving value for money and on improving their core competencies.

A typical charter aircraft in the mid 1990s is configured for more than 200 passengers, and it is a certainty that on every revenue flight its passengers will board the plane with a wide range of feelings and expectations. There will also be clients of a variety of tour operators on most flights, together with others who have purchased seat-only flights, preferring to arrange their own accommodation at the destination. The significance of this variety in passengers' backgrounds, interests and expectations is increasingly recognized as presenting a managerial opportunity to distinguish one charter carrier from its competitors, and has led to the branding of charter operations associated with the development of distinctive on-board service features. However, to do so effectively, it is necessary to recognize the complexity of charter airline management and, as Table 7.3 indicates, the range of factors which affect their quality.

RELATIONSHIPS BETWEEN TOUR OPERATORS AND CHARTER AIRLINES

The Spanish Civil Aviation Authority defined charters as 'special remuneration flights . . . in which the entire capacity is engaged by a limited number of tour operators' (cited in Frew, 1994). The general requirements for the leisure market are 'a low cost, efficient product which appeals to tour operators, and, through them, to leisure passengers'. However, as clients, tour operators present three distinct types of demand for charter airlines (although each could be found on a single flight). The major tour operators are driven by the need to publish their brochures with full costings as early as possible, and to offer their clients the most convenient departure dates and schedules. Charter airlines can therefore charge them the highest rates, as schedule A in Figure 7.2 indicates. The next most important tranche of business (schedule B) comes from the medium-sized tour operators who contract their capacity according to actual market demand, while most specialist tour operators contract their requirements early on. There are also opportunistic companies which often put their programmes together taking advantage of the remaining seats and times after most airline capacity has been contracted (schedule C). This business provides the airline with marginal revenue. Thus, the tradeoff for tour operators is between the degree of certainty in their flight arrangements against the charter rate they are prepared to commit to.

One indication of the significance of the transport element for the other members of the holiday industry can be seen in the growth of ownership of charter airlines by major tour operators. Of the 117 aircraft in Britain's charter fleets in 1991, vertically integrated companies

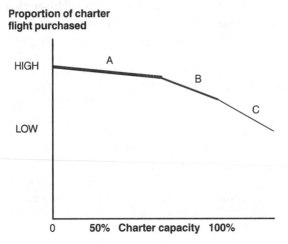

Proportion of charter flight purchased

A **Premium rate charterer**: priority in negotiating flight details, brochure details can be fixed long in advance of season.
B **Medium rate charterer**: spare capacity purchased on existing flight arrangements, details can be published in brochure, or low frequency *ad hoc* flights.
C **Marginal revenue charterer**: remaining capacity purchased shortly before departure, brochures produced just ahead of sale and departure.

Figure 7.2 A risks segmentation of the market for charter flights.

had 93 aircraft; by 1995, they operated 112 of the 140 charter aircraft. Similarly, in 1991, 74% of charter capacity was controlled by vertically integrated companies; by 1995 this had risen to 95%. This form of vertical integration gives synergy for both companies – the airline is virtually ensured a programme of flying, while the tour operator is confident that it can obtain the routes, schedules, frequencies and costings which it requires to fulfil its holiday programmes, and both thereby contribute to the group's revenue, growth and profit targets.

However, major tour operators are generally unwilling to use each others' charter carriers, mainly because of handling issues. The lack of trust and competition between major tour operators resulted in them all trying to grow the market. This had been facilitated in the 1980s by the increasing residual value of aircraft, but in the 1990s they were readily available for leasing. Speaking to a meeting of CIMTIG in October 1995, the Director of Airworld Aviation said that as a rule of thumb, an aircraft was added to the fleet for each £1 million of summer revenue. These new aircraft with high costs of ownership need high rates of utilization, further adding to capacity in the market, but their operating costs are low.

Vertical integration also provides the opportunity to invest in quality and branding with a guaranteed passenger base. The vertically integrated companies had improved product quality, but had beaten down prices and were faced with a seasonal market: they had to purchase passenger bases overseas. (See also Case study 7.3 on Air 2000 later in this chapter.)

CASE STUDY 7.1

The acquisition of Caledonian

Caledonian is a long-established airline brand, originally an independent scheduled carrier which British Airways acquired in 1988. The brand name was retained as the charter arm of the major airline until, in 1994, BA decided to concentrate on scheduled services. Caledonian had been profitable but BA foresaw that charter airline profitability would decrease as the vertically integrated holiday companies grew further. Inspirations paid BA £16.6 m, including £11.7 m of assumed debt, repayable on a monthly basis over five years. Inspirations had earned pre-tax profits for the 12 months to September 1994 of £4.5 million (up 77% on the previous year) and had been floated on the Unlisted Securities Market in December 1993.

At the time of the acquisition, Inspirations was Caledonian's largest customer with 40% of its flying capacity. The tour operators' flying requirements were forecast to rise from 1.2 million seats to 1.5 million in the following year, and even with Inspiration's three leased A320s due in April, Caledonian was expected to supply less than 50% of Inspirations' flying in 1995. Caledonian's fleet of five Tristars represented about half a million seats for the season, while the three Airbus A320s would contribute another 200 000. The airline employed 400 permanent staff, with another 200 flight crew seconded from BA and an additional 350 seasonal staff.

Although it was recognized that the acquisition had been a quick way to start a charter airline, industry analysts criticized the move because the type of aircraft was suitable only for high density routes (the Tristars were configured for 393 passengers). Another concern was the imbalance between the parent and the charter airline in their own markets. The smaller size of Inspirations relative to its tour operator competitors (1.5% market share) contrasted with Caledonian's 7% of the charter market.

Based on Kapur (1994) and McNee (1994).

AIRPORTS

An ever widening network of airports is associated with the expanding holiday business, while the airlines themselves are dependant on airports' technical efficiency. Many destination (and some origin) airports are heavily reliant on charter traffic. Airports can best be understood as complex combinations of industrial and customer service enterprises. 'They act as a forum in which disparate elements and activities are brought together to facilitate, for both passengers and freight, the interchange between air and surface transport ...' (Doganis, 1992).

Their essential features are one or more runways whose characteristics determine the type of aircraft which can be accepted, and the flight distances for departing aircraft. In addition, a wide variety of technical activities take place at airports; for example, the aircraft are cleaned, fuelled and flight checked, amongst many other services required to turn them around. Airports can also be described in terms of the terminals where arriving and departing passengers (and their luggage) are processed, and services are provided for their enjoyment while they await flights. These activities form sources of revenue for the airport authorities, and increasingly many of them are provided by other organizations. 'Commercial facilities are provided by concessionaires . . . duty-free shops, restaurants, car hire kiosks and possibly other facilities such as hotels . . .' (Doganis, 1992).

Airport productivity is measurable by aircraft handled and volumes of passengers embarked. 'Runways and taxiways are related to aircraft movements, while the size and nature of the terminal facilities are dependant on the number of passengers . . . handled' (Doganis, 1992). Airport charges vary according to type of aircraft, peak and offpeak usage and between different countries. Studies show that the impact of airport charges as a percentage of total operating costs range from United Airlines at 1.6% to Air UK at 19.8%, reflecting the higher airport charges which prevail in Europe and the longer sectors operated by United decreasing the effect of airport charges. For British charter airlines it ranges between 14.6% and 17.7%. Doganis points out that many airports are beginning to impose charges separately for each of the facilities used in the process of embarking passengers such as airbridges, buses or mobile lounges.

As air traffic has increased, airports have come under increasing operational pressure, but at the same time, the communities within which they are located have become more able to express their resistance to both runway expansion (either extensions for larger aircraft or the construction of additional runways) and to increases in the hours of operation: many now impose night-time curfews or complete bans. However, a traditional feature of charter operations is night-time flights. This represents a logical exploitation of the lower charges offered by regional airports for night-time flying in order to extend their revenue opportunities while reducing pressure on the day-time slots which scheduled operators are willing to pay a premium rate for. It also means that charter airlines can obtain much more intensive use of their fleets and explains the higher utilization compared to scheduled carriers. Both of the foregoing factors are significant contributors to the charter carriers' lower operating costs, and in turn are reflected in the ability of tour operators to charge low prices to holidaymakers when compared to the total cost of purchasing each element on an individual basis. However, a corollary is that charter destinations are often unable to resist pressures from charter airlines to accept night traffic, simply because the destinations need the business which tour operators bring them on charter flights. This problem will be further exacerbated when Europe-wide bans on what are termed Chapter 2 aircraft which will fail to meet the forthcoming noise abatement criteria are implemented early in the twenty-first century.

CHARTER OPERATIONS

Although an individual aircraft such as a Boeing 757 can cost about $US30 million, fleet investment is actually regarded as a relatively low-risk commercial investment because aircraft are mainly standard and can usually be sold on. Furthermore, most airlines lease aircraft rather than purchase them.

Airline efficiency is measured in a variety of ways. The theoretical maximum utilization of an aircraft type depends on its maintenance and turnround characteristics. Of the 8760 hours in a year, the most efficient long-haul airlines attain about 4500 to 5000 hours utilization. Short-haul scheduled fleets operate at around 2500 hours but some charter airlines attain more. Charter operators benefit from a high utilization of their aircraft and ground facilities by operating throughout the day and night.

The second key measure for scheduled airlines is passenger load factor – the proportion of seats sold. However, because charter flights are sold on a fully committed basis, the proportion of seats actually filled is not as relevant to the success of their operations. Neverthelesss, because their clients are actually tour operators, who buy blocks of seats and then try to fill them by offering a range of holiday products on each flight, charter airlines regularly have much higher load factors than scheduled carriers.

A third measure is the yield per passenger carried. Generally charter operators are not able to obtain the levels of revenue which scheduled carriers command. This is because the essence of charter flying is its low cost, and their flights are usually single class and therefore do not provide an opportunity for premium products and fares.

Leisure travellers' requirements can generally be forecast well in advance (although they are subject to a number of disruptions – Laws, 1995). They are also concentrated on specific holiday routes or those where there is also often a significant ethnic market for VFR. Peaks are expected at weekends for social and business reasons, followed by a trough in demand early in the week. Pricing is a relatively weak tactical tool to alter these demand characteristics which reflect structural factors.

Airline managers tend to seek commonality in their fleets. To keep one aircraft operational, an airline requires nine appropriately qualified people in each of six and a half sets of crew in order to comply with CAA regulations on their working hours and rest days. In the light of these costs, it is natural that managers seek the utmost flexibility in their rostering arrangements, and the ability of staff to operate all the aircraft in the fleet ensures ease of scheduling. Captains who command a salary of about £50 000 (1995 rates) can only be switched from one aircarft type to another if the two have the same cockpit layout, as is the case with the Boeing 757s and 767s. Cabin crew earning £10 000 to £15 000 pa may be rated for three aircraft types. Thus, charter airlines benefit from minimizing the variety of aircraft they operate by obtaining more flexibility in crew rostering. Further key advantages are gained by rationalizing spares holding and by efficiencies in maintenance scheduling.

Regulations concerning aircraft safety are detailed and strict, and are applied by the licensing authorities in each country equally to both scheduled and charter carriers. A range of checks are also required before each take off, the captain taking responsibility for the decision to operate the flight based on an instrument check, a visual inspection of flying surfaces and tyres and the technical ground crew's report. Aircraft receive a more detailed 'A' check every two days, a 'B' check after a specified number of hours depending on the type of aircraft and 'C' checks at regular intervals. The 'D' check, taking place at intervals between five and ten years, amounts to a virtual strip down of the airframe, its electronics, avionics and engines. Case study 7.3 later in this chapter shows how Air 2000 copes with the need to arrange for each aircraft in its fleet to be positioned at Luton for its technical servicing.

Although aircraft used to be purchased outright by the airlines, contemporary practice is to arrange operating or finance leases on equipment . Typically, a lease is for three years, after which the airline has the option to terminate the arrangement, thus allowing it to upgrade its fleet regularly to take advantage of the latest technologies in aircraft manufacturing and the benefits they confer in terms of reduced noise and pollutant emissions, increased range or load capabilities or improved economics of operation.

Although there is now an excess of aircraft making it possible to negotiate a short lease for the summer peak, it is harder to recruit pilots on six-month contracts. Furthermore, the temporary aircraft usually have to be reconfigured and painted to be integrated into the fleet. The alternative strategy, that preferred by Air 2000, is to find work for the aircraft not needed for winter flying from the UK. Generally this means leasing them, complete with crew, to Canada, South America or Australia, which all experience peak demand during the winter months.

COSTING CHARTER FLIGHTS FOR INCLUSIVE HOLIDAYS

As many airline operating costs are calculated in dollars and tour operators face paying for hotels and other destination services in a wide variety of currencies, ABTA has an agreed base date for tour operator costings, including currency exchange rates, and this forms the basis for charter pricing. Table 7.4 shows the prices charged for a

Table 7.4 Rotation prices for *ad hoc* chaters, 110-seat BAC 111, 1993

Charter route	Charter price
Birmingham/Lourdes/Birmingham	£10 800
Manchester/Lourdes/Manchester	£10 800
Manchester/Lourdes/Glasgow/Manchester	£13 800
Exeter/Lourdes/Exeter	£ 8 500
Stansted/Lourdes/Stansted	£ 9 100
Positioning costs	
Manchester/Glasgow	£ 2 500
Stansted/Exeter	£ 2 600
Stansted/Manchester	£ 2 800

Source: Aviation Solutions

variety of routes in 1993 by a charter airline operating 110-seat jets. Prices for a particular route vary according to the day of the week and the time of operation, but the challenge is to sell all the capacity in blocks to tour operators. It is then the tour operators' problem to fill their seat allocations.

The following basic analysis relates to a notional (but realistic) costing for the London-Malaga route in 1995. The direct operating costs for a 233-seat Boeing 757 are about £12 000 per rotation. On this basis, a Saturday day-time departure in the summer is priced at a seat rate of £105, a seat on a Friday departure is sold to a tour operator for £100, midweek is priced at £98 and a night flight at £85 per seat. Realistically, however, tour operators have to accept two empty legs per charter route – the first homebound flight and the final outbound flight of a season cannot normally be sold as part of the charter series. In a 26-week season, this equates to a reduction of 3.25% of capacity, which can also be expressed as an increase in the cost of saleable seats. Furthermore, most tour operators anticipate less than full compliments of paying passengers, and typically assume a load factor of about 90%. It is up to the tour operator, whether chartering the full aircraft or a block of seats, to include the costs of empty legs and reduced load factors in their calculations, giving a base price for seats to Malaga of about £115.00, with reductions for mid week and night flights.

THE CHARTER CONTRACT

The main features of a charter contract are summarized in Table 7.5. This shows that there are other charges in addition to those just discussed. Passenger taxes levied by the authorities are passed on to the tour operator, who includes them in the tourist's final invoice. In 1995, the peak charge at Gatwick was £12 and at Malaga £7. These taxes are charged to the airline for each passenger actually carried, but for invoicing airlines assume a 90% load factor, invoicing their tour operators before each departure and conducting a reconciliation on the basis

Table 7.5 Selected charter contract details

- The identities of the two parties including registered addresses and tour operator's ATOL number.
- The number of aircraft and its seating configuration
- What is included in the charter agreement, typically:
  - fuel
  - oil
  - water/methanol
  - landing fees
  - handling fees
  - navigation fees
  - international route charges
  - security charges
  - push back
  - deicing
  - catering (specified as, for example, coffee and biscuits)
  - duty-free bar operated for cash
  - aircraft cleaning.
- 'The Captain of the aircraft shall have complete discretion concerning the load carried and its distribution, as to whether or not flight should be undertaken, and as to where landings should be made.'
- The charter specifies preferred alternative airfields in the event of diversions due to weather conditions, and the agreement states who bears the associated costs.
- The charterer is responsible for ensuring that every passenger is fully covered by the tour operator's licence specified in the agreement.
- 'The charter will comply with, and cause all passengers and owners of freight carried to observe and comply with, all Customs, Police and Public Health and other Regulations which are applicable in the United Kingdom and in the other States in which landings are made.'
- The charter is not entitled to assign the agreement to any other person, not to subcontract any part of the services without the consent of the airline.
- The airline is entitled to substitute another aircraft without giving any reason.
- It can also substitute alternative carriers.
- In the event of an increase in costs beyond the airline's control, it can give the charter 14 days' notice and furnish documentary evidence.
- Disputes will be referred to an agreed arbitrator in London.
- 'This agreement shall be constructed according to and governed by the law of England and the parties hereby submit to the non-exclusive jurisdiction of the English courts.'
- The carrier must provide the airline with a passenger manifest for each flight 48 hours before departure.
- The charter will indemnify the airline for any costs in respect of the charter's passengers not being in possession of the correct documentation resulting in refusal of entry at either departure or arrival airport.
- In the case of weather delays the airline will not provide refreshments or hotel accommodation
- In the case of unserviceability or commercial delays, the airline will provide:

over 2 hours:	light refreshment
over 4:	meal
cancellation:	alternative aircraft or overnight accommodation.

Source: Aviation Solutions.

of passengers actually carried, adjustments to the prepayment being made either way on a monthly basis. Although there have been notable exceptions (such as the Gulf War crisis), surcharges are seldom more than a matter of pence per seat, so these too are made on a monthly basis.

REGULATING CHARTER FLIGHTS

For both charter and scheduled airlines, self-regulation is based on the negotiated allocation between them of runway and terminal times (slots). Slots are generally negotiated on a historical basis at the twice yearly slots conference organized by IATA so that, year to year, the business is built on the pattern of previous years' flying with modifications reflecting new business opportunities and the trends in the market. Most airports also operate a scheduling committee to optimize airline schedules, but this requires compromises. Night-time restrictions and curfews at destination airports also constrain schedules as there are limited windows of time within which an aircraft can set out from its origin in order to arrive while the destination is able to receive it. However, once an airport scheduling committee has allocated slots, these can be exchanged amongst airlines. 'At London's airports . . . it is estimated that up to 10% of slots change hands every year as a result of decisions of the scheduling committee and subsequent exchanges between airlines' (Doganis, 1992). Charter airlines' needs tend to get rather lower priority than scheduled services for the following reasons:
- airlines usually keep slots previously operated (historic slots);
- year round services have priority over seasonal ones;
- services operated on more days of the week have priority over those operated on fewer days.

Operationally, the critical problem is to obtain slots at departure and destination airports, and this is likely to become more severe against the background forecasts that air traffic worldwide is likely to grow at 6% per annum or more, resulting in growing pressures on runways and terminals. At the same time, airline operations have become increasingly deregulated. But as peak-time slots are used up, the system becomes increasingly anti-competitive. The alternative mode of regulation is through government controls on types of traffic; for example, time series charter flights were totally excluded from Heathrow until 1991.

A further set of problems results from the need to supervise aircraft during their flights. Air traffic control in certain areas comes under severe pressure from aircraft overflying en route between the industrial, cold northern countries from which most tourists originate and their sunbelt destinations. Air traffic controllers often claim that they work unsociable hours with outdated equipment and at very high levels of concentration and stress. If they express their anger by withdrawing from work, they rapidly disrupt a great many flights and ground many other aircraft until alternative routes can be organized.

Table 7.6 The roles of the CAA

- **Air safety**
  Airworthiness of aircraft; licensing flight crew, aircraft engineers, air traffic controllers and aerodromes; certifying UK airlines and aircraft; and maintaining air traffic control standards.
- **Economic regulation**
  Licensing of routes; approval of airfares for journeys outside the EU; regulation of certain airport charges; and licensing of air travel organizers.
- **Air traffic services**
  Air traffic control services; radio and navigational aids. Also:
  – advice to government on aviation issues;
  – represents consumer interests;
  – provides technical services to the industry.

In Britain, there were 114 135 000 passenger movements in 1993/94 (passengers are counted onto and off aircraft so the actually number of travellers was half the figure given above). The Civil Aviation Authority (CAA) is responsible for the safety and the economic regulation of British aviation: it also provides air traffic services in UK airspace and carried out 22 048 medical examinations of professional air crew and air traffic controllers in 1992 (24 crew were denied renewal of their medical certificates). Its main functions are summarized in Table 7.6. The CAA also regulates travel organizers whose tours are based on journeys by air, as Case study 7.2 indicates.

CASE STUDY 7.2

Air Travel Organizer's Licence

From the perspective of the holiday industry, the CAA's chief function is its role in issuing licences to sell holidays by air (ATOLs). 'The primary purpose of the ATOL system is to protect the public from financial loss arising out of the failure of a tour operator.' Applicants are examined for financial resources and fitness. Each licence holder provides an irrevocable bond which will be available in the event of failure for the benefit of customers. Shortfalls are met from the Air Travel Trust if bonds prove insufficient.

The Air Travel Organizer's Licence is a consumer protection scheme based on the Civil Aviation (Air Travel Organisers' Licensing) Regulations 1972. This made it a legal requirement (with a few exceptions) for travel organizers selling air seats to hold a licence. Financial protection for the customers of licence holders is provided by the bond which each company has to lodge before being granted a licence. If the company then goes out of business, the bond money is used to repatriate passengers from abroad and to refund those who have booked but not travelled. The bond system is underpinned by financial screening to ensure that each company has a reasonable margin of solvency at the time the licence is granted and the individual bonds are backed up by a reserve fund managed by the Air

Travel Trust. During 1992/93, twenty licensed companies failed. The CAA repatriated 10 600 passengers and gave refunds totalling £4.9 million to 22 300 people, £1.8 million of which was paid from the Air Travel Trust.

When applying for an ATOL, the applicant must specify the number of seats which it is sought to sell to the public. This is expressed as single journeys. The applicant must also state the turnover in connection with those seats, including hotels, car hire and other elements of the holiday package. In judging an application for an ATOL, the CAA uses a fitness criterion which includes the past activities, competency and fitness of the applicant and their employees. The applicant's financial position is evaluated, usually based on the latest audited accounts, and a surplus of free assets in the balance sheet is required to support the projected business. Free assets means recoverable net assets and the net value of fixed assets (mainly buildings, but not those abroad). This test includes consideration of non-licensable activities and the accounts of related companies such as holding companies, subsidiaries and those of associates linked by common directors or shareholders. The notes of guidance state that for new applicants the surplus of free assets 'is unlikely to be less than 5% of total income, and may be much more . . .' The notes also warn that the surplus required will be even greater for new companies since a new company incurs setting-up costs.

During the licence period, usually one year, a company can apply for a variation of its original licence for additional capacity, but must obtain the CAA's approval before entering into a commitment for extra business.

The CAA's regulations state that a minimum of £10 000 is required for a bond, and above that basic level 10% of licensed annual turnover. However, for their first two years of operation, new entrants are required to provide 15%. If the CAA considers that a venture is particularly risky, 20% (25% for new entrants) may be required.

The bond must be signed and sealed by an obligor, checked by the CAA and forwarded to the Trustees, the Green St branch of National Westminster Bank Plc. Obligors are generally banks (members of the British Banking Association), or approved insurance companies, while for a bond greater than £1 million, they are approved individually.

Applicants have to pay charges before an ATOL is granted. The CAA then issues an identifying number which must be put on all advertisements and brochures. The ATOL rules insist that the ATOL holder must send customers confirmation of booking within 14 days, giving details of the ATOL and the booking details. Confirmation may be sent via the travel agent but it must be passed to the client.

New package tour regulations were issued in 1994 following a European Union Directive. Tour operators using scheduled flights also now need a bond and as a result the CAA granted 346 licences to firms which had not previously held a licence. The number of licence holders rose by 60% over the previous year to 947, although the increase in the number of holidays licensed was less, since many new entrants offered small programmes. A total of 16.7 million holidays were licensed with a value of £6 billion.

In 1994, the CAA was granted a Citizen's Charter. As an enforcement agency, a body charged with the task of ensuring compliance with government regulations, it was expected to improve on the statutory requirement to consider an ATOL application within six months. The aim is a decision on 90% of applications within three months, with renewals in two months. Its ability to do so depends on applicants providing the relevant information. The CAA also undertook to publish clear and easily understood licensing criteria, guidance and information, including statistics about the number of licences granted and the business authorized, and to explain why an applicant failed to meet the licensing criteria.

The framework of holiday regulation has become more complex, and the public were less certain what questions to ask about ATOLs when booking a holiday. The CAA therefore introduced a leaflet explaining the system, 415 000 of which were distributed in seven weeks after its launch at the Holiday Live exhibition.

CASE STUDY 7.3

Air 2000

Air 2000, the UK's third largest charter airline, began operations in 1987, flying charter flights from Manchester to holiday destinations in the Canaries, Portugal, Spain, Greece and Turkey for over 40 tour operators. The airline is a wholly owned subsidiary of First Choice Holidays Plc, a company quoted on the Stock Exchange, and the third largest tour operator in the UK. In the winter of 1994, it was relaunched as three brands: First Choice, Freespirit and Sovereign. It also owns the largest direct-sell brand in the UK, Eclipse Holidays, and a company based in Canada, ITH. In 1994, it sold over 2.5 million holidays, accounting for 15% of the market.

In its first year of operation, 1987, Air 2000 operated two 757 aircraft purchased new from Boeing. In the summer 1987 season (April to October) it achieved 15 hours per day utilization of its aircraft, and 70 flights a week. This was the highest utilization rate for any aircraft type operated by a British airline. During the ensuing winter season, Air 2000 leased one of its aircraft to British Airways and operated charter flights from Manchester with the other.

Air 2000's management philosophy

Air 2000 differs from the air charter market's typical domination by in-house flying for an airline's tour operator-owner. Both Britannia, owned by Thomson, and Monarch, owned by Cosmos, operate about 95% of their capacity for their owner, whereas Air 2000 provides only 65–70% of its seats to First Choice. The philosophy underlying Air 2000 is that it should operate as a business in its own right, seeking clients for its spare capacity.

Traditionally, in-flight catering specifications had been determined by tour operators, but airlines were the target of passengers' complaints about limited or poor quality meals on their flights. From a passenger's perspective, the flight is an important element of their package, and as it is the first real experience of their holiday, any dissatisfaction with the flight can spoil their holiday. Air 2000's management took a strategic decision to provide a high standard of service and catering on its flights, and this has resulted in many awards. Special meals (vegetarian, kosher, etc.) are available by pre-request on any flight. For *ad hoc* charters the airline also provides an upgraded meal service on request, and kosher catering is standard on flights to and from Isreal. Their reputation for quality provides a strong point in attracting good tour operators. One of its managers defined these as 'tour operators who pay on time, operate a full season, and whose operating pattern is harmonious with Air 2000's'.

Fleet management

The airline's planning cycle is geared to the tour operators' brochure and sales cycle, with two distinct seasons as illustrated in Table 7.7. The strength of the summer season pinpoints one of the keys to success – the need to start an independent airline for the summer, to carry the fleet through the winter and build it up for the following summer season through planned incremental growth. Table 7.8 shows the record of passenger and fleet growth by Air 2000, which had achieved a mature fleet profile with 14 757 series 200 aircraft and four A320 series 180s at the time of writing in late 1995.

Table 7.7 Seasonality in Air 2000's operations

	Summer 1994	Winter 1994/95
Period	1 May–31 Oct	1 Nov–30 April
Turnover	£250m	£70m
Passengers	1.85m	625 000
Rotations	8300	2 900
Hours operation	3000	1 500
Aircraft operated	14 × B757 (233 seats) 4 × A320 (180 seats)	11 × B757 4 × A320
Aircraft leased out	0	3 × B757

Table 7.8 The development of Air 2000's fleet

	Fleet	UK bases	Passengers carried	Winter fleet disposition
1987	2 × 757	Manchester	423 846	1 leased to BA
1988	4 × 757	Manchester Glasgow	863 730	2 in Canada leased to Air 3000
1989	6 × 757 1 × 757		1 418 071	2 new 757s operated in Australia 3 leased in Canada to Air 3000
1990	9 × 757 1 × 737 (returned to lessor in October)	Manchester Glasgow Gatwick	1 848 825	3 leased in Canada
1991	12 × 757	Manchester Glasgow Gatwick Birmingham	2 443 512	3 leased in Canada
1992	14 × 757 2 × A320	Manchester Glasgow Gatwick Birmingham Bristol	3 404 843	3 leased in Canada
1993	14 × 757 4 × A320	Manchester Glasgow Gatwick Birmingham Bristol Newcastle Belfast		3 leased in Canada

Tour operators increasingly demand quiet and comfortable aircraft for their holidaymaking clients, and Air 2000 sees this as a business opportunity. It has invested in a modern fleet and prides itself on the quality of its service. It emphasizes its punctuality, the good food offered to its passengers, the cleanliness of aircraft interiors and good airport handling, as well as its safety record.

The types of aircraft an airline operates is determined by a number of factors, chiefly the market constraints for its particular routes and any operational limitations at specific airports. Most European resorts can sustain aircraft of about 200-seat capacity, and the 757 satisfies Air 2000's needs in this respect. However, it is not able to operate into Funchal within safety limits, whereas the A320 can cope safely with the technical constraints of this airport's unusually steep approach route and short runway. Funchal is an important destination for First Choice, but even so, these operational limitations mean that this and similar routes command a premium.

Air 2000's engineering base is at Luton, and consequently the airline needs to arrange the flying schedule for each aircraft so that it can be available for its 24-hour long service there on a regular basis, whichever airport it operates from. This is achieved by flying passengers from the aircraft's base to Paphos, returning with a previous complement of passengers completing their holiday to Luton, and after a 24-hour service, flying another outbound group to Paphos, returning to the aircraft's base with an earlier group of passengers. The scale of First Choice's programme to Cyprus makes this possible, allowing customers an unusual combination of days to stay in the resort. The alternative would be to fly the planes empty to and from Luton, which for the Manchester based aircraft would cost about £4000 each time.

Planning the season's charter operation

First Choice, as Air 2000's major client (rather than as its owner), specifies what routes it expects to operate the following year as early as May, and indicates how many seats it will require on each. The airline then considers what parts of this business match its own abilities and objectives, bearing in mind the airline's historic commitment to other clients. Negotiations result in Air 2000 itself operating about 65–70% of First Choice's flying programme. The airline's managers then buy in the additional requirements for the tour operator and sell their own excess capacity to other tour operators. The timing of these negotiations is driven by the market for inclusive holidays and the lead time required to print and distribute brochures ahead of sales.

For the May to October 1995 season, First Choice had their brochures ready by August of 1994, with all prices and surcharge guarantees. This required costings by June of 1994. First Choice is typical of major UK tour operators in this respect, and the Federation of Tour Operators has developed the concept of base dates for charging, using the third week of July for the following summer. The exchange rates published in *The Financial Times* on that date are used for all currency transactions by all tour operators. This simplifies the calculation of any subsequent surcharging resulting from currency fluctuations as permitted in current ABTA rules for holiday components charged in overseas currencies. As Table 7.9 indicates, charter airlines are affected by the need to pay in foreign currencies for a variety of services, while nearly all revenue is in sterling, the exception being any routes operated on behalf of tour operators based in, and operating from, other countries.

Most major holiday routes are characterized by what is termed 'market days'. For example, the market days for flights to Greek resorts are Tuesdays, Wednesdays and Thursday nights, for Arrecife the market day is Thursday and for Tenerife it is Tuesdays and Fridays. The rationale for this grouping of departures by UK tour operators is the resultant ability in a price sensitive market to consolidate flights and to take advantage of one charter's excess capacity without the need to operate another aircraft with 200 or more seats to fill. The concept of market days is an industry strength because tourists are relatively amenable to the offer of a later or earlier flight,

Table 7.9 Foreign currency payments incurred by Air 2000 (London–Malaga–London, 1995, Boeing 757)

Operating costs	Currency and conversion required	Approximate notional cost (1995)
Fuel	US$ to £ sterling	£2400
Landing fees	£ (Gatwick) Pesetas (Malaga) to £	£1056
Airport fees	£ (Gatwick) Pesetas (Malaga) to £	£1400
International route charge	ECU to £	£2300
Catering	£ (Gatwick) Pesetas (Malaga) to £	£1700
Crew allowances (not salaries)		£ 200
Overheads		£400 000 month + engineering

but they are more resistant to attempts to shift their departures to different days.

A manager of the airline commented as follows:

> The market in which airlines operate is highly structured, and it is further controlled by the CAA through the tour operators' ATOL licensing arrangements and requirements for airlines to deposit financial bonds. The CAA itself now has to ensure that its regulations conform to European Union regulations, but at the same time, deregulation has opened the European market to competition by airlines based in the loosely aligned countries of the old Soviet block, utilizing older aircraft with different overheads and operating costs and enabling them to service the established, high margin markets for charter flights within Western Europe. The effect has been felt indirectly through pressures on UK charters' rates. The problem for charters is that they are responding to the demand for overseas package holidays by supplying services to the tour operators – theirs is a derived demand and their product forms part of the holidaymakers' dream. They cannot directly influence the size of the market, nor can they set their own prices as the charter transport element is traded on routes and schedules. The competition between charters also focuses on punctuality, safety, airport handling, good catering and the cleanliness of aircraft. The ability to compete on these criteria depends on having a reliable fleet, and on good planning providing some fleet flexibility at peak periods.

Unlike scheduled carriers, charters are not permitted to cancel a flight for which they are contracted, as the extracts from a charter contract indicate. If they are unable to operate it themselves they must instead buy in *ad hoc* capacity. Air 2000 took a policy decision to station an aircraft at both Gatwick and

Manchester every Saturday night in order to cope with the following day's schedules in the event of a delayed inbound flight resulting either from technical problems or air traffic control and airport congestion whether on the runways or the terminals. However, over the summer season, this equates to taking 52 flights out of the airline's potential revenue earning programme.

Table 7.10 Information for tour operators

- Details of passenger loads are required by telex 24 hours before flight departure. The charterer is responsible for ensuring that all its sharers' clients have been included. The lists (known as manifests) are required for departures from overseas airports although rules vary, and are the basis for in-flight catering.

- In Cyprus, charter operators are obliged to provide the Department of Civil Aviation [within 24 hours] with passenger lists which give the name of each arriving passenger and the name of CTO (Cyprus Tourist Office) licensed premises where that passenger will be accommodated. The names of passengers travelling on outgoing IT charter fliths must be provided to the Department of Civil Aviation at least 48 hours before departure.

- In Malta, master manifests must be submitted to Air Malta at least 48 hours before departure. They must first be cleared through the Malta International Airport Duty Officer and must be stamped accordingly. Additional manifests not exceeding 6% of the aircraft configuration must be handed in no later than 2 hours before scheduled departure. The main charter is responsible for shared flights, and the airline warns that split or separate manifests will not be accepted.

- Kosher and vegetarian meals are provided at 24 hours' notice. Hot kosher meals are charged at £10, payable in advance. Birthday cakes, complimentary drinks and use of first-class lounges at airports (when available) can be arranged at additional costs.

- Passengers with valid tickets will be checked in until the flight is full. The flight is then closed and any remaining passengers will become the responsibility of the appropriate tour operator's representative.

- Tour operators are asked to notify the passenger services department of any traveller requiring special assistance. Air 2000 will then arrange for a wheelchair to be available at check in, and special handling can be arranged for groups of handicapped passengers. If a stretcher is required (for example after a skiing accident) it has to be fitted in the aircraft before operating the outbound sector. It occupies the space of three rows (nine seats), and in addition, a suitably qualified medical attendant must travel with passengers on a stretcher.

- Special arrangements can be made to carry sub aqua equipment (tanks must be empty and valves open), golf clubs, bicycles, windsurfers, prams and skis.

- Any company mail that charters wish to send must be handed to handling agents packaged so that contents can be verified, and is sent as baggage loaded in the hold.

Once the pattern of its operations is known the airline begins negotiations for the necessary operational slots – permission to land and take off. The basis of the negotiation is the historic pattern of flying, and year on year about 80% of a charter's operation is broadly similar. They also negotiate at this time for one of their major expenses, typically arranging for delivery of two million or more gallons of fuel paid for immediately at current prices, to be provided at all (or most) airports they operate to. The basis for pricing each route is now set, and a range of discounts is offered for weekdays while weekends are charged at premium rates. This structure provides the context to negotiations with a multitude of tour operators, with the objective of arranging the most profitable flying for the airline.

Information for Tour Operators

Whereas scheduled airlines sell individual seats to individual passengers through the retail travel agency network supplemented by consolidators, the charter airlines' unit of sale is the flight, the rights to sell seats on this being purchased by one or several tour operators who are themselves responsible for payment. The charter airlines therefore have to specify terms and requirements with their tour operator clients, both formally through contracts, and in detailed operational manuals which Air 2000 provides for its tour operators, as Table 7.10 indicates.

Based on interviews with Air 2000 managers and company documents.

CONCLUSION

In this chapter, it has been argued that the growth of overseas holidays has been intimately involved with that of the charter airline industry. It has been shown that this has itself evolved from basic, low-quality services as the charter airlines and their customers, the tour operators, have come to see them as key elements in the holiday industry. Charter airlines also provide the physical link between origins and destinations. As the demand for long-haul holidays grows, it may be doubted whether the charters' role will continue to be so dominant, as scheduled services offer a greater variety of destinations and, more flexibility in schedules, and as they gain in efficiency they are increasingly able to compete on price with the charter operators.

FURTHER READING

Corke, A. (1986) *British Airways – The Path to Profitability*, Pinter, London.

Doganis, R. (1985) *Flying Off Course: The Economics of International Airlines*, Allen & Unwin, London.

Page, S. (1994) *Transport in Tourism*, Routledge, London.

Wheatcroft, S. (1994) *Aviation and Tourism Policies*, Routledge, London.

Wheatcroft (1994) analyses air transport issues and policy choices for the tourism industry, while Page (1994) provides a theoretical introduction to the significance of transport generally for tourism. Doganis (1985) presents a critical appraisal of airline strategies during the 1980s, providing additional insights into aspects of their operations. Corke (1986) reviews the developments at British Airways which resulted in its emergence as one of the world's leading airlines in terms of financial performance and customer focus under the leadership of Lord King and Sir Colin Marshall.

SUGGESTED EXERCISES

1. Taking the roles of the airline negotiator, the airport manager, the destination's Minister for Tourism and the Prime Minister, debate the issues which a small tropical island with a declining sugar industry must resolve in permitting large-scale resort developments which would attract night charter flight movements.

2. Using the figures provided in this book (or more up-to-date data if available) calculate the costings for a programme of charter-based holidays to Spain and set up a brochure price matrix, explaining your reasons for seasonal and other supplements and any assumptions you have made.

3. Argue for and against the introduction by an established charter airline of a reconfiguration of its aircraft so that it could offer some clients a premium level of service.

The timeshare industry

PART 5

This part provides a profile of one of the most innovative product developments in the holiday industry. Certain bad practices by some members of the timeshare industry have attracted a great deal of adverse publicity, and they are also examined in this part. The sector is interesting because of further innovations, notably the timeshare exchange concept which is discussed in Chapter 9. The exchange companies depend on consistent high standards in all participating resorts as a basis for the holiday products which they offer owners. This gives them a base from which to provide leadership in the further development of a complex, expanding sector of tourism.

The timeshare industry | 8

INTRODUCTION

Timeshare can be defined as 'a system by which consumers purchase the right to use a resort's accommodation and facilities at regular intervals for their future holidays'. It is one of the fastest growing sectors of the holiday industry, and is also one of the most distinctive additions to the repertoire of holiday products since the introduction of charter-based inclusive holidays.

> Resort timeshare means that a number of buyers purchase a luxury accommodation and divide residency into increments of one week or more. Each buyer shares in maintenance and repair costs, thereby reducing the overall expense of owning a vacation home.
> (Masterton, 1993)

Tourists often form a strong affinity to a particular destination, becoming attached to the scenic qualities of a place, its culture, people and climate, or a particular hotel. They return for subsequent holidays, and as their knowledge of the area increases, they may prefer to make their own travel and accommodation arrangements, and ultimately invest in a second home there for their regular visits or when they retire. Many other people may be attracted by the idea of owning a property in their regular holiday area, but without the burden of responsibility for taxes, maintenance and so on, or they may be unable to afford the full costs of property purchase and maintenance. Time-share offers them an appealing solution: some 3.1 million households now own timeshare in more than 4000 developments around the world and between 9 and 10 million people take timeshare holidays each year (Ragatz, 1995).

Recently, a number of issues have been identified in this new and still developing industry. These relate to the structure of the industry, the relationships between its elements, and its economic significance. Another area of interest is the relationship between this sector and the established players in the wider holiday industry, particularly (but not exclusively) self-catering villas and hotel accommodation, and tour operators arising from timeshare's potential to attract holidaymakers from traditional package holidays. Already, Club Med has invested in timeshare operations, while other operators rent unsold units to include in their brochures alongside existing hotels. From the early days of the industry, hotel groups have recognized the advantages of converting properties to timeshare operations.

A further major concern is the relationships between timeshare organizations and their clients. Two researchers have described the present state of the industry as 'a sound concept suffering from a poor image'. (Goodall and Stabler, 1990).

THE DEVELOPMENT OF TIMESHARE

The timeshare concept began in 1963 when a Swiss company, Hapimag, offered shares for sale, using the proceeds to buy holiday properties throughout Europe, ownership of the shares conferring the right to holiday in the properties. An alternative form, which became more popular, was introduced by the French company Superdevoluy, trading under the slogan 'Stop hiring a room, buy the hotel – its cheaper!' This somewhat overstated the case, because what timeshare purchasers really buy is the right to use fixed weeks each year in that hotel for their holidays. Timeshare resorts are generally high-quality developments. Typically, in the UK, they offer large apartments, with accommodation for up to six people. They are well equipped, and the resorts provide a wide range of amenities, discussed in detail in the case study of RCI which follows in Chapter 9.

Table 8.1 shows the rapid growth in timeshare resorts and the increase in ownership of timeshare intervals, while Table 8.2 provides an analysis of timeshare activity and potential in Europe. This table contrasts the proportion of population in various countries who own timeshare (in any country), thus indicating both differential market penetration rates (highest in the UK) and the potential for the industry to grow further. The proportion of owners with units in any country is also stated in this table as a proportion of total tourism visits to that

Table 8.1 Trends in the timeshare industry

	Resorts	*Owners*	*Intervals sold*	*Value of sales ($)*
1980	506	155 000	100 000	490 million
1985	1774	805 000	245 000	1580 billion
1990	2357	1 800 000	405 000	3240 billion
1991	2678	2 070 000	440 000	3740 billion
1992	3050	2 363 000	500 000	4250 billion
1993	3653	2 760 000	530 000	4505 billion
1994	4145	3 144 000	560 000	4760 billion

Source: Ragatz (1995).

Table 8.2 Patterns of timeshare ownership and use in Europe (selected countries 1994)

	Timeshare resort projects in country	Timeshare owners owning in country	Timeshare owners in country per 1000 visiting tourists	Timeshare owners resident in country	Timeshare owners residing in country per 100 households
UK	108	62 169	3.35	286 259	1.43
France	143	15 971	0.27	54 259	0.25
Italy	152	41 884	1.6	56 986	0.29
Germany	43	68 735	4.54	40 000	0.24
Spain	407	327 064	8.25	51 214	0.48
Total (all European countries)	1188	657 591	n/a	669 571	n/a

country, thus Spain has the highest percentage (0.8%) of timeshare activity.

FORMS OF TIMESHARE

Originally, timeshare was often advertised and sold as an investment in real estate. Later the right-to-use holiday accommodation was emphasized, linked to suggestions that timeshare provided a cost-effective alternative to renting equivalent accommodation. Innovations were developed, giving owners more flexible ways to use their fixed-location, fixed-time purchase, especially through exchanges, 'untethering the purchaser from having to vacation during the same week each year' (Goodall and Stabler, 1992). Another innovation, floating weeks, was introduced to give owners more flexibility in choosing their holiday week each year within the seasonal price band they purchased.

Holiday ownership takes the following three main forms (Goodall and Stabler, 1990):

- fixed-week schemes giving the right to occupy for a specific week each year;
- revolving week schemes giving a guaranteed allocation which changes in a predetermined manner each year;
- floating week schemes in which owners book on a first come, first served basis.

TIMESHARE TYPOLOGY

Like most specialized activities, a range of terms has been developed for the technical aspects of timeshare, and to distinguish between the varied groups involved in the industry. These are explained in Table 8.3.

STRUCTURE OF THE TIMESHARE INDUSTRY

As Table 8.3 indicates, the timeshare industry consists of organizations providing a variety of functions for their proprietors and clients. The basic service of the industry is the provision of accommodation and facilities by resorts to timeshare purchasers, but many other elements contribute to generating a sound financial return to the investment required, to selling timeshare intervals and to ensuring the continuing satisfaction of clients.

Timeshare developers

Before the public can purchase timeshare intervals, developers have to take the risk of funding the construction of a resort (or the conversion of a suitable existing property such as a hotel or a large country house). The timeshare industry attracts investment from resort, construction and leisure companies against the revenue from subsequent sales of the resort units. The potential profit from a timeshare development is

Table 8.3 Typology of timeshare terminology

Timeshare	Purchase of the right to stay in a particular resort during a fixed week (or weeks) every year.
Purchaser	A person (or more usually, a family) which buys timeshare.
Timeshare resort	A development which operates on a timeshare basis.
Unit	An apartment or room in the resort to which the owner and family are entitled to exclusive use during their occupancy.
Interval	The period of ownership time, usually a week.
Developer	The individual or company which builds a timeshare resort.
Finance company	Either the source of funds for construction, or the institution lending to purchasers.
Marketing company	The organization contracted by a developer to sell timeshare intervals.
Trustee	An independent company which provides protection to purchasers by holding their funds and the property title until transactions have been completed.
Owner	The person or family who owns the right to occupy a timeshare unit for a particular week on a recurrent annual basis.
Exchange company	The company to which a timeshare resort is affiliated in order to provide its owners with the ability to exchange their week for a similar period in another affiliated resort.
Maintenance charge	The charge for resort maintenance and planned upgrading which all owners are required to pay annually. (The problem is that a proportion default.)
Owners' association	The elected owners who undertake the management responsibilities for the resort or delegate them to a specialist company. A management committee is formed when a previously agreed proportion of timeshare units have been sold.
Resale company	An organization specializing in the sale of weeks which owners wish to dispose of.
Management company	A company specializing in the running of resorts and employed either by the developer or the owners' committee or a combination of the two.

impressive as developers typically aim to sell 50 weekly blocks for each accommodation unit, reserving two weeks for maintenance of the property. In effect, they sell each room 50 times!

The developer selects the site for a new resort, commissions architectural plans, arranges planning permission and finance, and undertakes the construction. During the development and construction phase, parallel activities have to be carried out to enable the resort to be sold to the purchasers of timeshare weeks. For example, it is necessary to establish methods of marketing the timeshare weeks and to set up appropriate legal frameworks both to protect their funds during the purchase procedure and for their subsequent ownership of the resort.

Increasingly, developers are major corporations, including hotel groups such as Marriot, Sheraton and Stakis. It has been pointed out that Marriott, through its MORI (Marriott Ownership Resorts), and Hilton through Hilton Grand Vacation Partnerships benefit from 'an ever renewable source of potential sales clients amongst their guests'. They can also offer exchanges amongst their own locations, flexibility of use and special guest privileges.

TIMESHARE PURCHASE AND OWNERSHIP

Marketing timeshare

Originally, timeshare was promoted as an investment opportunity, but now developers and marketers encourage their purchasers to regard their expenditure as capital invested in the purchase of future holidays. The benefits offered include opportunities to take independent holidays in a range of accommodation through exchanges. The variety of resort locations and styles offers marketers opportunities to segment the market 'for example, according to socio-demographic characteristics in which timeshares based on hotel conversions are targeted at the over-50 age group while those with integral sporting facilities are intended for families with children'.

Timeshare purchase is measured in weeks and price. The average owned is 1.7 weeks, since many families invest in second purchases, demonstrating the satisfaction of most timeshare owners with their first purchase of a week. At an average price of £6000 per week, the value of timeshare sales in Europe in 1994 was approximately £1.3 billion, and UK sales were worth about £240 million (Haylock, 1994).

Ownership

Timeshare ownership has a number of characteristics of varying significance to each potential purchaser, depending on his or her financial situation and personal preferences. However, almost all of the factors listed in Table 8.4 entail complex financial calculations whose validity is

Table 8.4 Financial aspects of timeshare purchase

- An investment asset
- Inflation-proof means of securing future holidays
- Cost advantages compared to other holidays
- Resale value
- Rental potential
- Terminal value
- Management and maintenance costs

affected by the assumptions (such as future rates of interest) on which they are based.

Table 8.5 provides a profile of UK timeshare owners. They tend to be married, and most have no children at home, although the recent trend is more family oriented, and the average age of owners has been falling, being between 40 and 45. Their financial outgoings are therefore minimized, while their incomes are generally higher than average, as can be seen from the occupations of heads of households.

Purchase of a timeshare implies a long-term commitment to the responsibilities of ownership. For most families, this takes the form of making annual maintenance payments and the majority are content to delegate the management functions. However, the legal structure of timeshare resorts generally passes responsibility to the owners after the developer has sold an agreed proportion of the units. They therefore assume full responsibility for the day-to-day and strategic long-term running of their property during the term of their ownership. In practice, this requires the establishment of an owners' association to represent the long-term interests of the timeshare owners.

Table 8.5 Profile of UK timeshare owners

Age of head of household	%
< 35	12.4
35–44	21
45–54	28.6
55 >	38
Married	86.4
No chidren at home	70.3
Median number of weeks purchased	2
Ownership of more than one week	14.4
Occupation of household head	
Professional	28.2
Management	12.1
Government	2.7
Technical	22.5
Sales	7.9
Other	8.7
Retired	17.9

Source: Ragatz Associates.

Timeshare owners' committee

There are four difficulties in forming an owners' committee; two relate to the practicalities of arranging meetings amongst the international owners, and two are about recruiting members to serve on the committee. Given the large number of owners (up to 50 times the number of apartments) and the potentially worldwide spread of their residence, the difficulties of spatial and time coincidence limit the number of owners who can attend regular committee meetings. Furthermore, many owners regard their purchase as an investment in holiday facilities, and consequently are reluctant to undertake quite onerous committee duties as part of their leisure. The fourth issue is that of the technical expertise required to form an effective committee. The range of skills found amongst owners is largely a matter of chance, although as Table 8.5 indicated many owners do have appropriate professional backgrounds.

The owners elect a management committee which functions according to published regulations setting out detailed responsibilities and duties, and is re-elected annually (Jenkins, 1987). In general, the committee has two main tasks,

- setting the annual maintenance fees to be paid by owners;
- the day-to-day management of the resort.

Factors in setting the annual maintenance fee

While it is relatively simple to appoint a company to manage the resort on a daily basis, the maintenance charge is a key and complex issue. The problem is to minimize the expense of ownership while providing a fund which not only covers day-to-day running costs such as cleaning and reception services, but also enables the standards of the resort to be maintained and, over time, enhanced in line with the rising standards of an industry driven by competition for sales by new developers. Without this upgrading, owners potentially lose value as their resort becomes less popular as an exchange destination, and units become less easy to resell.

Setting a rate which satisfies these long-term obligations is made more sensitive by a practice identified (and condemned) by the Office of Fair Trading (OFT). It found that to make resorts more marketable developers often subsidize running costs in the early years, particularly where a significant number of units are unsold. The effect of this is two-fold. It makes a purchase appear more affordable, thereby expanding the market for timeshare ownership, and it masks from buyers the true extent of their long-term financial commitment. Commenting on this, the OFT noted:

> Running costs included in the maintenance fee cover cleaning and maintenance of accommodation and facilities, energy, water, insurance, rental, and exchange services . . . What is less clear is whether

Table 8.6 Reasons for selling timeshare weeks

Reason for sale	%
Financial pressure	40.2
Health problems in family	22.8
Divorce, or spouse deceased	5.9
Used it frequently, want some money back	5.6
Redundancy	5.6
Long ownership, expect a profit	3
Others	17

Source: Primeshare, cited in OFT (1990).

a sinking fund for replacement of equipment, furniture and refurbishment also includes more fundamental structural repairs and amortisation of the buildings themselves ...

(OFT, 1990)

In 1994, the average maintenance charge in UK resorts was £228, with a range from about £100 to £300 per week's ownership. In Europe, according to RCI data, the average was £175, with a range from £110 to more than £300.

Resales

Timeshare owners have the right to sell the weeks which they purchased, just as do home owners, although the resale market in Europe is not yet as developed as in America. Lifestyle changes as owners age may cause them to cease making use of their timeshare, and financial pressures and a variety of personal misfortunes account for many other sales, as Table 8.6 indicates. This poses a risk to developers since the personal urgency of obtaining capital from a resale (or of paying off a debt which requires interest payments) suggests that individual vendors are likely to accept lower offers. This potentially undermines the value of the remaining unsold weeks at the resort, and is a matter of concern to developers since up to 40% of the sales price is accounted for by the costs of marketing the resort (Mendoza, 1986). Consequently some resort companies retain the right to buy any weeks back, offering them for resale through specialist magazines.

REGULATING THE TIMESHARE INDUSTRY

In its rapid growth, the way some of the timeshare industry's activities have been performed has caused concern, both to the public and the industry. Table 8.7 identifies a range of problems related to the elements in the timeshare industry and their influence on the ownership of timeshare. Public concerns resulted in official enquiries into the industry's practices, the beginning of self-regulation, and the imposition of measures to regulate it from outside. Several surveys have indicated that while the majority of owners are satisfied or very satisfied with their timeshare and the overall operation of the majority of resorts (Table 8.8), adverse publicity and concern centres mainly on aspects of the industry's marketing and sales practices.

Table 8.7 Problems related to elements in the timeshare industry

Element in the timeshare industry	Problem identified in OFT report
Developers	They play a pivotal role. The care, or lack of it, in planning the resort, setting up its legal structure and the integrity of their financial dealings with clients are key factors.
Trustees	Their role may give a false sense of security to purchasers. Some are insufficiently independent, and because of the international nature of the industry, some are beyond the reach of the laws of the UK.
Finance companies	Few operate outside the UK, and the lack of easily available finance at the point of sale has hampered the ability to sell timeshare.
Owners' associations	They have sometimes encountered difficulties in managing the day-to-day affairs of the resort or in setting charges, and in some cases there is doubt about their true independence from the developer.
Exchange companies	'Have increased the popularity of timeshare by providing a greater variety of resorts for owners, and are able to exert a useful influence over the viability of schemes and standards within affiliated resorts. But their importance to the industry has led to an exaggeration or distortion of the benefits of exchange during sales presentations.'
Rental services	Are sometimes ineffective.

Based on OFT (1990).

Table 8.8 Satisfaction with timeshare

	%
Very satisfied	44.8
Satisfied	41.2
So-so	7.7
Dissatisfied	3.3
Very dissatisfied	2.9
Likely to purchase again	67

Source: Ragatz.

Criticisms of timeshare sales methods

Despite the complexity of the timeshare product, its financial significance to the owner and the long-term commitment implied, timeshare selling has often been subjected to criticism from consumer groups and from other elements of the industry. Consumer criticism focuses on the misleading, harassing and high-pressure techniques used to attract prospective purchasers and to convert these prospects to buyers, but there are also longer-term, structural problems which can detract from purchasers' enjoyment of timeshare. The following excerpts from the OFT report and Table 8.9 summarize the views expressed to the OFT about timeshare presentations.

> Over 50% of a sales presentation ... focuses on ... facilities such as swimming pools or beaches, tennis courts, golf courses and skiing and activities such as children's programmes, evening entertainment, trips to local entertainment ... The sales approach used most frequently involves creating the image of a 'dream vacation' for the entire family, and problems usually arise in the actual delivery of these programmes ... High pressure sales techniques are used ... to get a purchase commitment the first time individuals look at a property ... Techniques to encourage signing ... include price savings that won't be equalled if customers decide to come back at a later time ... creative methods are used [to attract people to tour the properties] ... Premium or free gifts are offered as incentives. These can include vacation packages, clocks, jewellery, cameras or sporting goods. Mini vacations ... are also used to encourage interested purchasers to view the property.
>
> (OFT, 1990)

There are two ways to sell timeshare: through off-site presentations or by persuading people who have visited the resort to purchase there. In both cases, the initial problem is to attract potential buyers. The

Table 8.9 Experiences of timeshare presentations

	Attendees agreeing with statement (%)
I thought I would collect an award, and went just for that purpose.	37
I knew it was about timeshare, and went solely for that purpose.	31
I did not expect anyone would try to sell me anything.	15
I felt I was under pressure to buy.	44
I was not given enough information to make a decision on whether to purchase or not.	62
I received an award.	72
I was disappointed with the award I received.	34

Source: OFT (1990).

harassment to which holidaymakers have been subjected in many destinations to attend resort presentations has caused a high level of complaints against canvassers, often young people who are remunerated only by commission. Invitations to attend off-site presentations are criticized on the grounds of their intrusiveness, or that offers of high value gifts are seldom actually received because very stringent (or expensive) codicils are attached to the award. The presentations themselves are highly structured, and control over the session is deliberately retained by the presenter, who leads his or her prospect through a programme which minimizes the detailed factors a client should evaluate but emphasizes the benefits (usually a once-only offer of a discount) of an immediate decision.

The OFT report points out that the majority of owners who wrote to the Office 'were entirely content with what they have bought and had enjoyed trouble-free holidays for a number of years.' However, 'it is the methods used to sell timeshare which have generated most controversy and concern.'

One issue is that, although there were then 200 000 British timeshare owners, 'The marketing of timeshare affects many more people – a survey revealed that nearly 50% of those over 16 had received direct mail about timeshare during the year to November 1989. Six per cent of these had attended timeshare presentations.' The report levelled five criticisms at the methods often used to sell timeshare, summarized in Table 8.10.

The OFT report pointed out that the fundamental weakness of these tactics is that 'where they are used, timeshare is not bought on its merits.' The report called for increased care and responsibility in the industry's marketing, arguing that: 'The potential buyer is being asked to make a major financial decision and a commitment about future holidays for years ahead.' It then considered the nature of the long-term relationship between timeshare owners and the industry. Problems arise when an owner's personal or economic circumstances change.

Table 8.10 Criticisms of timeshare sales practices

Direct mailshots	Often misleading about their purpose and the awards offered
Canvassing	Aggressive or deceptive behaviour by canvassers
Advertising	Often entices people to attend sales presentations without being clear about the purpose of it
High-pressure sales techniques	'Seek to contol the buyers' behaviour and suppress rational decision-making'
Information given orally	Often incomplete, untrue or misleading, given to induce people to make an 'unduly hasty buying decision'

Based on OFT (1990).

Since the Office of Fair Trading report in 1990, the 1992 Timeshare Act has given protection to consumers in the form of a cooling-off period following initial intention to purchase and the situation has improved. The European Union has issued a Directive requiring national legislation to be in force by 29 April 1997 ensuring, amongst other conditions of timeshare sale, that consumers receive a detailed brochure describing the resort, that they can withdraw without giving a reason during a ten-day cooling-off period and that there should be no advance payment (Jenkins, 1994). While many reputable timeshare organizations endorse this protective framework, there was criticism of the intention to prohibit acceptance of a deposit (even when it could be returned if the purchaser changed his or her mind within a specified time).

An alternative sales method used by many established resorts is a referral programme. This encourages existing timeshare owners to bring friends and relatives to tour the property, relying for an interest in purchasing based on positive word-of-mouth recommendations by satisfied owners.

The Timeshare Council

The Timeshare Council (TC) was established as the official body of the timeshare industry, to provide consumers with 'peace of mind in holiday ownership'. Its members, drawn from all supply sectors of the industry, must operate within its code of conduct. In particular, this ensures that purchasers have secure occupancy rights and that sound arrangements are made to protect their money prior to completion of the property purchase. Importantly, the trade association for owners' committees is not part of the TC structure. The Timeshare Council provides a free advisory and conciliation service for everyone who deals with its member organizations and issues advisory leaflets to intending purchasers. The TC is the trade association for the UK industry; similar associations exist in most European countries.

THE COMMUNITY AND ECONOMIC BENEFITS OF TIMESHARE

The community benefits of timeshare

Timeshare benefits the surrounding communities in a number of ways. It provides new uses for redundant buildings linked to the reclamation of derelict land. Langdale in the English Lake District is an example, where the resort is based on a converted watermill, gunpowder works and caravan site. Because of the need for developers to sell units (rather than merely renting them), resorts usually have high standards of construction and landscaping and are blended into the area, often using local materials. They have extensive leisure facilities attracting ownership from the local population, and the multiple ownership concept for each unit reduces the demand for second homes in attractive rural areas. (The problems created by second and vacation home ownership have been discussed in Laws, 1995.)

The economic benefits of timeshare

The following sections summarize a number studies on the impacts of timeshare resorts, highlighting their economic consequences. They have created additional spending in the area, and consequently created employment opportunities through direct and indirect multiplier effects, spread more evenly through the year than the typically peaked hotel seasonality.

Timeshare in the Canary Islands

Studies of timeshare in the Canary Islands have been carried out for the industry by Ernst & Young in 1985 and by Ragatz & Associates in 1995. In 1990, there were 85 resorts with a total of 7985 rooms (completed or planned) – this represented a total investment in construction of £373 million. A further £443 million was spent in the islands promoting and advertising the resorts and resulted in 239 550 households purchasing timeshare property there. With an average party size of 2.5 persons, the report concluded that 598 875 timeshare visitors travelled to the Canary Islands in 1990. Table 8.11 shows the pattern of their spending.

Spending and jobs in Britain

A survey by Ernst & Young in 1991 found that 42 000 timeshare holidays are taken annually in Britain, generating about £30 million of expenditure. Table 8.12 shows how this was calculated. This reported level of spending was sufficient to support 1500 full-time jobs. Overall, the industry created an additional 13 400 jobs through resort purchases, and the report projected the equivalent of 50 000 full-time jobs in Britain by year 2000.

Table 8.11 Average spending in the Canary Islands by timeshare families (1989)

	Average spent (£)	% budget
Car rental	111.75	19
Tours, sightseeing	78.13	13
Gifts	81.13	14
Postcards	3.29	1
Self-catering	120.85	21
Eating out	186.63	32
Total	£582.23	

Source: Ernst & Young (1991) cited by ETF (1994).

Table 8.12 Calculating the value of timeshare expenditure in Britain

Annual cost	£227
Travel	£35
Expenditure on site	£133
Expenditure off site	£319
Total individual family expenditure	£714
Number of timeshare holidays	42 000
Approximate total value	£30 million

Source: Ernst & Young (1991), cited by EFT (1994).

The significance of timeshare in Malta

A study in Malta found that timeshare contrasted in important ways with the island's hotel sector. Timeshare had significantly higher occupancy levels, as well as year round occupancy. At 70% occupancy of 574 timeshare apartments by two persons, this is equivalent to 293 000 visitors, that is nearly 30% of Malta's tourist arrivals (Dean, 1993).

Return visits and length of stay

Other surveys have indicated that timeshare owners express the intention to return to their 'home' resort about twice as often as vacationers who do not own timeshare there. Timeshare ownership also encourages the spending of longer vacation time in the resort, a 34.4% increase being noted by Ragatz.

CONCLUSION

Timeshare is a new and rapidly developing sector of the holiday industry. It is unique in offering clients a financial stake in their future holidays through part ownership of vacation units. In addition to the normal benefits of tourism, timeshare also benefits destination areas in terms of an increased level of spending by timeshare visitors, greater length of stay, a more even spread of holidaytaking throughout the year, and a greater propensity to return. Generally, timeshare resorts are high-quality developments, thereby adding to the appeal of a destination.

However, the rapid growth of the sector coupled with the opportunities for developers and marketers to make fast profits from the sale of units has led to criticisms of the industry's sales methods and doubts about its long-term relationships with purchasers. These issues are being addressed in a number of ways, particularly by trade membership bodies which are seeking consensus for more ethical trading methods, and by the implementation of consumer protection methods through the introduction of new legislation.

Another approach is considered in the case study presented in Chapter 9 which examines the way timeshare exchange companies such as RCI add value to the initial purchase of timeshare, and their leadership roles in coordinating the industry and giving direction to its further development.

FURTHER READING

Bolwell, R. (1988) *Timesharing in Australia*, Paladin.

Irwin, R. (1991) *Time Share Properties: What Every Buyer Must Know*, McGraw.

Jenkins, C. (1994) *Practical Timeshare and Group Ownership*. Butterworth.

Office of Fair Trading (1990) *Timeshare*, OFT, London.

SUGGESTED EXERCISES

1. Interview several people who have attended timeshare presentations and critically evaluate the methods adopted. Interview others who own timeshare units and discuss their reasons for purchasing timeshare and their experiences of ownership.

2. Taking the role of a timeshare developer, draft a presentation to local councillors of the case for building a new resort in or near a national park such as the Lake District, contrasting its impact with those of second home ownership, caravan parks or hotels able to accommodate an equivalent number of visitors.

3. Interview the managers of hotels, tour operators and travel retailers and report on their views of the business opportunities and threats to them presented by timeshare.

9 RCI – adding value to the timeshare industry

The concluding chapter of this book takes the form of an extended case study based on RCI documents and conference presentations, and personal communications with Malcolm Wood, Head of Resort Services and Market Development, RCI UK and Ireland.

INTRODUCTION

The distinguishing feature of the timeshare holiday market is the opportunity it provides people to purchase an 'affordable interval of ownership' in high-quality holiday accommodation without the added burdens of full responsibility for the property. However, this implies a fixed location for future holidaytaking and contrasts with the general desire to visit new and exotic locations for one's vacation. Recognizing this conflict, specialist companies have been established which give additional value to timeshare owners by enabling them to exchange the weeks which they purchased in a specific resort for a similar period in an alternative resort.

In his introduction to a conference of timeshare industry leaders and resort managers in 1995, Malcolm Hewitt, then Managing Director of RCI UK & Ireland (Resort Condominiums International), stated firmly that '[our] business is about providing good holidays.' As this case shows, the company, which trades in the UK and throughout Europe simply as RCI, is in a unique position to provide coordination and a sense of direction to the many elements which make up the timeshare industry.

ORIGINS AND SCOPE OF TIMESHARE EXCHANGE

The exchange concept was introduced into timeshare in the 1970s in Florida, after the oil crisis caused the collapse of the market there for holiday condominiums. In response to a rapid fall in the outright sale of apartments, a modification was introduced to the contract allowing the sale of holiday homes by the week, so that one apartment could be sold 50 times, each of the owners being entitled to return for that week every year. (The remaining two weeks have traditionally been reserved for annual maintenance or longer-term upgrading by the property

Table 9.1 Distribution of RCI affiliated resorts, 1995

North America	1247
Europe	939
Africa	150
Latin America	410
Asia/Pacific	237

Source: RCI audited data.

managers.) Subsequently, it became apparent that Americans were not attracted by the idea of returning to the same hotel year after year, and observing this, a private swap system for condominiums was established by Jon and Cristel DeHaan from their home in Indianapolis. This early scheme enabled a network of 12 friends to exchange weeks in each other's apartments, located in Colorado, Florida and Indianapolis.

In 1974, the couple widened the scheme and put it on a business footing by founding Resort Condominiums International (RCI), a privately owned corporation. This took the form of a club which anyone purchasing good quality timeshare could join in order to exchange the weeks they owned in specific resorts for weeks in other approved resorts. RCI took responsibility for recruiting resort developers into their exchange system, and undertook to organize the exchanges for owners. (A competitor, Interval International (II), was established in 1976.) Meanwhile, in Europe, timeshare developments were begun in Scotland, France, Italy and Scandinavia. Some of these resorts were signed up by RCI, thus introducing an international dimension to the menu of exchange possibilities for members. This feature has become increasingly important. Table 9.1 shows the spatial distribution of RCI affiliated resorts.

Similarly, the majority of member families were American (1 074 476) or European (516 845). Of the total 1350 timeshare resorts in Europe in 1995, 939 were affiliated to RCI, an estimated 350 to Interval International, 45 to Hapimag and 23 to Holiday Property Bond while only 70 resorts were unaffiliated. While RCI organized 450 000 European exchanges, II accounted for 60 000. RCI's membership had grown every year, rising from about half a million in 1986 to one million in 1990. In 1995, there were about 4 000 timeshare resorts worldwide, and RCI's 1996/97 brochure offered a choice approaching 3000 affiliated resorts in 80 countries. In 1995 it organised 1 562 594 exchanges for a total of 2 048 804 members worldwide (RCI data).

MEMBERSHIP AND MEMBERSHIP SERVICES

People who purchase timeshare at affiliated resorts are enrolled by the developer who includes their initial period of membership in the purchase price. Subsequently members pay subscriptions for one, three or five years when they come to renew their initial terms. This enables them to exchange weeks they own for similar accommodation in other affiliated properties. It has been pointed out that timeshare is an international business; for example, the purchasers at some Spanish resorts come from many European countries. The timeshare sales report which RCI receives from its affiliated resorts includes a note of the client's native language, so that when a Belgian family purchases a week in a Spanish resort, they will receive a welcome pack within two weeks from RCI's Brussels office. Their pack, and ensuing correspondence, will be in Flemish, one of 18 European languages (and about 30 worldwide) in which RCI regularly communicates with its members.

Members receive a Directory containing descriptions of all resorts and details of the exchange system. In 1995, the 380 pages of the Directory listed some 2700 resorts. Since less than 25% of the pages and relatively few resorts change each year, RCI provides members with a 100 page supplement to the directory annually. Changes result from the addition of newly recruited resorts, the occasional withdrawal of affiliation status, and from the regular upgrading of resort or accommodation facilities. The European directory is printed every two years, and members also receive a quarterly magazine with articles of interest, information on the latest resorts to become affiliates and a variety of special offers.

The Member Benefits Handbook provides details of exclusive worldwide deals with leading airlines. The flights offered are on airlines (whether charter or scheduled) selected for their quality of in-flight service and the convenience of their schedules rather than lowest fares, thereby ensuring consistent quality standards in each element of the exchange system. RCI sold 165 000 flight seats in 1995. At one time, RCI also offered telex information on current flight prices to its resort areas. However, although company research showed that members were using this information service, not enough bookings were generated by this medium to justify the cost (over £100 000).

In addition to the accommodation exchanges which form the core of its business, RCI offers its members related services such as air travel, airport parking, or cross channel ferries, motor breakdown cover, and overnight stays en route to European resorts. RCI also offers the services of a tour operator to its members, providing cruise offers, city breaks and other packages which are likely to appeal to them, as indicated in Table 9.2. The scale of these activities is such that in 1994 the number of travellers buying RCI's products accounted for about 9% of the UK overseas inclusive holiday market (Haylock, 1995).

With the rapid growth of timeshare exchange, RCI's policy has been to open an office in each country when the size of the existing membership and the market potential make it financially attractive to have a presence in the local market. Previously this has been done without drawing up a formal business plan, although in the case of their Moscow office opening in 1996, a full feasibility study was carried out because of the complex local trading and political conditions. With

Table 9.2 Services provided by RCI
to its members

- Exchanges
- Organized holidays
  - concert breaks
  - great train journeys
- US phone cards
- Holiday insurance
- Sightseeing tours
- US accommodation vouchers
- Avis car hire
- Emergency contact phone number
- Cruises

Source: RCI.

11 000 member families by the end of 1995, it had become apparent that a large number of Russian families were potential timeshare purchasers, having capital (sometimes held overseas) and desiring to travel outside the old USSR's boundaries. By the end of 1995, RCI had established offices in 70 countries, and others were being planned for South America and the Far East.

THE EXCHANGE CONCEPT

RCI's core function is similar to the role of a banker, with members depositing and withdrawing 'exchange values'. Members deposit the weeks which they do not wish to use at their own resort into a pool of space, which RCI calls 'Spacebank', a term to which the company holds copyright. The trading value of each week is then calculated on the basis of the size and location of their unit, the season, the history of demand for the interval, and the length of time between when the deposit is made and the start date of the holiday. A computer search then matches the value of a week deposited against what is available at those resorts and times which the member requested. The result of this search procedure may be a match or the offer of an alternative, and a booking can be confirmed immediately the member accepts. Alternatively, an exchange request which was not fulfilled is kept on a 'confirmation pending' status, as what was originally requested may become available later. The exchange value of the week deposited is set at the time of deposit, and does not change no matter how long it takes for that deposit to become a confirmed exchange. The trading power reduces, however, the later that the member leaves it to deposit his or her week in relation to the date of travel required. At the 45-day margin, it falls into the late exchange category when all members can access it, irrespective of the trading power of their own deposit.

Exchange requests can be returned to members (i.e. refused) if they fail to deposit vacation time in the Spacebank, fail to pay exchange fees or do not submit it within minimum time requirements. More than

97% of 'properly submitted exchange requests, including alternatives' are fulfilled, although not all members receive an exchange into the resorts which they requested. In 1993, the number of exchanges represented 75% of the membership. Some members take more than one holiday, and in any one year a significant proportion of RCI members decide to return to their own resort.

The concept of exchange trading power or value embraces several elements including season, the size of a unit 'most easily expressed as numbers of bed spaces', the quality of the particular resort and the demand for it. RCI divides holiday time into three seasons, for example a 13 week high season, 18 week shoulders and a low season of 19 weeks (although the seasons and their relative lengths vary greatly from one country to another). The allocation of seasons to a particular resort reflects the popularity of its location at different times of the year. For resorts in the Mediterranean, the 'red' season stretches from May to September, whereas in a skiing centre, the 'red' or high period coincides with the skiing season there. These three seasons are further divided by RCI to reflect the higher trading power of weeks available during the school holidays.

The purchase price for a week's timeshare in a particular resort reflects this seasonal structure both because of the seasonal variation in the demand for the property and also because ownership of a week in the most expensive and sought after time, the 'red season', allows an exchange into any season. Similarly, the 'white' or shoulder season owners can exchange into 'white' or trade down into the 'blue' (regular) times, while those who own 'blue' weeks can normally only exchange into other resorts during the least popular 'blue' season. However, another sophistication built into the exchange system is a late exchange facility which overrides the season banding. This provides members with access to higher value resorts and dates for any week deposited for an exchange which has not been taken up by other RCI members 45 days prior to departure.

Another major factor in valuing an exchange is the size of the unit offered, and RCI evaluates this in two ways. The maximum number of people which each unit can accommodate is the starting point. This is based on a count of bed spaces, including any roll-aways and sofa beds in the unit. Consideration is also given to the number who can enjoy privacy in it. This is defined as 'direct access to a bathroom without passing through another sleeping area such as a sitting room with a convertible sofa bed'. The concept of trading power encompasses both of these aspects and is calculated for each individual unit in a resort.

Spacebank

Given the large number of interval owners, the high proportion who make an exchange each year and the range of resorts, units and time intervals on offer, RCI depends on real-time access by each of its international offices to a sophisticated computer system to enable fair exchanges to be arranged rapidly. Poon has pointed out that 'the very concept of timeshare, without technology, is inflexible.' She argues:

> An owner would be committed to spending his or her holidays in the same week each year in the same room in one resort. However, through the use of computers and communications technology, it is possible to facilitate . . . exchange(s) amongst timesharing vacationers. Information technology has thus increased the flexibility, choice and variety with which timeshare vacations can be produced, marketed and consumed.
>
> (Poon, 1993)

RCI's system consists of two IBM AS400s in the UK, connected to 16 European offices and to the IBM 3090 mainframe in Indianapolis. It contains details of all affiliated resorts and their accommodation, and members' records, as well as providing links to standard travel industry CRS systems whereby travel arrangements can be provided for members at the time they book an exchange.

Special offers

The size and variety of the entire exchange market inevitably leads to a number of weeks and resorts being less popular, and RCI copes with this difficulty by producing special offers to soak up otherwise surplus weeks. Bonus weeks provide members with the opportunity of taking a holiday in selected resorts without the need to deposit their own time, thereby encouraging second or additional holidays. This facility has been available for many years to some parts of the US and Venezuela. Bonus weeks have also been used to increase familiarity with less well known areas. For example, members wishing to holiday in Mexico and South Africa in 1995 were offered a 2 for 1 arrangement which doubled the standard holiday period available for the exchanger's deposit.

ALTERNATIVE EXCHANGE SYSTEMS

RCI is the major player in the exchange industry, but its competitors provide alternatives to its exchange trading value and Spacebank system. Typically the approach is that of a holiday club. These are either companies with their own resorts or which rent inventory. Clients buy points with an exchange value, calculated on season, unit size and location. This gives more flexibility in access, allowing weekend stays and other combinations in contrast to RCI's week-long exchanges, and it has the advantage of simplifying the need to balance inventory and its allocation. However, the points-based system provides a 'first come, first served' solution for clients, and it depends on a level of use smaller than the total exchange capacity. Typically, 10 to 15% of space is left as a reserve to ensure sufficient availability, and a further safeguard for points club members is that the clubs have to produce a disclosure document which states what proportion of space is available for use by members.

Colin Collins, Group Marketing Director for Global Group, speaking at the RCI New Horizons conference in Istanbul, commented that: 'The public want more choice. They don't want to be tied to fixed or floating weeks . . . Some wish to add part of a week onto another week and make a 10- or 11-day holiday.' However, splitting occupancy into finer time slices also increases the costs of operating a resort since clients have to be checked in and out more frequently, accommodation has to be prepared for each newly arriving set of guests and the increased complexity of bookings imposes more demands on the reservations system.

RCI'S POSITION IN THE TIMESHARE INDUSTRY

The creation of opportunities for holiday exchanges enhances the satisfaction obtained by timeshare owners from their purchases, and represents one of the key values added by RCI to the timeshare sector's product. Another contribution is the leadership role which the company takes amongst the industry's member organizations, thereby creating an effective network as illustrated in Figure 9.1.

RCI, although a large player in the timeshare industry, does not have direct control over the core elements, the resorts. However, the demand for its exchange service is derived from timeshare ownership and this has two consequences. Members expect high standards of accommodation, amenities and facilities from the resort into which they exchange and RCI monitors their satisfaction with each exchange. Secondly, a resort developers' primary need is to sell ownership of the units and increasingly this is determined by the exchange value attached to them.

A RESORT MARKETING PROBLEM

One example of the difficulties which can occur is the development in 1991 within Spain of a domestic ownership market. Previously, holidays in the main Spanish resorts had been purchased from overseas, typically by residents of the colder, Northern European industrial countries. However, Spaniards' holiday behaviour is characterized by a very strong August peak demand, and when the sale of timeshare to Spanish families began to take off, the marketing companies claimed that any week bought in a Spanish resort could be exchanged for an August week. Many Spanish member families bought on the basis of wishing to go away in August to resorts in their own country. Of the 20 000 families who enrolled during one year in RCI, 19 000 requested August weeks, and there was insufficient time available. What had

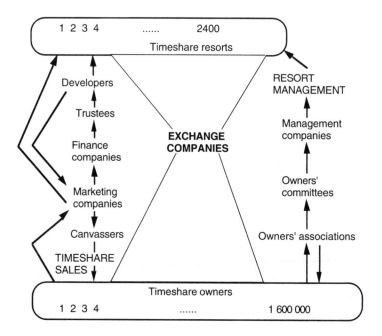

Figure 9.1 Elements in the timeshare industry.

happened was that the resort developers, with whom RCI had a contractual relationship, had engaged a marketing company to sell timeshare weeks which included membership of RCI. However, RCI had no contractual relationship with the marketer or its claims. Its influence over the marketer was via the developer, once it became aware of the problem.

COMMUNICATING WITH INDUSTRY PARTNERS

RCI publishes a monthly Review for the industry dealing with current topics of interest, and stages an annual European conference, thus acting as a forum for the exchange of views and discussion between all sectors of the timeshare industry. In 1995 the annual conference was held in Istanbul, and attracted delegates representing timeshare resort developers, vendors, trustees, finance houses and resale companies. The programme, entitled 'New Horizons', was introduced in the following way:

> More than ever before, the timeshare industry must adapt itself to change: changing markets, changing laws, changing public perceptions. The days of quick sales and instant return are gone for good: long-term thinking, innovative and creative ways of doing business

are the order of the day. All sides of the industry must expand their horizons.

The keynote address was given by Jan Carlzon, former Head of the Scandinavian Airlines Group and author of *Moments of Truth*. His presentation focused on delivering first-class service in the global marketplace.

MANAGING QUALITY STANDARDS IN THE TIMESHARE INDUSTRY

A characteristic of tourism, which is also a significant factor in the timeshare sector, is the fragmented nature of an industry which is composed of many independent and often quite small companies. One potential consequence is the difficulty of setting and maintaining consistent standards of service and quality amongst the 4000 timeshare resorts: the exchange companies have a particularly prominent role in this respect.

RCI resort recognition scheme

RCI's claim to be the major force for quality in the timeshare industry stems from the effort it puts into ensuring fairness in their exchanges for its two million strong membership. Since exchange is the key benefit which RCI offers its members, it must ensure that they receive accommodation of equal standard to the week which they deposited in the timeshare exchange bank. This is not to say that all resorts are expected to provide near-identical facilities: the Directory encompasses a wide range and style of timeshare resorts. These include converted country houses and castles, hotels in city centres and purpose-built, new resorts in country, mountain and seaside locations throughout the world. Table 9.3 gives details of the facilities required of RCI's affiliate resorts. This varies according to their location, while additional features are expected of Gold Crown Resorts.

RCI does not evaluate a resort as such other than to offer the Resort Recognition Awards for the top two tiers, namely Gold Crown Resorts and Resorts of International Distinction. The majority of resorts are standard resorts, and these are not evaluated except that the way in which their trading power is calculated by computer takes into account the quality rating of each resort by members exchanging into it and the overall demand for it.

A key factor in RCI's success in promoting consistent quality standards amongst timeshare resorts is that the resort recognition scheme is entirely driven by members' comments. RCI sends satisfaction questionnaires to every member's home during the holiday. It received back

Table 9.3 Facilities required of affiliated resorts

Beach resort	Downhill ski resort	Urban resort	Regional resort
REQUIRED Beach area – 1 mile Pool – on site	Ski area –5 miles	Cultural event – 5 miles Urban shopping – 5 miles	Pool – on site Amenities pack – 1 item
ADDITIONAL 3 of the following	4 of the following	3 of the following	3 of the following
Cultural event – 10 miles Entertainment – 5 miles Golf, 18+ 5 miles Grocery shopping – 3 miles Health club – on site Public parking – half mile Tennis – 1 mile Sauna/whirlpool/steamroom – on site	Cultural event – 10 miles Entertainment – 5 miles Golf, 18+ 5 miles Grocery shopping – 3 miles Health club – on site Pool – on site Public parking – half mile Tennis – 1 mile Sauna/whirlpool/steamroom – on site	Entertainment – 5 miles Golf, 18+ 5 miles Grocery shopping – 3 miles Health club – on site Pool – on site Public parking – half mile Tennis – 1 mile Sauna/whirlpool/steamroom – on site	Cultural event – 10 miles Entertainment – 5 miles Golf, 18+ 5 miles Grocery shopping – 3 miles Health club – on site Public parking – half mile Tennis – 1 mile Sauna/whirlpool/steamroom – on site

Also considered:
additional unique amenities, e.g. horseback riding, water activities, etc.

Hotel unit	Studio unit	1-bedroom unit	2-bedroom unit
REQUIRED	REQUIRED	REQUIRED	REQUIRED
Appropriate heating, ventilation and air conditioning Telephone Television	Appropriate heating, ventilation and air conditioning Telephone Television	Appropriate heating, ventilation and air conditioning Telephone Television	Appropriate heating, ventilation and air conditioning Telephone Television
ADDITIONAL 2 of the following	2 of the following	3 of the following	3 of the following
Alarm clock/clock radio Balcony/terrace Iron/ironing board available Oversize bath Stereo Video recorder/player or cable	Alarm clock/clock radio Balcony/terrace Iron/ironing board available Oversize bath Stereo Video recorder/player or cable	Alarm clock/clock radio Balcony/terrace Iron/ironing board available Electric sweeper/vacuum Washer and drier Oversize bath Stereo Video recorder/player or cable	Alarm clock/clock radio Balcony/terrace Iron/ironing board available Electric sweeper/vacuum Washer and drier Oversize bath Stereo Video recorder/player or cable

Kitchen
Detailed requirements increasing with the size of unit.
For example, a 1 or 2 bedroom unit is required to have:
2 or 4 burner stove top, conventional oven or microwave, full or mini refrigerator, matching table service, and 3 of the following:
mini refrigerator, full refrigerator with freezer, conventional oven, microwave oven, kitchen grill, dishwasher, trash compactor, toaster, coffee maker, tea service, blender/mixer, food processor, electric can opener, electric citrus juicer, kettle, ice maker, service bar, kitchen courtesy kit, wetbar, room service.

Bathroom
Minimum size required, increasing with occupancy rating of unit.

The units and fitments, for example cabinets, counter tops, upholstery and window coverings, are required to be in good condition.

Source: RCI.

more than a quarter of a million comment cards, a 60% response rate in 1994. The company's literature states:

> Working in partnership with resort affiliates, RCI is committed to strengthening the resort timeshare industry by ensuring that timeshare owners enjoy quality holiday experiences. Towards that end, we have sought to affiliate resorts that adhere to high standards of product quality and service delivery.

Table 9.4 indicates the five major factors which each exchanger is asked to evaluate and shows the minimum score which an affiliate resort is required to attain under each heading to gain the Gold Crown status. Resort recognition is significant in another way, as it helps timeshare marketing companies to sell weeks since their exchange potential is an increasingly important factor in the client's decision to purchase timeshare at a particular resort.

Table 9.4 Members' resort evaluation criteria

	Minimum score required (out of 5)
Quality of unit	4.2
Housekeeping	3.9
Maintenance	3.9
Hospitality	4
Check-in	3.9

Source: RCI.

Gold Crown resorts

To honour those resort affiliates which consistently exceed these high standards and provide exceptional holiday experiences to both owners and exchange guests, RCI has created two levels of distinguished award: 'Gold Crown Resorts' and 'Resorts of International Distinction'.

RCI Gold Crown Resorts represent 'the highest level of excellence in resort accommodation and hospitality'. Some 36 000 of the total 180 000 UK timeshare member families own space in Gold Crown Resorts either in the UK or abroad. The documentation circulated to resort managers states that:

> Recipients . . . will have met stringent standards in five RCI Member Comment Card categories over a 12-month period. Resorts meeting these standards will then undergo an independent evaluation of its resort amenities, unit amenities/interiors, and guest services facilities.

Table 9.5 shows the additional range of criteria required for an affiliate resort to attain the highest category of award – the Gold Crown.

Table 9.5 Criteria required of Gold Crown resorts

- Emergency (non-medical) – 24 hours a day
- Front desk – 8 hours a day on site
- Laundry facilities or service – 7 hours a day on site
- Maid or linen service – daily or mid week

And 2 of the following:

- Activities coordinator/concierge on site
- Equipment rental on site
- Health club arrangements off site within 5 miles
- Multilingual staff
- Restaurant within half mile
- Security on site

Source: RCI.

Recognition and quality control

It is a basic tenet of the exchange system that timeshare owners expect to be able to bank their weeks with RCI in order to benefit from an exchange to another resort. But if standards have slipped at their own resort and it has not been possible for RCI to obtain improvements through negotiation, the company can impose various restrictions on the resort. These include barring incoming or outgoing exchanges until the problem has been remedied. The ultimate sanction is to disaffiliate a resort which fails to maintain acceptable standards. This is a real threat, but the computer logging of members' comments flags up problems at an early stage. These are notified to resort managers and this stimulates remedial action. As an example, a resort in Malaga has had consistently low card ratings regarding unit quality and resort maintenance. An RCI manager made a thorough inspection of the resort and produced a list of requirements to avoid disaffiliation. The facilities at the resort were subsequently upgraded, but it was agreed that some problems could not be resolved as suggested due to structural considerations, and alternative action was taken for these matters.

INFLUENCING FUTURE DEVELOPMENTS IN THE TIMESHARE INDUSTRY

Timeshare is characterized by ever-improving product specifications. Each newly built resort incorporates additional features and the latest kitchen, entertainment and activity facilities since their developers are driven by the need to sell weeks quickly in order to recover the capital invested. Recently opened resorts provide microwave ovens, sophisticated entertainment facilities in apartments and well equipped fitness centres amongst their many other amenities. As a result, although timeshare in Europe is less than 20 years old, and much of what was built in the beginning was of a higher standard than virtually all other types of holiday accommodation available at the time, there is a need for older products to be improved to meet increasing customer expectations. This investment in improvements is largely driven by their owners wish to retain their timeshare exchange trading power in the evolving market conditions, because without continuous improvements they risk slippage in the relative value of their exchange. Timeshare properties, as a result of the need to sell the property, must incorporate the best quality amenities, and therefore accommodation and site standards in the sector tend to improve faster than amongst the quality self-catering villas. This arises from the key distinguishing feature of the timeshare sector of the tourism industry – although villas and hotels also invest in improvements, guests have no real stake in the property as they are renting rather than owning rooms or apartments.

RCI's detailed knowledge and understanding of timesharers' holiday requirements can also form the platform for an advisory service for future resort developments. The critical issues for developers are how to optimize the size and configuration of resorts (the mix of one, two or larger bedroom apartments), and the design of infrastructure and amenities. RCI's understanding of these issues is based on its continuing analysis of its members' booking preferences and their views as expressed through surveys, and is enshrined in the specifications for the award of Gold Crown.

A consequence of the expanding number of resorts coupled with the improvement of others is the trend towards ownership of multiple weeks in different resorts. One in three British owners and one in five Europeans have subsequently bought additional timeshare weeks. The pattern is for each additional purchase to be of higher grade units in terms of exchange value than that previously bought, thus confirming the significance to purchasers of the exchange value of the timeshare concept.

INDUSTRY LEADERSHIP

Against the background of a new and rapidly growing sector of tourism characterized by many small organizations and a high degree of adverse publicity attracted by a minority of elements, RCI has taken the high ground in identifying common interests and coordinating the strategic development of the timeshare industry. It is only able to achieve this by acting in partnership with resort developers, resort managers and owners' committees, and by providing a platform through conferences for discussion between the industry's stakeholders.

RCI stages annual conferences for resort developers, financiers and management companies. The company regards these as a way in which it can fulfil its responsibility to owners through teamwork to attain the efficient running of all resorts affiliated to its exchange network, thereby endeavouring to ensure its members' satisfaction whatever resort their exchange takes them to.

THE CLUB ELECTA CONFERENCE

One of the key issues emerging in the mid 1990s is the future management of resorts as they become fully sold and the responsibility passes to the timeshare owners. RCI established a club to provide a forum for owners' committee members, Club Electa, and in 1995 hosted the first conference at its European headquarters for owners who are members of their resorts' management committees.

During a weekend of intensive technical presentations they heard expert views on the legal and financial responsibilities which this role implies, and were also introduced to the scope and philosophy of RCI's own operations. Introducing the conference, the Managing Director of RCI UK said that the objective was 'to ensure the continuity of quality holidays on which RCI's business is based, through responsibility towards timeshare owners to be ensured through teamwork by all industry members'. He defined RCI's approach to business as based on five factors:

- delivering the promise of high-quality resorts portrayed in its brochure;
- listening to its members and responding to them;
- investing in sales improvements;
- investing in service improvements;
- investing in the people, infrastructure and technology which enable RCI to serve its members effectively.

One indication of RCI's ability to deliver its promise was the low rate of complaints by its members: only 1.5% had complained about any aspect of their holiday or exchange, while ABTA received an average of eight complaints for each one hundred holidays sold by its member companies. RCI also wanted to achieve a seamless service for its members with consistent service standards delivered by all organizations contributing elements to their holiday, and it aimed to achieve this goal through training and by a reasoned approach to the margins which it earned.

During the conference, Club Electa members were invited to adopt a different approach to their ownership of timeshare intervals: what had begun as the purchase of a 'holiday week' had taken on aspects of a 'second job' as their minimum responsibility was to ensure that the standards in their resort did not slip or that they were improved, thereby increasing the value of all owners' investments. It is a stipulation in some timeshare resort sales contacts that, after a proportion of the resort is sold, the owners would form an owners' committee. The constitution of many timeshare resorts, particularly those selling to the British market, have a provision made for the formation of an owners' committee, but in several other European countries there is no process for the individual owners to gain eventual control of their resort. A study by RCI indicated that about 150 out of some 900 resorts in Europe had owners' committees in 1995. Yet each had to establish its own methods of working in the best interests of the many individuals who had purchased ownerships. The challenge was about financial planning, with an adequate provision for long-term improvement balanced against owners' wishes to minimize their expenses.

STAFF POLICY

Although the exchange system depends on computerization, the variety of holidays, resorts and units on offer means that RCI's members rely on its staff to obtain the best use of the company's range of services. As an example of this, a special helpline was established to provide additional advice to new members. The philosophy behind this investment in service enhancement was that a member's first experience of RCI must be good. Experienced staff were allocated to the special desk and dedicated phone lines, spending time with novice clients to ensure that they obtained the exchanges which they desired and explaining the finer points of RCI's services. Between February and December 1994, the service dealt with 20 000 callers. On the basis of its success, the new member support was further developed and extended to help newly recruited resorts and developers.

RCI's own staffing policy is designed to ensure a fair effective resourcing of personnel taking account of current employment legislation and equal opportunity policy. It has set out a detailed procedure for recruitment and for training 'to encourage the maximum utilization of employees' potential'. This is achieved within a partnership between the individual and her/his immediate manager, supported by the Human Resource department through the provision of training services and specialist advice.

To encourage the highest standards of professionalism in its affiliated resorts, RCI introduced a Resort Recognition Programme in 1991, and followed this in 1995 with a Resort Employee Recognition Programme for staff who have 'gone that extra mile'. This is open 'to all operational staff, regardless of rank or role'. In a letter to each Resort Manager, RCI's Managing Director invited them to nominate one employee for each of six categories – housekeeping staff and porters, reception and reservations staff, back-office staff, bar, restaurant and kitchen staff, maintenance staff and gardeners, and leisure care staff including hairdressers and beauticians. RCI's Board of Directors then choose an overall winner for each of the categories based on a résumé submitted by the Resort Managers explaining why staff had been nominated. The overall winner was presented with a two-week exchange holiday for two to any European or US resort, including flights, at a gala dinner during the December 1995 UK conference. A keepsake was presented to the six category winners, and a certificate was awarded to all of the team members in their category. RCI's Managing Director stated in the letter: 'We at RCI are very enthusiastic about the new scheme. We feel that it will motivate staff to strive to improve standards, which can only be of benefit to the industry as a whole.'

SUGGESTED EXERCISES

1. Interview timeshare owners who participate in exchanges and report on their reasons for so doing.
2. Taking the role of the representative of a timeshare exchange company, outline to the managers of a new timeshare resort developer and its marketer the advantages of joining its scheme.
3. Evaluate the leadership role of the timeshare industry taken by the exchange companies and consider why no equivalent power has yet been exercised by any member of the inclusive holiday industry system.

Glossary

		Related terms
Courier	The tour operator's staff member who escorts holidaymakers during a multi-destination itinerary.	Guide, resort representative
Client	A person (or group of people) buying an inclusive holiday or experiencing their holiday.	Holidaymaker
Destination	The location in which holiday experiences occur	Resort
Ground handling agent (GHA)	A destination-based organization providing services to a tour operator or charter airline and to their clients.	
Guide	A destination-based person who accompanies holidaymakers during local excursions and who interprets aspects of local culture and other points of interest.	Courier, resort representative
Holidaymaker	A person experiencing an inclusive holiday.	
Holiday shop	A retailer specializing in the sale of inclusive holidays and certain allied products such as holiday insurance.	Travel agent
Inclusive tour (IT)	A holiday organized for clients by a tour operator, consisting of travel and accommodation together with other destination benefits, sometimes including several destinations.	Inclusive holiday, packaged holiday
Independent holidaymaker	A person who buys some elements of a holiday from a tour operator (usually the air travel) and makes his or her own arrangements for activities during the destination stay.	Unpackaged holiday
Leisure traveller	A person travelling and staying away from home for leisure, including independent travellers and those whose holiday arrangements have been organized by and purchased from a tour operator.	Tourist
Origin country (or origin market)	The country where holidaymakers reside or in which the tour operator is based.	Destination
Principal	The hotel companies and charter airlines from which tour operators purchase service to package for resale to their holidaymaker clients. Also the tour operators for whom travel retailers act as agents when selling holidays.	
Resort	Alternative term for destination	Destination
Resort representative	A person employed in a destination by a tour operator to liaise with local organizations and to manage the arrangements for their clients' stay and activities.	Courier, guide
Tour operator	A company specializing in packaging the elements of inclusive holidays for sale to clients.	
Tourist	The general term for travellers, including those on business or family visits as well as leisure travellers.	Holidaymaker, leisure traveller
Travel agent (or travel retailer)	A retailer specializing in selling travel services on behalf of principals.	Holiday shop

References and select bibliography

ABTA (1994) *Members Handbook*, Columbus Press, London.

Ansoff, H.I. (9168) *Corporate Strategy*, Penguin Books, London.

Ashworth, G. and Goodall, B. (eds) (1990) *Marketing Tourism Places*, Routledge, London.

Asseal, H. (1987) *Consumer Behaviour and Marketing Action*, Kent Publications, Boston, Mass.

Atherton, T. (1994) 'Package holidays: legal aspects', *Tourism Management*, Vol. 15, No. 3, pp. 193–9.

Bailey, M. (1988) 'Tour wholesaling in Japan, Hong Kong and Taiwan', *Travel and Tourism Analyst*, No. 4, pp. 57–74.

Baker, M. (1985) *Tourism for All*, English Tourist Board, London.

Bathurst, (1995) 'Sick drunks and rock 'n' roll', *Observer Review*, 26 November, p. 11.

Baumol, W. and Willig, R. (1981) *Fixed Costs, Sunk Costs, Entry Barriers and Sustainability of Monopoly*; Quarterly Journal of Economics, August, p. 405–431.

Beaver, A. (1993) *Mind Your Own Travel Business: A Manual of Retail Travel Practice*, 3 vols, 3rd edn, Allan Beaver, Radlett, Herts.

Berry, T.H. (1991) *Managing the Total Quality Transformation*, McGraw-Hill, New York.

Bolwell, R. (1988) *Timesharing in Australia*, Paladin Publishing Pty Ltd, Sydney.

Boniface, P. and Fowler, P. (1993) *Heritage and Tourism in the Global Villag*, Routledge, London.

Bonn, M.A. and Brand, R.R. (1995) 'Identifying market potential: the application of brand development indexing to pleasure travel', *Journal of Travel Research*, Fall, No. 2, pp. 31–5.

Brendon, P. (1990) *Thomas Cook, 150 Years of Popular Tourism*, Secker and Warburg, London.

Bucklin, L. (1967) 'The economic structure of channels of distribution', in Mallen, B.E. (ed.), *The Marketing Channel*, Wiley, New York.

Bull, A. (1991) *The Economics of Travel and Tourism*, Longman Cheshire, London.

Burkhart, A.J. and Medlik, S. (1974) *Tourism, Past, Present and Future*, Heinemann, London.

Burns, P.M. and Holden, A. (1995) *Tourism: A New perspective*, Prentice Hall, Hemel Hempstead.

Buzzel, R.D. and Gale, B.T. (1987) *The PIMS Principles*, Free Press, New York.

Bywater, M. (1992) *The European Tour Operator Industry*, EUI Special Report 2141, London.

CAA (1994) *ATOL Business*, Issue 5, December.

Carlzon, J. (1989) *Moments of Truth*, Harper & Row, New York.

Carr, H. (ed.) (1993) *Travel Trade Gazette 40th Anniversary Supplement*, Morgan Grampion, London.

Carter, J. (1985) *Chandler's Travels*, Quiller Press, London.

Checkland, P. and Scholes, J. (1990) *Soft Systems Methodology in Action*, John Wiley & Sons, Chichester.

Chisnall, P.M. (1985) *Marketing: A Behavioural Analysis*, McGraw-Hill, Maidenhead.

Christopher, M., Payne, A. and Ballantyne, D. (1991) *Relationship Marketing: Bringing Quality, Customer Service and Marketing Together*, Butterworth-Heinemann, Oxford.

Cockrell, N. (1987) 'Credit cards, cash and travel vouchers in Europe', *Travel and Tourism Analyst*, No. 4, pp. 38–48.

Cohen, J.B. (1986) 'Involvement, separating the state from its causes and effects', quoted in Wilkie, W.L., *Consumer Behaviour*, John Wiley & Sons, Chichester.

Cooney, M. (1995) 'Airtours plots a course for a growing market', *Travel Weekly*, March, p. 6.

Cooper, C., Fletcher, J., Gilbert, D. and Wanhill, S. (1993) *Tourism Principles and Practice*, Pitman, London.

Corke, J. (1988) *Tourism Law*, Elm Publications, Huntingdon.

Cowell, D. (1986) *The Marketing of Services*, Heinemann, London.

Davidson, J. (1989) 'Strife begins at 40 for the jaded package', *Sunday Times*, 3 September.

Davidson, W.E., Sweeney, D.J. and Stampfl, R.W. (1988) *Retailing Management*, 6th edn, John Wiley & Sons, New York.

DCTPB (1993) *Dubai Tourism Survey, 1992/93*, Dryland Consultants, Dubai.

Dean, P. (1993) *Timeshare Opportunities For The Hotel Sector*, Travel and Tourism Analyst, Vol. 4, pp. 74–94.

Doganis, R. (1985) *Flying Off Course: The Economics of International Airline*, Allen & Unwin, London.

Doganis, R. (1992) *The Airport Business*, Routledge, London.

Donnelly, J.H. Jr (1976) 'Marketing intermediaries in channels of distribution for services', *Journal of Marketing*, January, pp. 55–70.

Downes, J. (1993) 'Legal liabiliteis in the European travel trade: the EC Package Travel Directive', *Travel and Tourism Analyst*, No. 1, pp. 81–97.

Duke, C.R. and Persia, M.A. (1993) 'The effects of distribution channel level on tour purchasing attributes and information sources', in Uysal, M. and Fesenmaier, D.R. (eds), *Communication and Channel Systems in Tourism Marketing*, Haworth press, Binghampton, NY.

Echtner, C. and Brent Ritchie, J. (1993) 'The measurement of destination image: and empirical assessment', *Journal of Travel Research*, Vol. XXXI, No. 4, pp. 3–13.

Edgington, J.M. and Edgington, M.A. (1990) *Ecology, Recreation and Tourism*, Cambridge University Press, Cambridge.

Embacher, E. and Buttle, F. (1989) 'A repertory grid analysis of Austria's image as a summer vacation destination', *Journal of Travel Research*, Winter, pp. 3–7.

Engel, J.F., Blackwell, R.D. and Miniard, P.W. (1986) *Consumer Behaviour*, Dryden Press, New York.

Euromonitor (1988) *International Outlook: The World Package Holidays Market, 1980–1995*, Euromonitor, London.

Farrell, B.H. (1982) *Hawaii, the Legend that Sells*, University of Hawaii Press, Honolulu.

Fayol, H. (1949) *General and Industrial Administration*, Pitman, London.

Featherstone, M. (1982) 'The body in consumer culture', *Culture and Society*, Vol. 1, pp. 18–33.

Festinger, L.A. (1957) *A Theory of Cognitive Dissonance*, Stamford University Press, Stamford.

French, Y. (1994) *PR in Leisure and Tourism*, Pitman, London.

Frew, E. (1994) 'International charter travel – a new opportunity for Australian tourism', in Seaton, A.V. *et al.* (eds), *Tourism: The State of the Art*, Wiley, Chichester.

Garvin, D.A. (1988) *Managing Quality: The Strategic and Competitive Edge*, Free press, New York.

Gee, C.Y., Choy, D.J.L. and Makens, J.C. (1984) *The Travel Industry*, AVI Publishing, Westport, Conn.

George, W.R. and Gibson, B.E. (1988) *Blueprinting: A Tool for Managing Quality in Organizations*, QUIS Symposium at the University of Karlstad, Sweden, August.

Go, F. (1993) 'Development of new service products for the leisure travel market: a systems review', *Revue de Tourisme*, Vol. 2, p. 81.

Goodall, B. (1990) 'Opportunity sets as analytical marketing instruments: a destination area review', in Ashworth, G. and Goodall, B. (eds), *Marketing Tourism Places*, Routledge, London.

Goodall, B. and Stabler, M. (1992) 'Timeshare: the policy issues', in Johnson, P. and Thomas, B. (eds), *Perspectives on Tourism Policy*, Mansell, London.

Goossens, C.F. (1994) 'External information search: effects of tour brochures with experiential information', *Journal of Travel and Tourism Marketing*, Vol. 3, No. 3, pp. 89–108.

Grant, D. and Mason, S. (1993) *The Package Travel, Package Holidays and Package Tours Regulations*, University of Northumberland Travel Law Centre.

Grönroos, C. (1980) *An Applied Service Marketing Theory*, Working Paper No. 57, Swedish School of Economics, Helsinki.

Grönroos, C. (1990) *Service Management and Marketing: Managing the Moments of Truth in Service Competition*, Lexington Books, Lexington, Mass.

Guiltinan, J.P. and Gordon, W.P. (1994) *Marketing Management*, 5th edn, McGraw-Hill, New York.

Gummesson, E. (1988) 'Service quality and product quality combined', *Review of Business*, Vol. 9. No. 3.

Gummesson, E. (1990) 'Service design', *The Total Quality Magazine*, Vol. 2, No. 2, pp. 97–101.

Haylock, R. (1994) 'Timeshare, a new force in tourism', in Seaton, A.V. et al. (eds), *Tourism: The State of the Art*, Wiley, Chichester.

Heape, R. (1994) 'Outward bound', *Bulletin of the Tourism Society*, Vol. 83, Autumn, pp. 4–5.

Heggenhougen, H. (1987) 'Traditional medicine (in developing countries): intrinsic value and relevance for holistic health care', *Holistic medicine*, Vol. 2, pp. 47–56.

Hobson-Perry, J.S. (1993) 'Increasing consolidation within the cruise line industry', *Journal of Travel and Tourism Marketing*, Vol. 2, No. 4, pp. 91–6.

Hodgson, A. (ed.) (1987) *The Travel and Tourism Industries: Strategies for the Future*, Pergamon, Oxford.

Hollins, G. and Hollins, B. (1991) *Total Design: Managing the Design Process in the Service Sector*, Pitman, London.

Holloway, J.C. (1994) *The Business of Tourism*, 4th edn, Pitman, London.

Holloway, J.C. and Robinson, C. (1995) *Marketing for Tourism*, 3rd edn, Longman, Harlow.

Hooper, P. (1995) 'Evaluation strategies for packaging travel', *Journal of Travel and Tourism Marketing*, Vol. 4, No. 2, pp. 65–82.

Howard, J.A. (1963) *Marketing Management*, Irwin, Homewood, Ill.

Hughes, R. (1993) *Culture of Complaint*, Warner Books, New York.

Hunt, J.D. and Layne, D. (1991) 'The evolution of travel and tourism terminology and definitions', *Journal of Travel Research*, Vol. XXIX, No. 4, pp. 7–11.

Irwin, R. (1991) *Timeshare Properties: What Every Buyer Must Know*, McGraw-Hill.

Jansen-Verbeke, M. (1991) 'Leisure shopping, a magic concept for the tourism industry?', *Tourism Management*, March, pp. 9–14.

Jenkins, C. (1987) *Practical Timeshare and Group Ownership*, Butterworth, London.

Jenner, P. and Smith, C. (1993) *Tourism in the Mediterranean*, Economist Intelligence Research Report, London.

Johnson, P. and Thomas, B. (eds) (1992) *Choice and Demands in Tourism*, Cassell, London.

Kapur, U. (1994) 'Caledonian: an inspired acquisition?', *Travel Weekly*, 21 December.

Kaspar, C. (1989) 'Recent developments in tourism research and education at university level', in Witt, S.F. and Moutinho, L. (eds), *Tour-*

ism Marketing and Management Handbook, Prentice Hall, London.

Kirk, D. (1995) *Hard and Soft Systems: A Common Paradigm For Operations Management?*, International Journal of Contemporary Hospitality Management, Vol. 7, No. 5, pp. 13–16.

Klien, Lewis and Scott, (1989)

Kotler, P.H. (1992) *Principles of Marketing*, Prentice Hall, Englewood Cliffs, NJ.

Kotler, P.H. and Armstrong, G. (1987) *Marketing: An Introduction*, Prentice Hall, Englewood Cliffs, NJ.

Kotler, P., Haider, D.H. and Rein, I. (1993) *Marketing Places*, Free Press, New York.

Krippendorf, J. (1987) *The Holiday Makers*, Heinemann, London.

Lamnert, C.U., Lambert, J.M. and Cullen, T.P. (1989) 'The overbooking question, a simulation', *Cornell HRA*, August, pp. 15–20.

Laws, E. (1986) 'Identifying and managing the consumerist gap', *Service Industries Journal*, Vol. 6, No. 2, pp. 131–43.

Laws, E. (1991) *Tourism Marketing, Service and Quality Management Perspectives*, Stanley Thornes, Cheltenham.

Laws, E. (1995) *Tourist Destination Management: Issues, Analysis and Policies*, Routledge, London.

Laws, E. (1996a) 'Health tourism, a business opportunity analysis', in Clift, S. and Page, S. (eds), *Health Issues in Tourism Management*, Routledge, London.

Laws, E. (1996b) 'Perspectives on pricing decisions in the inclusive holiday industry', in Yoeman, I. and Ingold, T. (eds) *Yield Management – A Strategy for Service*, Cassell, London.

Lehtinen, U. and Lehtinen, J.R. (1982) *Service Quality. A Study of Service Dimensions*, Service Management Institute, Helsinki.

Leiper, N. (1990) *The Tourism System*, Massey University Press, Palmerston North, New Zealand.

Leith, E. (1995) 'The holiday's over', *Mail on Sunday Review*, October.

Le Pelley, B. and Laws, E. (1995) *PATHS toward PEACE: a stakeholder-benefits approach to city centre tourism management in Canterbury*. Paper presented at the Urban Environment: Tourism Conference, South Bank University, London.

Leppard, J. and Molyneux, L. (1994) *Auditing Your Customer Service*, Routledge, London.

Levitt, T. (1969) *The Marketing Mode*, McGraw-Hill, London.

Lewis, B. and Outram, M. (1986) 'Customer satisfaction with package holidays', in Harris, B. (ed.), *Are They Being Served?*, Philip Allen, London.

Likorish, L.J. and Kershaw, A.G. (1958) *The Travel Trade*, Practical Press, London.

Locke, E.A. and Schweiger, D.M. (1979) 'Participation in decision-making – one more look', in Straw, B.M. (ed.), *Research in Organizational Behaviour*, Vol. 1, JAI Press, Greenwich, Conn.

Lockyer, K.G. and Oakland, J.S. (1981) *The Quest For Quality, How to sample success*, Management Today, July, pp. 41–48.

Lovelock, C.H. (1992) *Managing Services Marketing Operations and Human Resources*, 2nd edn, Prentice Hall.

MacCannell, D. (1976) *The Tourist: A New Theory of the Leisure Class*, Macmillan, London.

Mallen, B. (1978) *Channel Power, A Form of Economic Exploitation* European Journal of Marketing, Vol. 12, No. 2, pp. 194–202.

McCarthy, E. and Perreault, W.D. (1988) *Essentials of marketing*, Irwin, US.

McCracken, G. (1990) 'Information technology changes the way you compete', *Harvard Business Review*, pp. 98–103.

McFarlan, W.F. (1994) *Information Technology Changes The Way You Compete*, Harvard Business Review, January/February, p. 98–103.

McKenna, R. (1991) *Relationship Marketing: Successful Strategies for the Age of the Customer*, Addison-Wesley, Reading, Mass.

McNee, A. (1994) 'Business update', *Travel Weekly',* 21 December.

Mallen, B. (1978) 'Channel, power, a form of economic exploitation', *European Journal of Marketing*, Vol. 12, No. 2.

Marsh, P. (1994) 'Customer retention: a strategy for travel agents', *Journal of Vacation Marketing*, Vol. 1, No. 1, pp. 75–80.

Marti, B.E. (1993) 'Cruise line brochures: a comparative analysis of lines providing Caribbean service', *Journal of Travel and Tourism Marketing*, Vol. 2, No. 1, pp. 31–52.

Mastenbroek, W. (ed.) (1991) *Managing for Quality in the Service Sector*, Blackwell Business, Oxford.

Mayo, E. and Jarvis, L. (1981) *The Psychology of Leisure Travel*, CBI Publications, Boston, Mass.

Medlik, S. (1993) *Dictionary of Transport, Travel and Hospitality*, Butterworth-Heinemann, Oxford.

Mendoza, A. (1986) 'A decade in timeshare', *Leisure Management*, Vol. 6, No. 2, pp. 41–2.

Middleton, V.T.C. (1988) *Marketing in Travel and Tourism*, 2nd edn, Heinemann, London.

Middleton, V.T.C. (1991) 'Whither the package tour?', *Tourism Management*, Vol. 12, No. 3, pp. 185–92.

Mill, R.C. and Morrison, A.M. (1985) *The Tourism System: An Introductory Text*, Prentice Hall, Englewood Cliffs, NJ.

Milligan, S. (1971) *Adolf Hitler: My Part in His Downfall*, Penguin Harmondsworth.

Monopolies and Mergers Commission (NMC) (1986) *Foreign Package Holidays*, Cmnd 9879, HMSO, London.

Morgan, M. (1994) *Homogeneous Products, The Future of Established Resorts*, in Theobald, W.F. *Global Tourism, The Next Decade*, Butterworth-Heinemann, Oxford, p.378–396.

Morgan, M. (199) 'Dressing up to survive: marketing Majorca anew', *Tourism Management*, March, pp. 15–20.

Moutinho, L. (1987) *Consumer behaviour in tourism*, European Journal of Marketing, Vol. 21, No. 10, pp. 5–44.

Moynahan, B. (1983) *Fools Paradise*, Pan Books, London.

Murphy, P. (1985) *Tourism: A Community Approach*, Methuen, London.

Noakes, G. (1995) 'Unijet beats its main rivals to launch second edition series', *Travel Trade Gazette*, 13 December.

Normann, R. (1991) *Service Management, Strategy and Leadership in Service Business*, John Wiley, Chichester.

Office of Fair Trading (1990) *Timeshare*, OFT, London.

Page, S. (1994) *Transport for Tourism*, Routledge, London.

Parkinson, L. (1989) 'Direct Sell', in Witt, S. and Moutinho, L. (eds), *Tourism Marketing and Management Handbook*, Prentice Hall, London.

Patching, D. (1994) *Practical Sodt Systems Analysis*, Pitman, London.

Payne, A. (1993) *The Essence of Services Marketing*, Prentice Hall, Hemel Hempstead.

Pearce, D. (1987) 'Mediterranean charters – a geographical perspective', *Tourism Management*, December, pp. 291–305.

Pearce, D. (1989) *Tourist Development*, Longman Scientific, Harlow.

Peisley, A. (1989) 'UK tour operators and the European market in the 1990s', *Travel and Tourism Analyst*, No. 5, pp. 56–67.

Peters, M. (1969) *International Tourism: The Economics and Development of the International Tourist Trade*, Hutchinson, London.

Pimlott, J.A.R. (1947) *The Englishman's Holiday*, Faber & Faber, London.

Pi-Sunyer, O. (1989) 'Changing perceptions of tourism and tourists in a Catalan resort town', in Smith, V. (ed.), *Hosts and Guests. The Anthology of Tourism*, 2nd edn, University of Pennsylvania Press, Pennsylvania.

Pompl, W. and Lavery, P. (eds) (1993) *Tourism in Europe: Structures and Developments*, CAB International, Wallingford.

Poon, A. (1993) *Tourism, technology and Competitive Strategies*, CAB International, Wallingford.

Porter, M. (1980) *Competitive Strategies: Techniques for Analysing Industries and Competitors*, Free Press, New York.

Porter, M. (1987) *From competitive Advantage to Corporate Strategy*, Harvard Business Review, pp. 43–59. May-June, 1987.

Prus, R.C. (1989) *Pursuing Customers. An Ethnography of Marketing Activities*, Sage, London.

Ragatz (1995) *Timeshare Purchasers: Who They Are, Why They Buy*, Ragatz Associates, Eugene, Oreg.

Relihan, W. (1989) 'The yield management approach to hotel pricing', *Cornell HRA*, Vol. 30, No. 1, pp. 40–5.

Ries, A. and Trout, J. (1986) *Positioning: The Battle for Your Mind*, Warner Books, New York.

Riley, C. (1983) 'New product development in Thomson Holidays: the use of research', *Tourism Management*, December, pp. 253–61.

Rogers, P. (1993) *A Practical Guide to the Package Travel Regulations*, Landor Travel Publications, London.

Rothschild, M.L. (1987) *Marketing Communications*, D.C. Heath, Lexington Mass.

Ryan, C. (1995) *Researching Tourist Satisfaction*, Routledge, London.

Ryan, C. (1991a) 'UK package holiday industry', *Tourism Management*, March, pp. 76–7.

Ryan, C. (1991b) *Recreational Tourism: A Social Science Perspective*, Routledge, London.

Sahlberg, B. (1995) 'Information systems and the quality of tourism', in Teare, R., Olsen, M.D. and Gummesson, E. (eds), *Service Quality in Service Organizations*, Cassell, London.

Sales, H.P. (1959) *Travel and Tourism Encyclopaedia*, Blandford Press, London.

Sasser, E.W., Olsen, P.R. and Wycoff, D.D. (1978) *Management of Service Operations*, Alleyn & Bacon, Boston, Mass.

Selwyn, T. (1992) 'Peter Pan in South East Asia – views from the brochure', in Hitchcock, M.J., King, V.T. and parnwell, M. (eds), *Tourism in South East Asia*, Routledge, London.

Shaw, G. and Williams, A. (1987) *Firm formation and operating characteristics in the Cornish tourist industry – the case of Looe, Tourism Management*, Dec. p. 344–348.

Shaw, S. (1987) *Airline Marketing and Management*, 2nd edn, Pitman, London.

Sheldon, P. (1986) 'The tour operating industry, an analysis', *Annals of Tourism Research*, Vol. 13, pp. 349–56.

Sheldon, P. and Mak, J. (1987) 'The demand for package tours: a mode choice model', *Journal of Travel Research*, Vol. 50, pp. 146–60.

Shostack, G.L. (1984) *Designing Services That Deliver*, Harvard Business Review, January–February, pp. 133–139.

Shostack, G.L. (1985) *Planning the Service Encounter*, in: Czepiel, J.A.; Soloman, M.R. & Surprenant, C.F. (eds) *The Service Encounter*; Lexington Books, Lexington, Mass ok.

Shostack, G.L. (1987) 'Service positioning through structural change', *Journal of Marketing*, Vol. 51, pp. 34–43.

Showalter, G.R. (1994) 'Cruise ships and private islands in the Caribbean', *Journal of Travel and Tourism Marketing*, Vol. 3, No. 4, pp. 107–18.

Skidmore, J. (1995) 'Airtours play down need for acquisitions', *Travel News*, April.

Smith, S.L.J. (1988) 'Defining tourism: a supply side view', *Annals of Tourism Research*, Vol. 25, pp. 179–90.

Stabler, M. (1990) 'The concept of opportunity sets as a methodology for selling tourism places', in Ashworth, G. and Goodall, B. (eds), *Marketing Tourism Places*, Routledge, London.

Stern, W.B. (1989) *The Aloha Trade. Labour Relations in Hawaii's Hotel Industry*, University of Hawaii Press, Honolulu.

Swinglehurst, E. (1982) *Cook's Tours: The Story of Popular Travel*, Blandford Press, Poole.

Towner, J. (1985) 'The history of the Grand Tour', *Annals of Tourism Research*, Vol. 12, No. 3, pp. 301–16.

Trend, N. (1994) 'Local airport blues', *BBC Holidays*, July, pp. 50–1.

Urry, J. (1990) *The Tourist Gaze*, Sage, London.

Uysal, M. and Fesenmaier, D.R. (eds) (1993) *Communication and Channel Systems in Tourism Marketing*, Haworth Press, Binghampton, NY.

Vellas, F. and Becherel, L. (1995) *International Tourism*, Macmillan, London.

Vlitos-Rowe, I. (1993) *The European Market for Very Expensive Holidays*, EIU Report No. 2, pp. 35–53.

Voas, R. (1995) *Tourism – The Human Perspective*, Hodder & Stoughton, London.

Walsh, V., Roy, R. and Bruce, M. (1988) 'Competitive by design', *Journal of Marketing Management*, Vol. 4, No. 2, p. 201.

Webster, F. and Wind, Y. (1972) *Organziational Buying Behaviour*, Prentice Hall, Englewood Cliffs.

Weitz, B.A. (1981) *Effective sales interactions: a contingency framework*, Journal of Marketing, Vol. 45, No. 1, pp. 85–103.

Wheatcroft, S. (1994) *Aviation and Tourism Policies*, Routledge, London.

Wild International Ltd (1994) *International Cruise Market Monitor*, launch copy.

Wilkie, W.L. (1986) *Consumer Behaviour*, Wiley, New York.

Witt, S., Brooke, M.Z. and Buckley, P.J. (1995) *The Management of International Tourism*, 2nd edn, Unwin, London.

Woodside, A.G. and Sherrill, D. (1977) 'Traveller evoked and inept sets of vacation destinations', *Journal of Travel Research*, Vol. 20.

WTO (yearly) *Annual Statistical Yearbook*, World Tourism Organization, Madrid.

Zeithaml, V., Parasuraman, A. and Berry, L. (1990) *Delivering Quality Service: Balancing Customer Perceptions and Expectations*, Free Press/Macmillan, New York.

Zemke, R. and Schaaf, D. (1989) *The Service Edge: 101 Companies that Profit from Customer Care*, NAL Books, New York.

Author Index

Subject Index